salty urbanism

salty urbanism

a design manual to address sea level rise and climate change for urban areas in the coastal zones

ORO EDITIONS

How can we retool architects, landscape architects, land developers and community stakeholders with a place-based design framework to address adaptation to sea level rise and climate change?

In the face of sea level rise and climate change, a new framework rooted in landscape architectural thinking for the built environment must emerge—one that unites landscape architects, architects, urban designers, planners, engineers, scientists, and others directly shaping our cities. Through policy and design, we must work together to create a more equitable, resilient, and sustainable future.

This manual is not only a resource for sea level rise adaptation—it is a call to action. It provides a framework for communities confronting a range of climate challenges, including chronic flooding, rising heat, intensified rainfall, and ecosystem disruption.

South Florida presents a particularly urgent case. Its porous limestone geology renders conventional flood control methods—such as levees, walls, and pumps—ineffective over time, as water seeps up from below. Flooding occurs through five interconnected pathways: storm surge, fluctuating groundwater tables, extreme rainfall, runoff, and tidal influence—all of which are being visibly and permanently reshaped by sea level rise.

Known as the "Venice of America," Fort Lauderdale—with 330 miles of shoreline and a seasonally swelling population—sits at the intersection of land and water. This edge condition presents a critical opportunity for creative, climate-conscious development. Salty Urbanism proposes a methodology grounded in reconciliation ecology, which supports biodiversity within human-dominated landscapes. These emergent green infrastructures—or nature-based solutions—provide essential ecosystem services such as flood mitigation, food production, temperature regulation, and geochemical balance.

Salty Urbanism anticipates new architectural and urban design patterns that integrate ecosystem services into the built environment. It challenges us to rethink our relationship with water and to embrace a future where designing for exceedance—planned, managed flooding—is the new norm.

Nothing else will change the built environment more than sea level rise over the next 100 years.

contents

Southeast Florida is a paradise; it is the only tropical region within the continental united states.

Over the next **hundred years** south Florida will **experience radical** changes to the built and ecological environment from

STOP
ITALICA

“the infrastructure we have is built for a world that doesn’t exist anymore”

Nicole Hernandez Hammer, 2015
Environmental Studies Researcher,
Union of Concerned Scientists

Seasonal high-tide flooding, commonly called **"King Tides,"** only occur about three times a year today, but such events could multiply over the next thirty years to become **the daily high tide as early as 2050.**

Storm surge, like that from Hurricane Irma, will **compound** with rising sea levels to **make floods more widespread and longer-lasting.**

DO NOT
ENTER

All types of flooding will become more frequent and more extreme as **stormwater has increasingly fewer places to drain to.**

intro- duction

current Florida coastline

"The most important line on this planet is the coastline, and we mistake it as something static, but understandably so because throughout recorded human history it has relatively remained the same, but it's now shifting and we need to adapt."

John Englander, Oceanographer

WEST PALM BEACH
FORT LAUDERDALE
MIAMI

future Florida coastline

By 2100 moderate projections show six feet of sea level rise will inundate the region, drastically changing the environment. Essentially South Florida will become the Upper Keys.

WEST PALM BEACH
FORT LAUDERDALE
MIAMI
Only six feet of sea level rise will cause profound alterations to the landscape

What if future development in the region served as a **flood adaptive asset**, rather than an environmental liability in the face of rising seas and climate change?

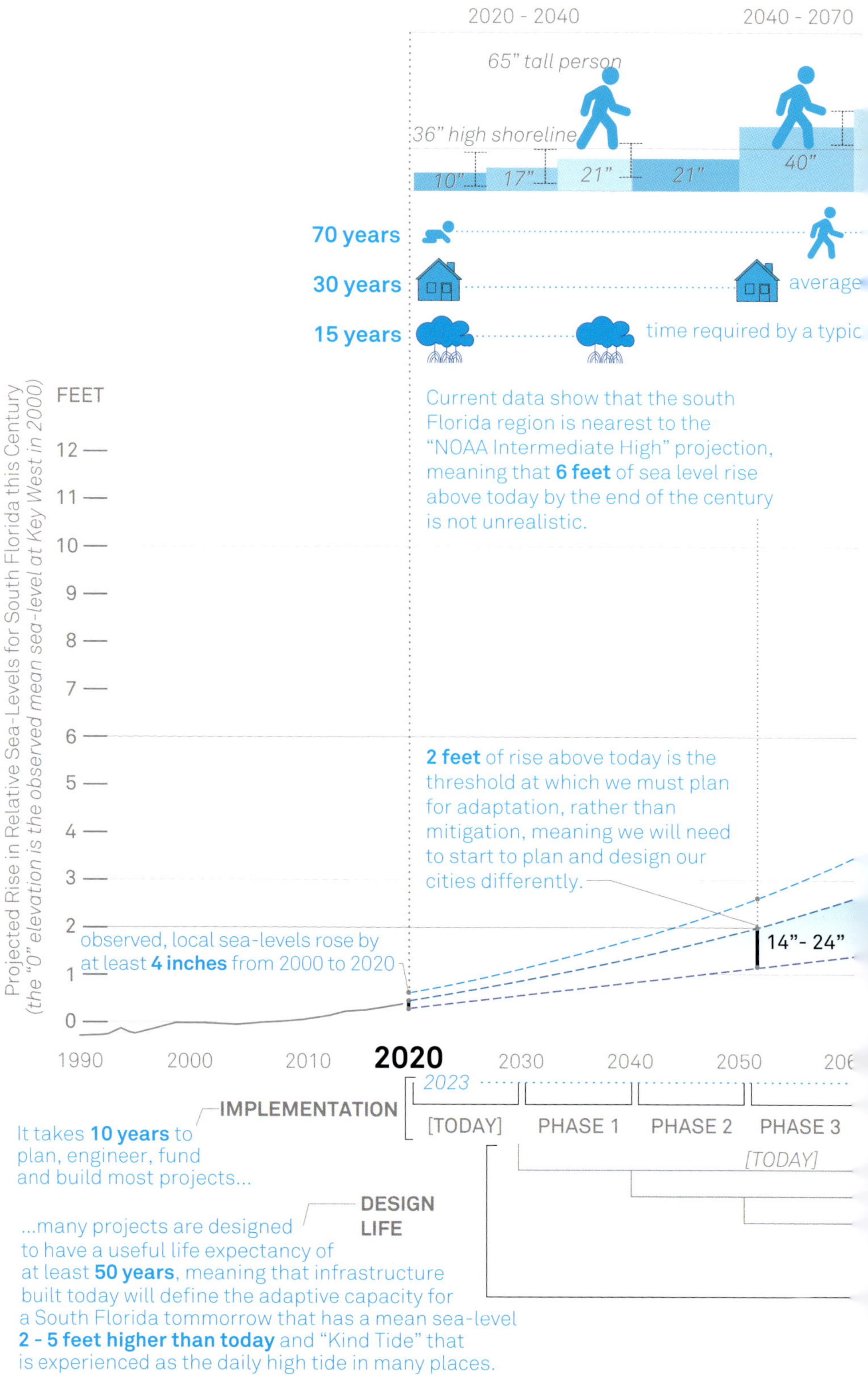
2020 - 2040
2040 - 2070
65" tall person
36" high shoreline
10"
17"
21"
21"
40"
70 years
30 years
15 years
average
time required by a typic
Current data show that the south Florida region is nearest to the "NOAA Intermediate High" projection, meaning that **6 feet** of sea level rise above today by the end of the century is not unrealistic.
Projected Rise in Relative Sea-Levels for South Florida this Century
(the "0" elevation is the observed mean sea-level at Key West in 2000)
FEET
12
11
10
9
8
7
6
5
4
3
2
1
0
2 feet of rise above today is the threshold at which we must plan for adaptation, rather than mitigation, meaning we will need to start to plan and design our cities differently.
14"- 24"
observed, local sea-levels rose by at least **4 inches** from 2000 to 2020
1990
2000
2010
2020
2030
2040
2050
206
2023
IMPLEMENTATION
[TODAY]
PHASE 1
PHASE 2
PHASE 3
[TODAY]
It takes **10 years** to plan, engineer, fund and build most projects...
DESIGN LIFE
...many projects are designed to have a useful life expectancy of at least **50 years**, meaning that infrastructure built today will define the adaptive capacity for a South Florida tommorrow that has a mean sea-level **2 - 5 feet higher than today** and "Kind Tide" that is experienced as the daily high tide in many places.

for a home mortgage cycle

produce a full range of potential benfits

nfrastructure and built
tures represent a balance
ween resilient function and
ts of construction, therefore,
tching the project scope with
ssumed projection is critical.

astructure projects have
esign life of 50 years and
uld use the shaded area
ow that best matches goals
funding.

Long-term infrastructure projects with a design life of more than 50 years should **plan for a minimum of 6 feet**.

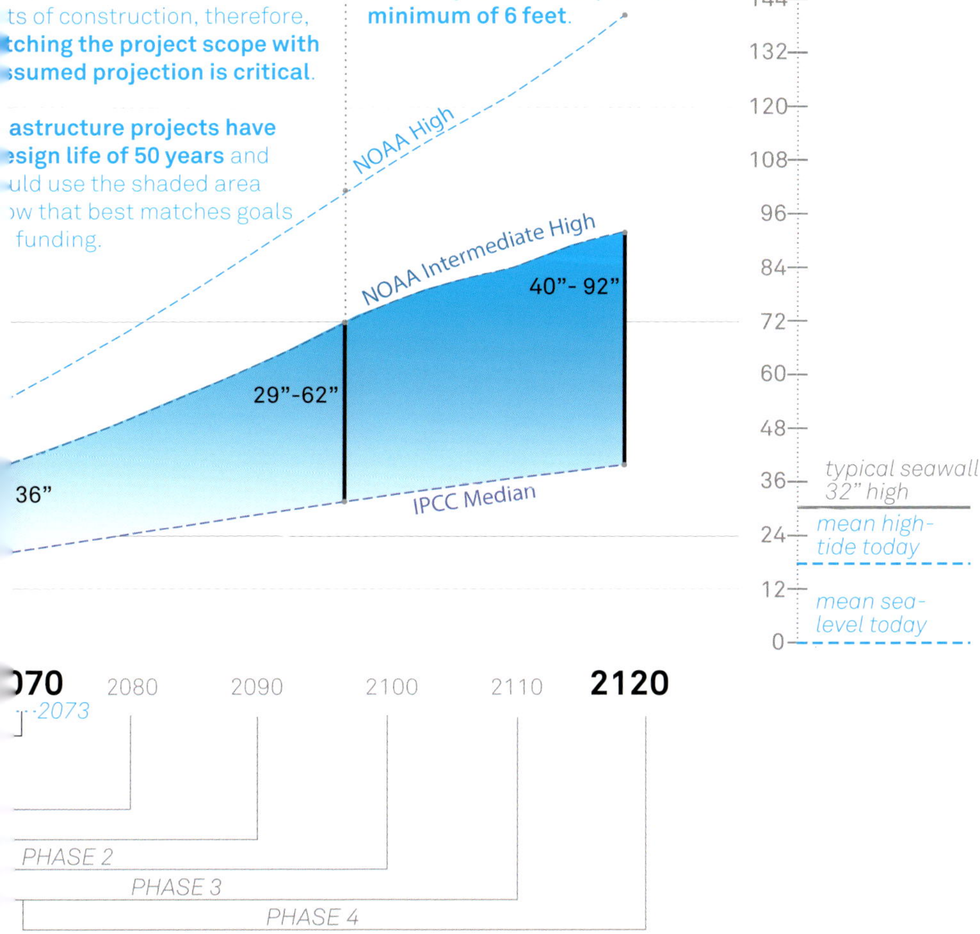

planning in **2023**
should include considering the conditions in **2073**

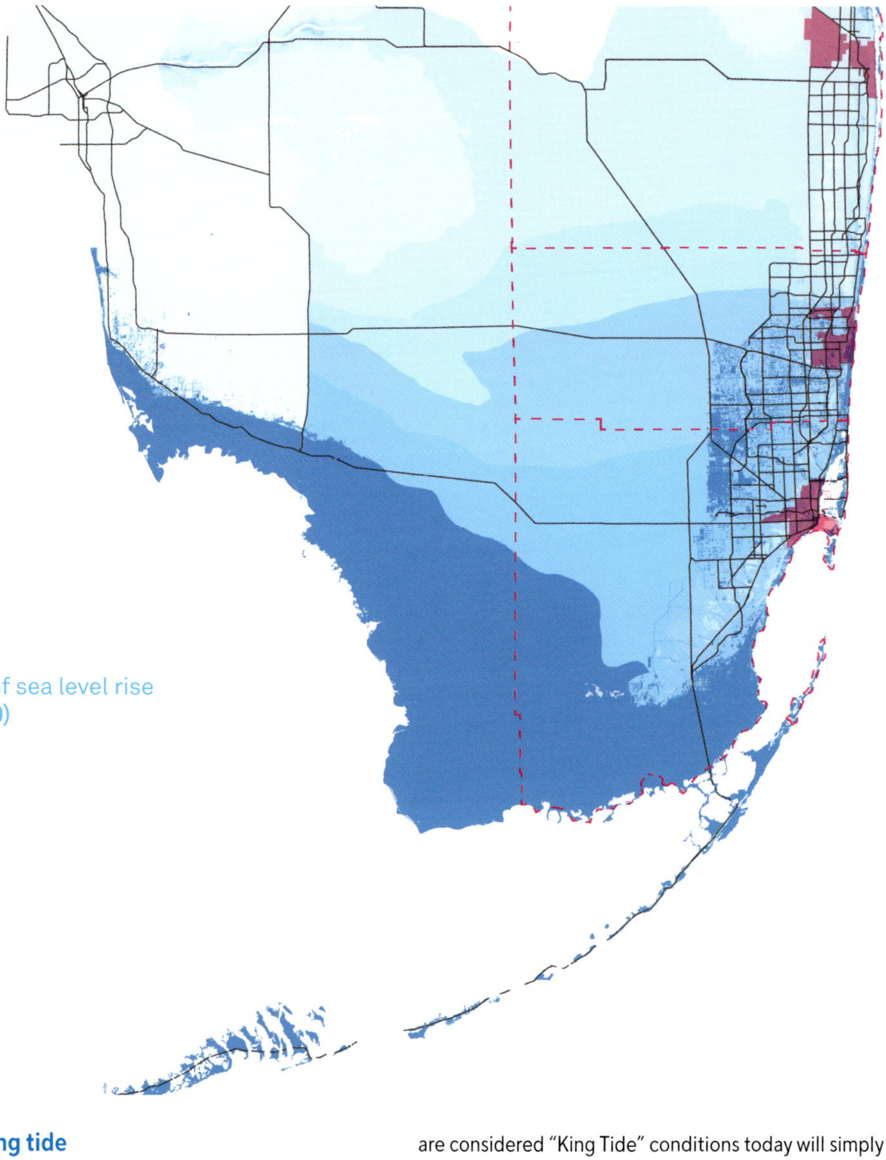

3 feet of sea level rise
(c. 2070)

The rising tide

Given that the rate of sea level rise is increasing, the pace of change will culminate over time. During the 2030s, the frequency of high-tide floods may only increase slightly above today, adding just a few more days of seasonal King Tides and just a few more inches to their maximum depths. But these increases could suddenly triple by the 2040s, with King Tide conditions occuring at high tide every day for an entire month or more[1] and at nearly double the current depths. As much as two feet of sea level rise above today is likely as early as 2050. At two feet of rise, what are considered "King Tide" conditions today will simply become the daily high tides, while seasonal high-tide flooding will become more equivalent to what is considered "major flooding" now.[2] However, way before this relatively dramatic shift, many much more subtle and chronic issues caused by elevated sea levels will have long strained communities. With as little as three to six inches in rise above today, saltwater intrusion into the porous aquifer will drastically reduce south Florida's drinking water supply.[3] At eleven inches of rise, direct damages to buildings and infrastructure caused by increasingly frequent sunny day floods will have outpaced the yearly costs associated with

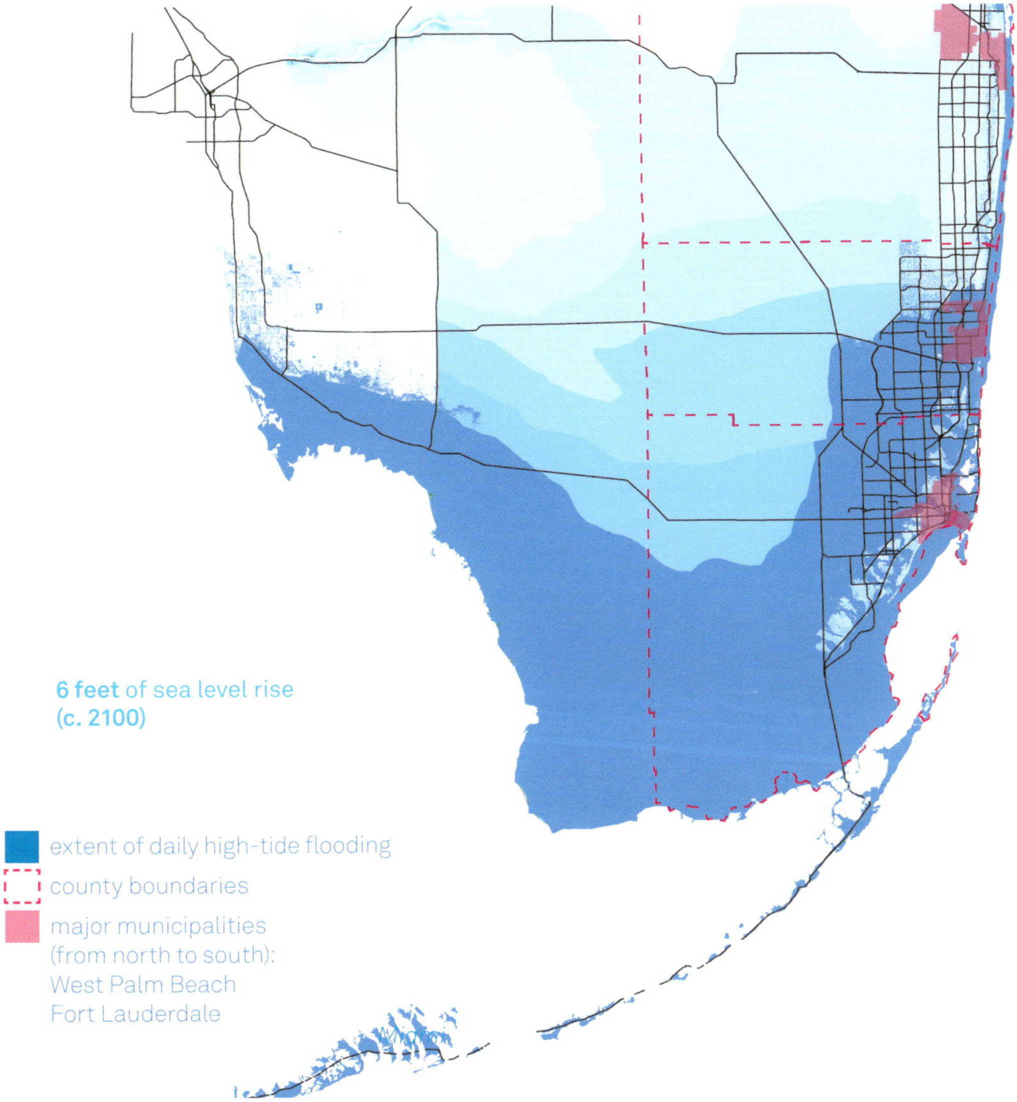

hurricanes and rain-driven floods.[4] At the same time, a warming climate will bring about other problems, many of which will compound and heighten the issues of a rising sea. While it is much more difficult to predict future changes in rainfall, current best estimates indicate that the overall climate will become far drier on average[5] while also experiencing increases in wet season flooding, in large part due to increasing urbanization.[6] Combined with regionally elevated water levels, these changes in local climate will likely push already strained urban infrastructure to its limits and excacerbate a wide variety of socio-economic issues. Looking out to the end of the century, south Florida faces an even more extreme shift with the potential for six feet of sea-level rise or more. At six feet of rise above today, the urban coast will shift to a fully marine paradigm, one where freshwater can only be stored aboveground and where tidewaters flow through most city streets on a daily basis. South Florida cities will need to radically re-conceptualize their relationships with flooding and water.

1. 2. 3. Heimlich and Bloetscher 2011 - sea level rise/climate change problems & drinking water.
4. McAlpine and Porter 2018 - direct damages of tidal flooding on south FL real estate.
5. Obeysekera et al. 2015 - future FL water/temp with climate change.
6. Mitsova et al. 2020 - impact of heat on health/social vulnerability

flooding landscapes

south Florida's five types of flooding

1. Storm Surge
Storm surge refers to a dramatic, but temporary, rise in sea level caused by pressure and/or wind displacement from a hurricane or other large storm offshore.

2. Rainfall
Heavy, seasonal rainfall can cause rapid flooding of low-lying areas within minutes or hours (typically less than six hours).

3. Urban Runoff
Once rain enters the urban landscape it flows downhill over impervious surfaces (i.e, roads and buildings) as "runoff," collecting speed, pollutants, and problems along its route.

4. Groundwater
Groundwater is, quite simply, water retained underground. Rainwater naturally percolates and soaks into tiny spaces in the earth, but where saturated earth (i.e, the "water table") rises too near the surface, groundwater can worsen and prolong flooding.

5. Tidal Flooding
Seasonal high tides can overtop shorelines and storm drains and cause "sunny day" flooding. Tidal flooding events only occur as much as three times a year today, generally during the months of October and November, but are expected to become ten to one hundred times more frequent over the next thirty years.

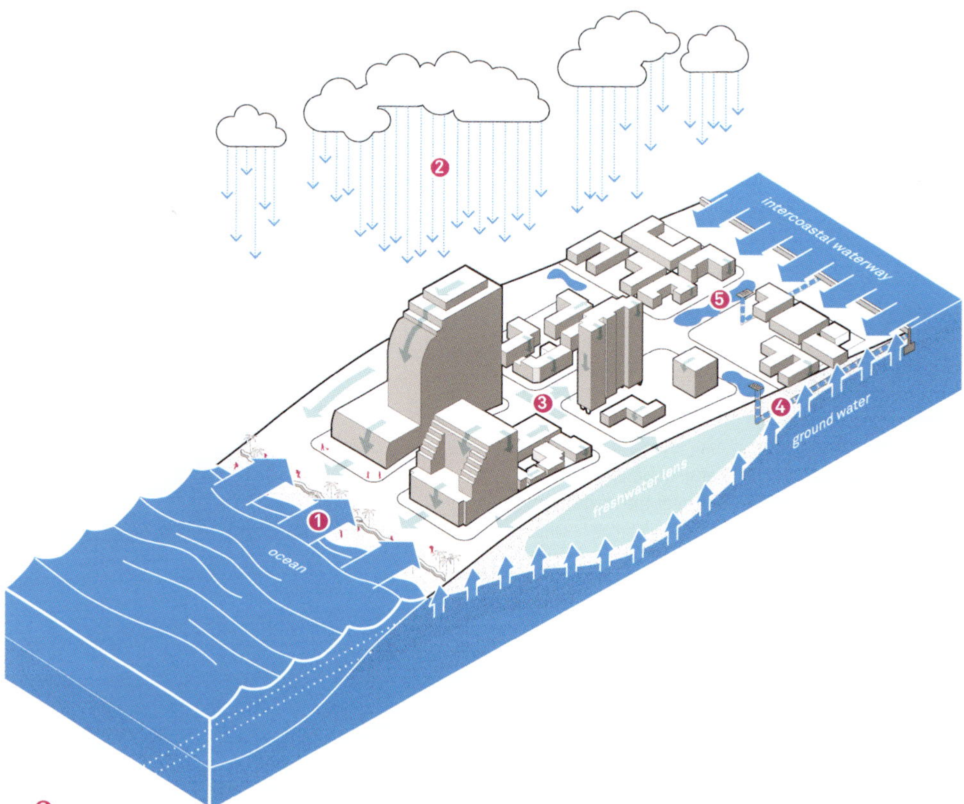

6

flooding and urban south Florida

South Florida's environment and abundance of waterways presents many economic and recreational opportunities to residents but also a variety of flood risks. Flooding can occur in south Florida by way of five distinct pathways, many of which tend to compound upon one another seasonally. While some of these are directly influenced by coastal exposure, others are more influenced by localized topography or by the behavior of water in the underlying geology. The urban landscape itself can be a cause for flooding as an over-abundance of "impervious surfaces" prevents stormwater from draining into soils, creates "runoff," and reduces the area where floodwaters can safely dissipate.

Historically, water and the efforts to control it have driven south Florida's development patterns. From the earliest settlements and trading posts to the luxurious resorts and urban landscapes of today, Florida's history is interwoven with flood management. For south Florida, specifically, the trajectory of the built environment is most closely linked to the series of projects meant to "drain the Everglades." Prior to these drainage projects, communities in south Florida were largely small, flood-adaptive hamlets situated on the relative elevation of islands or "hammocks" adjacent to riverine and coastal transportation routes.

Development skyrocketed once the regional drainage projects were completed in the 1950s and 60s, resulting in the sprawling metropolis of today. As of 2020, south Florida is the eighth most populace metropolitan area in the United States, accounting for nearly 30 percent of the entire state's population.[7] These numbers are expected to continue to increase, by as much as 80 percent in Palm Beach and Miami-Dade and by nearly 300 percent in Broward County, over the next thirty years.[8] Regardless of sea level rise, this growth will invariably result in more of all five types of flooding as more, non-adaptive development continues to cover flood-prone landscapes.

7. US Census, 2020 - FL population
a. https://www.census.gov/library/stories/state-by-state/florida-population-change-between-census-decade.html
8. Florida Office of Economic and Demographic Research - FL population growth
a. http://edr.state.fl.us/Content/
http://edr.state.fl.us/Content/population-demographics/data/MediumProjections_2020.pdf

problemscape

The combination of an ever-increasing population, rising sea levels, and a history of myopic development practices has resulted in a "problemscape" of interlocking urban issues across south Florida. One problem begets or worsen another, which affects yet another – and so on – resulting in a "cascade" of culminating issues across the urban landscape. Many of these issues, particularly erosion and pollution, exist in various chronic and acute forms irrespective of climate change and are instead attributable to development practices that prioritize local economic and recreational goals over environmental integrity. Climate change will only heighten these problems and expand their reach far beyond that of environmental policy, likely impacting every aspect of society, from the real-estate market to drinking water reserves. To address this problemscape, it is useful to first understand what the problems are and their connections.

erosion

Rising sea levels will erode beaches and aging seawalls, threatening inland infrastructure and building foundations.

tidal flooding

"Sunny day" flooding will worsen erosion and pollution rates while costing south Florida hundreds of millions in direct damages.

precipitation

More intense and erratic rain-events and droughts will increasingly challenge all aspects of water management.

elevated water tables

Saltwater intrusion will elevate groundwater, farther enhancing flooding potential while reducing regional drinking water reserves.

storm surge

Tropical storms and hurricanes are expected to become more frequent and more intense, causing many direct and indirect damages.

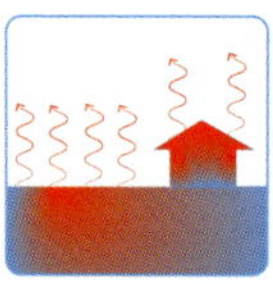

heat island effect

Increasingly higher average temperatures will enhance urban heat islands, damaging both human and ecosystem health.

pollution

Urban pollution will worsen with increasing floods, temperatures, and urbanization, degrading water quality and quality of life.

drinking water & saltwater intrusion

Most of south Florida's drinking water is pumped to the surface by wells tapping groundwater reserves located in the shallow Biscayne and Floridan aquifers. The porous limestone "karst" geology of these aquifers allows the ample surface waters of the Everglades to percolate and filter down into the aquifer, thereby "re-charging" the supply of fresh, clean, drinking water. However, the porous nature of this geology also means that rising sea levels cause saltwater to infiltrate into the aquifer through a process known as "saltwater intrusion." To date, saltwater intrusion has already made dozens of coastal wells in Miami-Dade and southern Broward too salty for human consumption. The rapidly increasing urban population in these same areas has prompted managers to take increasingly drastic measures to maintain regional freshwater reserves. As such, the sustainability of drinking water in south Florida is becoming increasingly complex and expensive.

saltwater intrusion

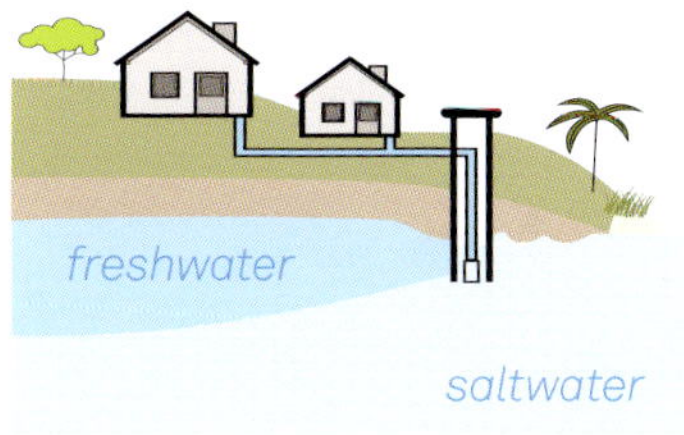

over-draw from aquifer

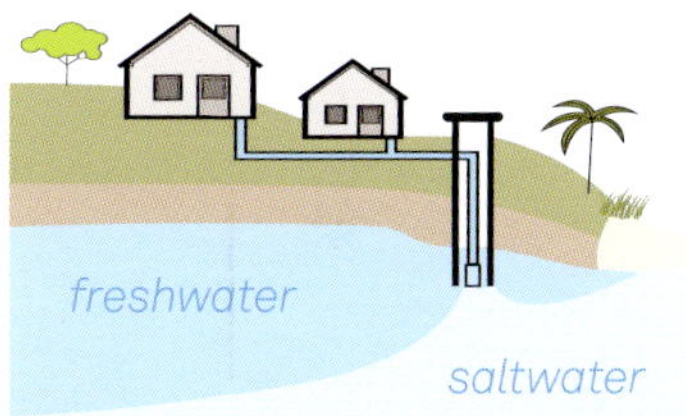

heat

Heat can be especially pervasive in urban areas due to the conductive/radiative/reflective properties of many common building materials, particularly asphalt, concrete, steel, and glass. In areas where there is an over-abundance of these materials and a lack of the cooling influences of plants and water, an "urban heat island effect" may take hold, enhancing the severity and persistance of extreme heat. This phenomenon is expected to increase substantially over the next fifty years, resulting in a greater incidence of heat-related illnesses and a reduction of dissolved oxygen in waterways, worsening pollution issues.

pollution

Urban areas produce a variety of toxic substances and wastes, many of which are directly released into the environment. These often fall onto surfaces like roads and buildings where they are eventually washed off into waterways with stormwater as runoff. Septic systems, releases from broken sewer pipes, and poor construction practices also contribute to water quality issues. At the same time, the absence of intact ecosystems along the urban coast means that the landscape has few opportunities to remediate this pollution, a combination that results in degraded water quality, causing "harmful algal blooms" that deplete oxygen in the water, kill fish, smell, reduce property values, and degrade quality-of-life generally.

Broward County case-study

While all of south Florida shares the problems and risks of climate change, Broward County is arguably one of the most perilous locations in the region. This largely stems from the fact that a majority of the County's area – roughly centered around the New River – was once a massive, eastward-flowing floodplain for the Everglades. In contrast to Miami-Dade or Palm Beach, major development in Broward was only possible after the successful channelization and drainage of the Everglades. Although few recall the connection today, the county was named for Napoleon Bonaparte Broward who, as governor of Florida between 1905-09, was among the first to seriously push for drainage of the Everglades. Today, Broward County is (mostly) dry and has realized the erstwhile governor's dream, but this was a dream built upon the foundation of a static sea level. Today's massive complex of canals, pumps, and dam-like control structures is a system that depends, at it's core, on the tendency of water to flow out to the ocean with gravity. On average, southern Broward's elevation is about three feet above sea level, and many of the county's key drainage canals rely on this meager elevation difference to move excess stormwater away from the inland cities and suburbs out to the coast. But as sea levels continue to rise, and water tables elevate nearer to the surface, this essential function will become increasingly challenged.

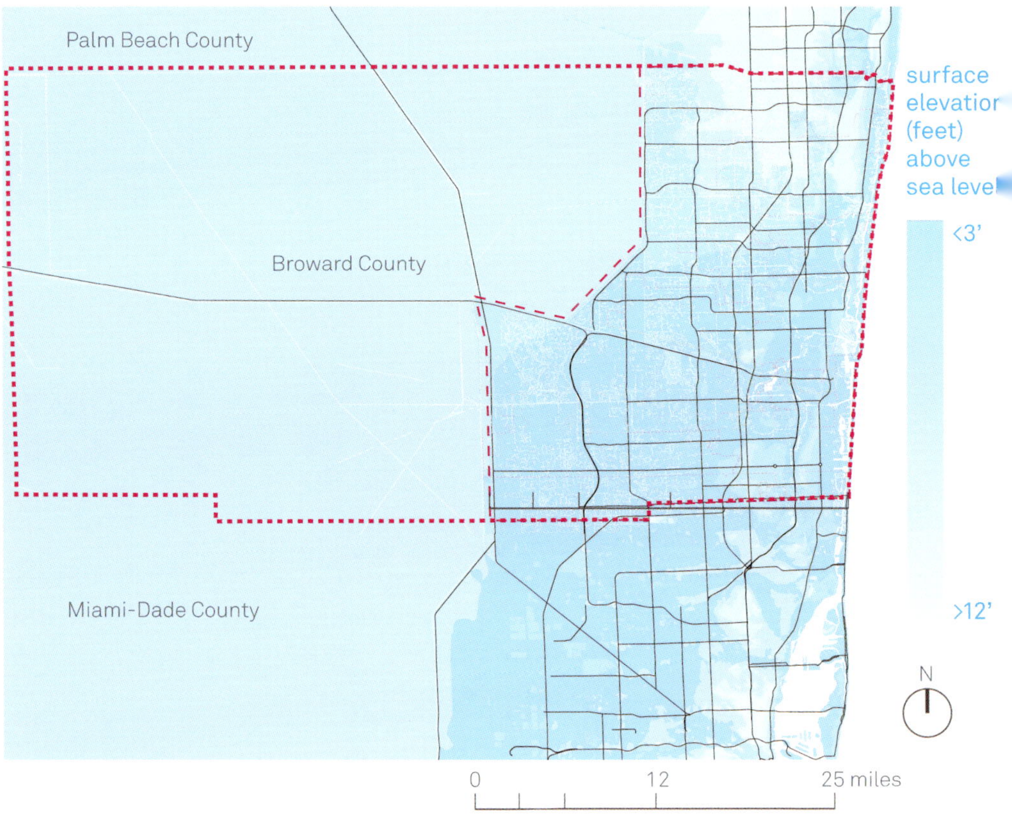

Broward County Land Elevation Map

While parts of coastal Miami-Dade may experience a greater frequency of tidal flooding, Broward has some of the worst rates and extents of saltwater intrusion in south Florida today. As of 2019, nearly all of the drinking wells east of I-95 have been closed, with those remaining operational having to increasingly contend with saline over-draw. Groundwater being closer to the surface also leads to a greater potential for "ponding" above the landscape after heavy rains, and this will become especially true if storms increase in frequency and intensity and if urban impervious surface cover expands. Given this confluence of factors, it is likely that inland Broward County will likely be among the first non-coastal urban areas impacted by sea level rise. If the control structures that meter the drainage of Everglades water to the coast reach an equilibrium with sea level, most of inland Broward County would experience widespread flooding every year. With no place to drain water as runoff, no room to store water in the ground, and no land area to safely hold water above ground, the only place left for this water is to flood the urban landscape. While this situation is by no means unique to Broward, the county will be among the first to feel its effects.

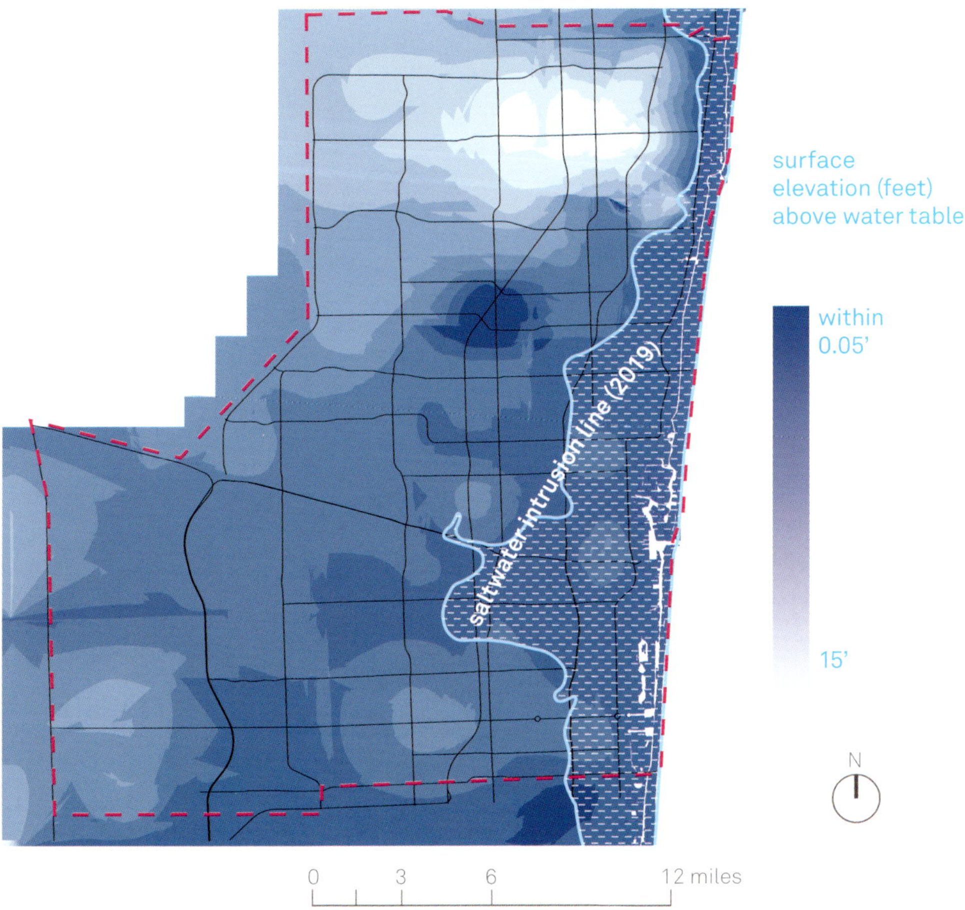

Broward County Water Table Elevation Map

2040 scenario

daily tidal flooding

A lower-to-middling range sea level rise projection (similar to the "NOAA Int-High" on pp. 22-23) for sea level rise this century is utilized for the following map series to highlight areas in Broward County that may experience an increase in tidal influence moving into the future. The dark blue color highlights increased flooding, but is not meant to indicate constant inundation. Rather, it simply indicates areas that are likely to be overtopped daily by high tides or areas that are likely to be flooded by the surge of a category 1 storm with a path and behavior similar to Hurricane Irma. Given the changes in sea level rise rates that have already been observed, an additional foot of rise above today's sea levels seems likely by the year 2040. What this map does not show is the accompanying rise of the water table and the effects this would have on flooding inland. It is likely that increases in rain-driven flooding wil also increase everywhere.

category 1 storm surge

By 2040, storm surge from a category 1 hurricane could inundate far more areas than a similar storm in the past. While Hurricane Irma itself caused significant amounts of surge flooding in relatively localized areas, the same kind of surge in Broward after an additional foot in sea level rise could inundate entire neighborhoods. An aspect of Hurricane Irma that was especially challenging for Broward and Miami-Dade was persistent flooding experienced across the region after the storm. This was the result of stormwater management facilties becoming overloaded by the shear volume of rain released over the region, and at a time of year when both rain volumes and sea levels are naturally elevated and when stormwater networks are already at capacity. This same kind of "compound flooding" would be both deeper and last significantly longer if sea level rise were to elevate the regional water tables by an appreciable amount.

2060 scenario

daily tidal flooding

By 2060, it is likely that over two feet of sea level rise will be impacting the region. In this scenario, high tides would begin to inundate entire neighborhoods almost every day. However, if present planning goals are met prior to 2060, most waterfront properties in both Broward and Miami-Dade Counties will have raised their shoreline elevations about twice above their heights now (i.e, >5 ft. NAVD88). If this change is successful, the daily tidal flooding experienced would likely be less than what is shown below. It is also important to remember that shorelines are not the only consideration as tidewaters can "back-up" through storm drains and other stormwater infrastructure and cause flooding inland of the shoreline itself. However, even if "tidal check valves" and other adaptive infrastructue are perfectly implemented across the county, flooding from ponding rain would still be common even after a relatively minor rainstorm.

category 1 storm surge

Surge from a category 1 storm in 2060 would likely cause extensive inundation and accompanying damage from erosion. Surge caused by Hurricane Irma in 2017 moved tons of sand off of beaches in Broward and spread it over roads and other urban areas. This sort of impact is likely to occur with storms only a fraction of Irma's strength after a sea level rise of more than two feet. Again, this assumes there has been no structural change to the elevation of shorelines. Similarly, if the "salinity control structures" – those dams that separate inland water from tidewater within the regional canal network – are over-topped by surge, then tidal-induced flooding will also likely occur much farther inland than ever before. If this were to happen, the possible damage and lost drainage capacity of these dams, combined with heavy rain from an Irma-like storm, would result in widespread and long-lasting flooding across the region and could persist for months.

2080 scenario

daily tidal flooding

Towards the end of the century, and after three feet of sea level rise, seasonal King Tide conditions overtop the salinity control structures at the heights they are today. This causes urban areas much farther inland to experience tidal changes for the first time and renders the regional drainage network effectively useless as the elevation differential required to drain excess stormwater from inland areas to tide equilizes, negating the use of gravity and requiring enormous and monstoursly expensive pumping to provide similar levels of service. SFWMD, USACE, and local partners are already working to expand the inland portions of these canals and to elevate key areas along the network, providing additional storage and attenuation capacity for inland stormwater volumes that may help up to this point. However, after three feet in sea level rise, even these improvements would struggle to keep up, and many coastal areas would regularly flood regardless.

category 1 storm surge

Assuming there has been no change to stormwater and shoreline infrastructure by 2080, surge from even relatively modest storms would inundate much of the region. With the regional control structures at equilibrium with high tides during the King Tide months, even normal conditions could result in most of Broward County experiencing perisistent flooding, with a thin layer of water ranging between a few inches to several feet deep covering the landscape after every rain event. Even if there were no hurricanes, the extent of high-tide flooding shown in the opposing map would likely be enough to overload most of the region's drainage capacity and would have elevated the underlying water tables to very near the surface in many areas. This combination would mean that most of Broward could expect to be flooded like this every summer, with water only subsiding well after the wet season rains have ended.

solutions

parks, not pipes

Just as these problems have synergistic causes there exist synergistic solutions able to address many of the root issues underlying compounding climate-urban cascades. Utilizing plants and "soft" landscapes for infrastructural purposes traditionally reserved for "hard" engineering has the potential to improve many urban-climate problems, enhancing the adaptive capacity of landscapes to climate change while also improving urban quality of life. This softer way of managing water with landscapes is known as "green stormwater infrastructure."

Conventional urban infrastructure treats water in the landscape as a waste to dispose of and as a threat to life and property, resulting in an "inputs/outputs" and "control/defend" mindset. While the power of water to destroy should never be underestimated, viewing water as only a nuisance and not as the life-giving substance that it is has resulted in urban landscapes that reflect this mindset with debilitating results. Where rainwater once fell onto trees and wetlands, percolating and infiltrating into the ground and evaporating into the air at zero cost, now stormwater runs off of buildings, lawns, and roads – gaining speed, volume, and pollutants along the way, creating new problems that did not exist before and that require costly management. This phenomenon is sometimes referred to as "urban stream syndrome" aptly referencing how a natural system replaced by engineering can force itself back onto the artificial as a disservice when extreme conditions occur.

Where plants and landscapes are used to manage urban stormwater instead of pipes and pumps, not only are runoff rates reduced and water quality improved, but a host of other benefits are enhanced as well, including reduced urban temperatures, improved mitigation of pollutants, and provision of wildlife habitat. Well designed urban tree cover alone can simultaneously reduce heat islands, reduce runoff-driven flooding, and increase access to quality urban green space, all of which are increasingly understood to be important aspects of urban public health.

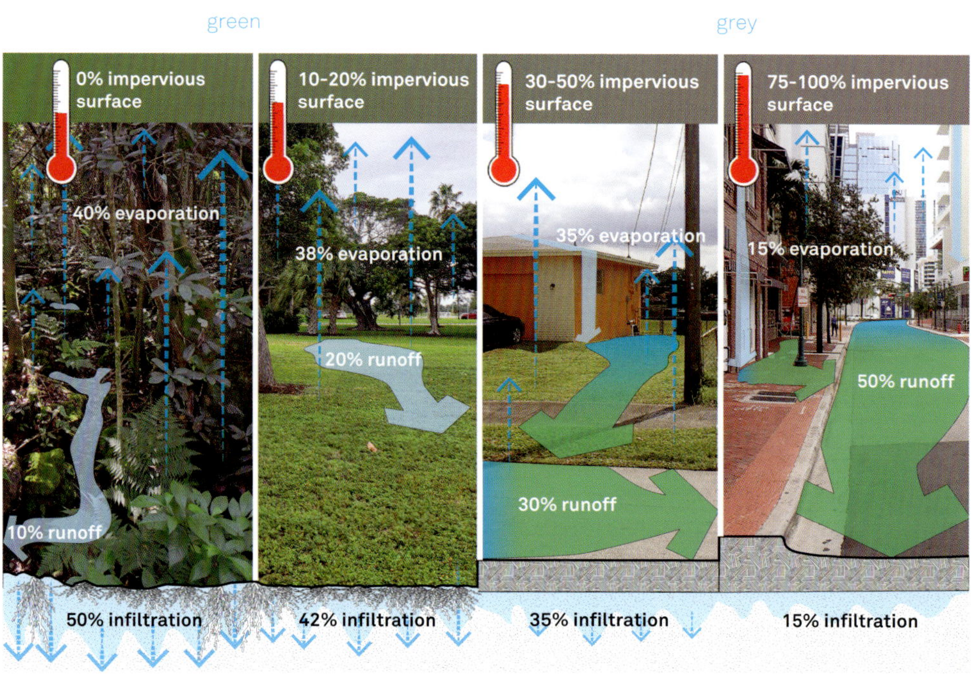

soft

hard

greenways, not giant walls

Armored walls known as "seawalls" are the mainstay shoreline of urban south Florida. This is mostly because they maximize buildable land area with waterfront while also preventing erosion and retaining inland soils. While convenient, this practice has become so widespread that precious few of the region's valuable estuarine habitats remain, causing and worsening a variety of environmental problems. But seawalls were never the only option. Shorelines that use the stabilizing power of plants and marine habitats, often called "coastal green infrastructure," have always been an equally suitable alternative.

As the sea rises, south Florida shorelines will continue to be on the frontline of adaptation efforts. Many of the seawalls throughout the region today were built nearly fifty years ago and would need to be replaced soon anyway, irrespective of elevated tidal stress. Simply raising shorelines would help to protect inland areas but at the continued cost of the region's unique coastal ecosystems, halting them from migrating with the rising tides. Seawalls also require continual restructuring with sea level rise, making them more expensive in the long term. Mangroves, on the otherhand, have the potential to grow and adapt to rising seas at minimal cost.

However, coastal ecosystems in southeast Florida are some of the most imperiled in the world due a host of pressures caused by the urban coast. Being stuck between rising seas and rising walls, many unique Florida habitats, like mangroves, seagrasses, and coral reefs, will be unable to adapt. The loss of these systems would not only present an aesthetic and moral crisis for Florida but a direct economic one as well. As these important ecosystems continue to decline, it will only become harder to leverage their unique adaptive benefits.

While coastal green infrastructure generally requires more land area to implement than seawalls, these nature-based solutions manage coastal resources much more holistically, resulting in a more cost-effective investment over time, imparting "cobenefits" and creating amenities that improve urban quality of life through living place-making.

salty urbanism

Salty Urbanism is a concept that focuses on the development of coastal cities and their relationship with the surrounding natural and economic systems. It recognizes the unique challenges and opportunities presented by flood-prone coastal areas and aims to create sustainable and resilient urban environments. Salty Urbanism takes into consideration the quality of life for residents, the economic systems in place, and the preservation and integration of the natural systems.

Quality of life is a fundamental aspect of Salty Urbanism. Coastal cities offer a distinct lifestyle with access to beaches, waterfronts, and natural beauty. Salty Urbanism aims to enhance this quality of life by designing cities that prioritize walkability, public spaces, and mixed-use developments. By creating vibrant and inclusive neighborhoods, residents can enjoy a high standard of living and have easy access to amenities such as parks, recreational areas, and cultural institutions.

Economic systems play a crucial role in coastal cities, especially those with active ports and tourism industries. Salty Urbanism recognizes the economic potential of these cities and seeks to leverage their natural assets. It promotes the diversification of the local economy, encouraging a balance between traditional industries and emerging sectors such as green technology, marine research, and sustainable tourism. By fostering innovation and entrepreneurship, Salty Urbanism helps create jobs, attract investment, and enhance economic resilience.

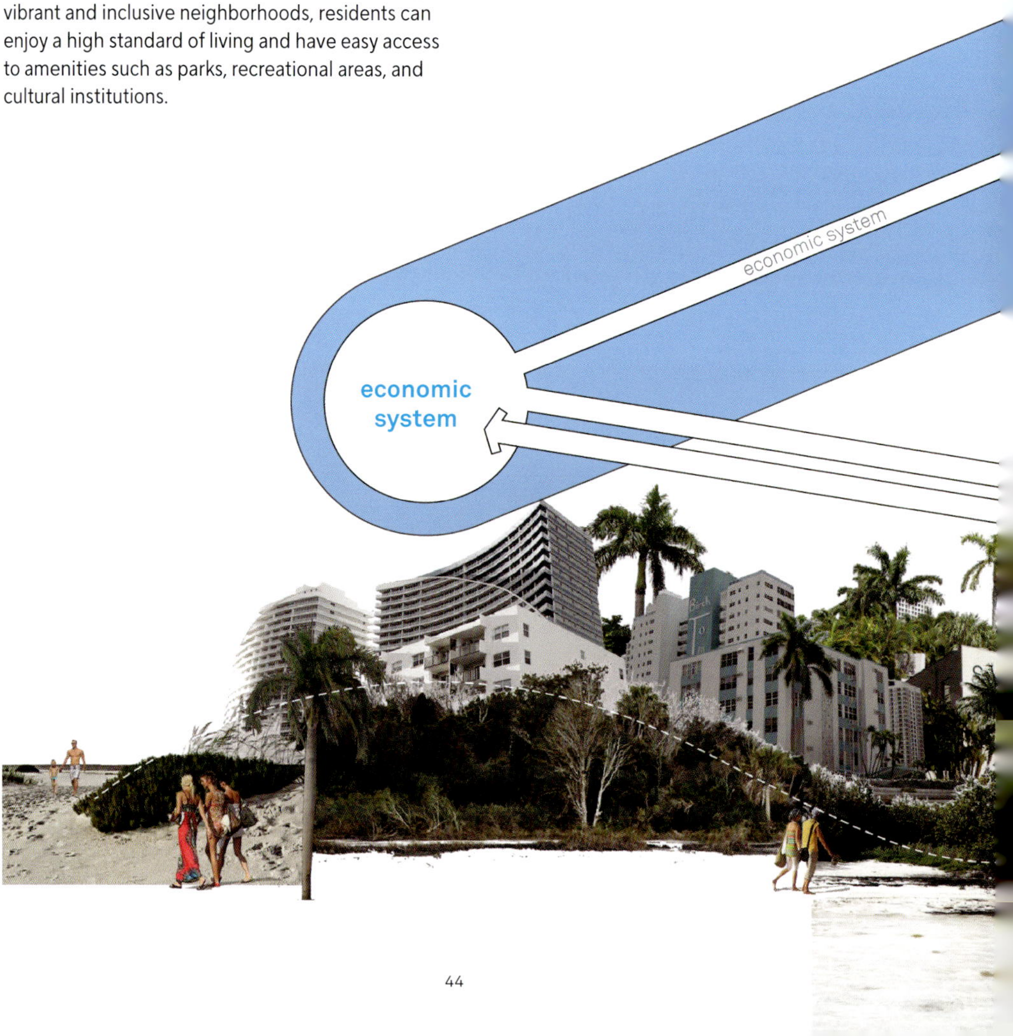

Natural system thinking is a key component of Salty Urbanism. Coastal cities are directly influenced by their surrounding ecosystems, including beaches, wetlands, and marine habitats. Recognizing the value of these natural systems, Salty Urbanism emphasizes their protection and integration into urban design. It promotes sustainable development practices that minimize the ecological footprint of cities and ensure the long-term viability of the coastal environment. This includes measures such as protecting and restoring coastal ecosystems, managing stormwater runoff, and implementing climate adaptation strategies.

Salty Urbanism also encourages collaboration between architects, landscape architects, urban planners, engineers, scientists, and local communities to develop holistic solutions. By adopting a systems thinking approach, it aims to address the interconnected challenges faced by coastal cities, such as rising sea levels, climate change, and population growth. This involves considering the social, economic, and environmental aspects of urban development and finding innovative solutions that benefit both humans and nature.

Overall, Salty Urbanism offers a framework for creating flood-adaptive coastal cities that prioritize the quality of life for residents, foster a resilient and diverse economic system, and promote the protection and integration of natural systems. By embracing the unique characteristics and challenges of coastal areas, Salty Urbanism strives to create vibrant, livable, and environmentally conscious urban environments.

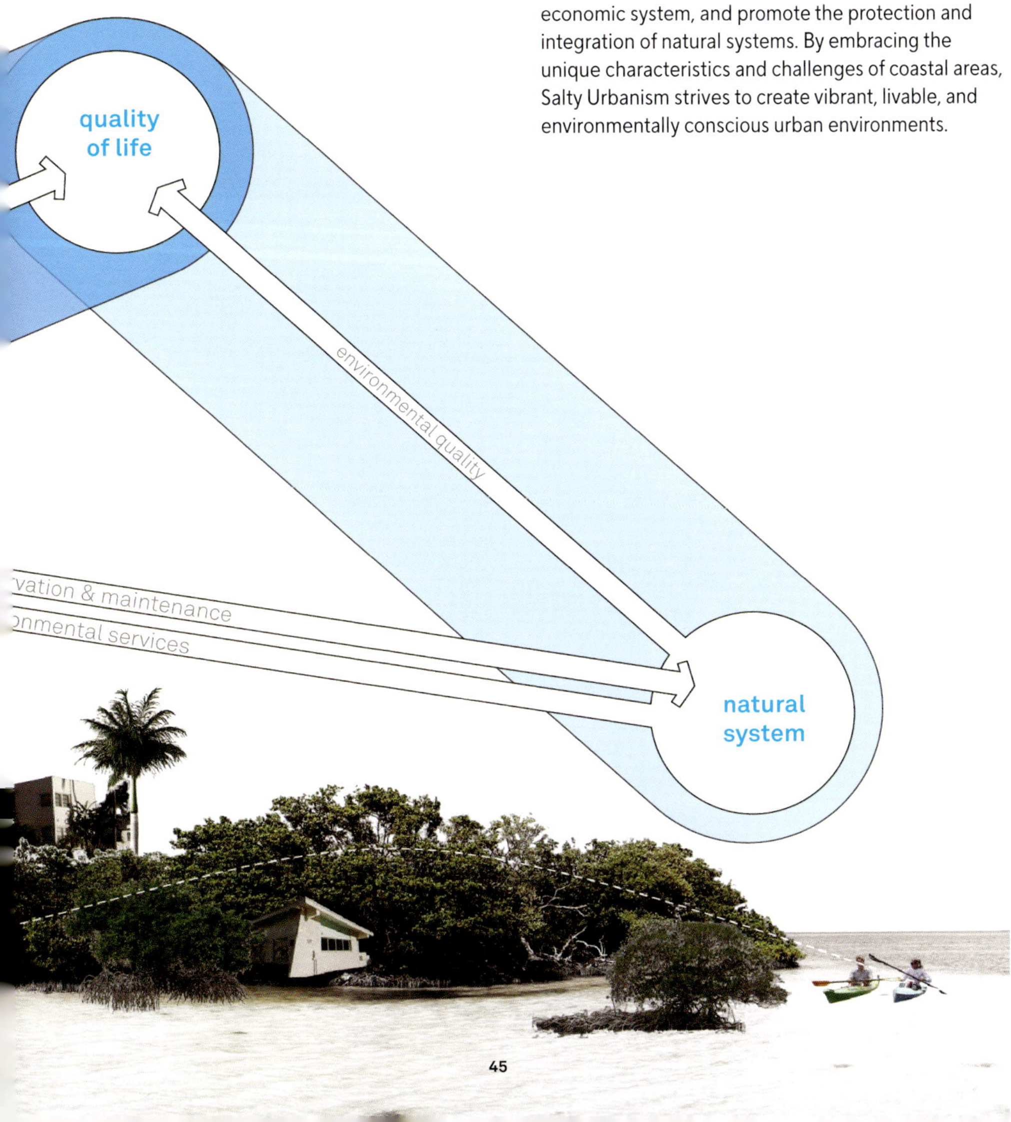

eco-
types

“any land west of I-95 was once the Everglades and when it rains, the land remembers that”

Tommy Strowd,
Former assistant executive director
South Florida Water Management District

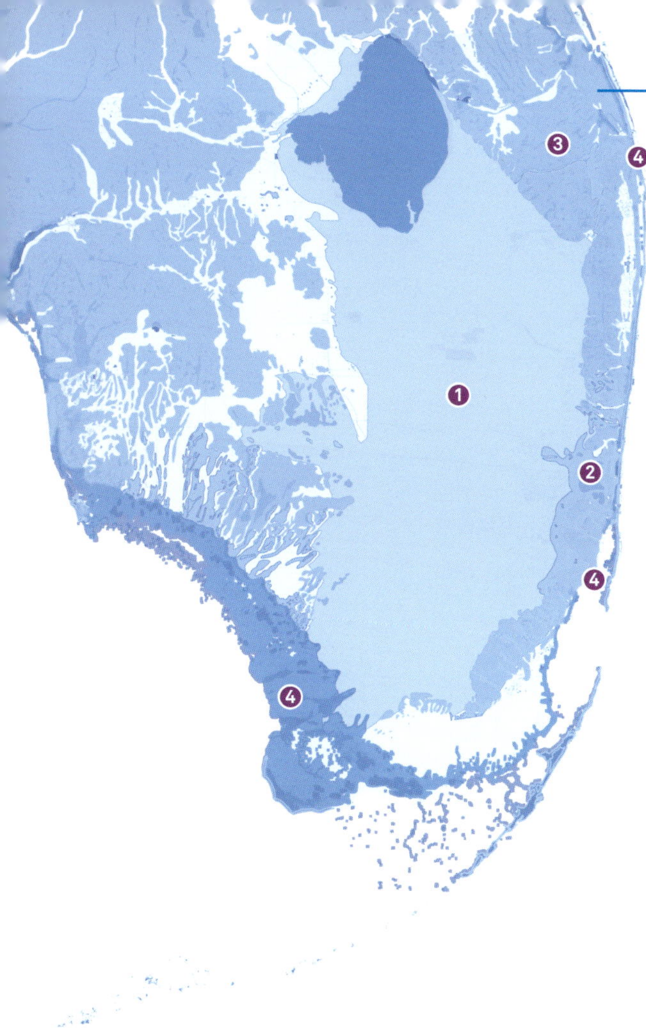

historic ecotypes

Nature-based designs are highly place and site-specific, with low-impact and green infrastructure approaches varying by site criteria like prevailing soils, water regimes, and appropriate native vegetation. The best designs try to replicate as much of the pre-development character of a site as possible. However, because south Florida has been so heavily developed, because the regional drainage system has changed the landscape so comlpetely, and because there is very little topographical variation to begin with, it can be challenging for designers to imagine what "pre-development" even looks like.

In ecology, the term "ecotype" refers to geographically distinct populations within a species that are specially adapted to the set of conditions unique to their region. With inspiration taken directly from this concept, this work seeks to pull together a wide variety of urban design and planning considerations with respect to the historic landscapes that produced unique species, what are called here "ecotypes." The hope is this will inform nature-based designs with respect to both low-impact development and climate adaptations.

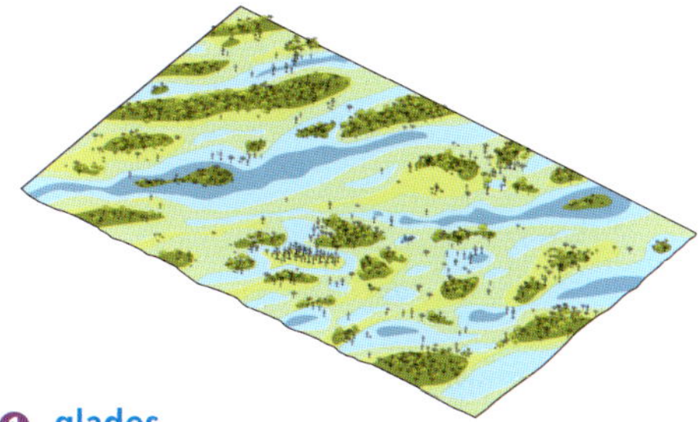

1 glades

The historic Everglades, or "Glades" represent one of south Florida's most iconic and valuable landscapes. Reconciling urban areas with glades landscapes could greatly improve coastal water quality and help the urban coastal zone to enhance regional and sustainable water reserves generally.

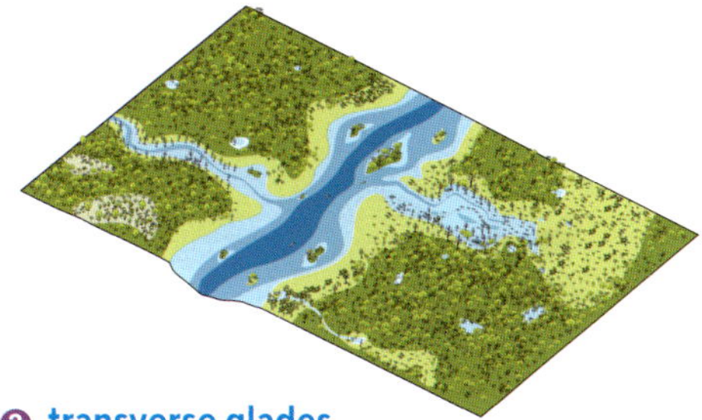

2 transverse glades

The "transverse glades" are a now extinct landscape where water from the glades once spilled to the ocean via the East Coast. Reconciling this fresh-salt "ecotone" may be invaluable to future salt-tolerant landscape designs using nature to adapt to increasing tidal influences inland with rising seas.

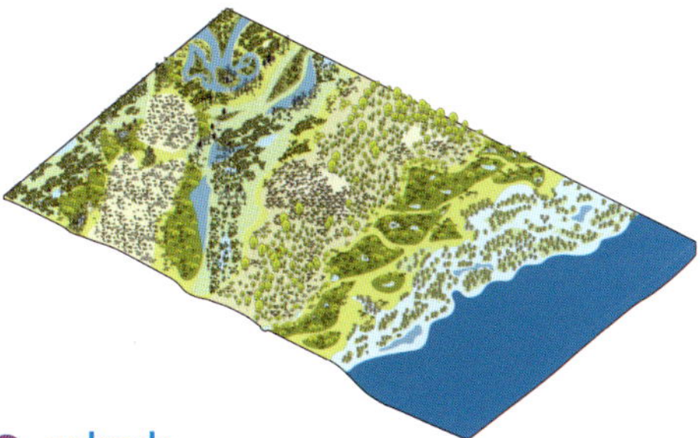

3 uplands

Upland areas in south Florida are the "top" of the urban watershed in many cases, and so attempting to replicate the pre-development conditions in these areas could greatly benefit the entire region as the effects of runoff on downstream areas would be reduced.

4 coastal-estuarine

These two closely related, yet highly distinct, landscapes – protected tidal estuaries and exposed marine coasts – represent the bulk of south Florida's "natural capital," collectively providing an aesthetic and environment that contributes tremendously to the state's economy. These valuable landscapes also happen to be the most at-risk landscapes to the various impacts of urban-climate cascades.

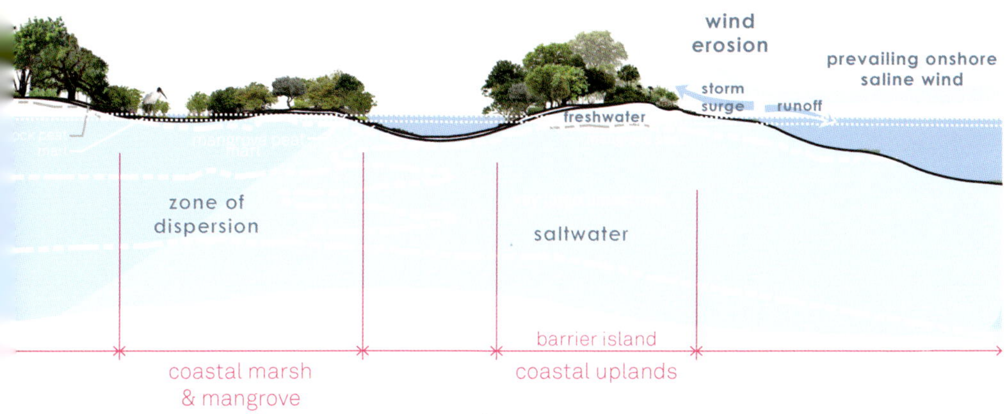

01. everglades

historic orientation

The famous "River of Grass," a massive basin of marsh-dominated wetlands, dotted with intermittent "tree islands" is a landscape that once covered nearly all of the Florida penninsula south of Lake Okeechobee. During wet seasons, water historically flowed unimpeded southward, over the edge of Lake Okeechobee, and down to Florida Bay as a shallow, slow-moving, "sheetflow" of water over the landscape. Seasonal and small-scale fluctuations in the water levels of this extremely shallow and wide river resulted in a mosaic pattern of topography called a "ridge and slough" landscape. Different vegetation communities are associated with these ridges and sloughs, respectively, but both are roughly oriented north-to-south.

modern orientation

Today, the remaining Everglades are contained by an extensive series of levees and canals, resulting in a highly compartmentalized landscape. "Stormwater Treatment Areas" and "Water Conservation Areas" sequester huge portions of the historic Everglades for water treatment and freshwater aquifer recharge purposes, respectively. To the north, these compartments result in water levels that are much higher than they were historically, effectively expanding the "slough" type habitats significantly. To the south, these compartments tend to be much drier and have lower water levels than they did historically, which can result in a change from sawgrass marsh to willow-marsh scrub.

attributes

1. soils - Mostly thin and extremely low in nutrients, glades soils are defined by deposits of peat and muck layered over top of calcareous limestone marl or sand. **2. water regime -** The water table in the 'Glades is seasonal and defined by rainfall. The porous nature of the

Willow Head Guild
cocoplum (*Chrysobalanus icaco* var. *pellocarpus*)
sawgrass (*Cladium jamaicense*)
red bay (*Persea borbonia*)
pickerelweed (*Pontederia cordata*)
coastalplain willow (*Salix caroliniana*)
cardinal airplant (*Tillandsia fasciculata*)
Fakahatchee grass (*Tripsacum dactyloides*)

Strand Swamp Guild
red maple (*Acer rubrum*)
giant leather fern (*Acrostichum danaeifolium*)
pond apple (*Annona glabra*)
strap fern (*Campyloneurum phyllitidis*)
stringlily (*Crinum americanum*)
dahoon holly (*Ilex cassine* var. *cassine*)
giant sword fern (*Nephrolepis biserrata*)
white waterlily (*Nymphaea odorata*)
royal fern (*Osmunda regalis* var. *spectabilis*)
Florida peperomia (*Peperomia obtusifolia*)
red bay (*Persea borbonia*)
goldfoot fern (*Phlebodium aureum*)
pickerelweed (*Pontederia cordata*)
royal palm (*Roystonea regia*)
arrowhead (*Sagittaria lancifolia* subsp. *lancifolia*)
pond cypress (*Taxodium ascendens*)
bald cypress (*Taxodium distichum*)
swamp fern (*Telmatoblechnum serrulatum*)
alligator flag (*Thalia geniculata*)
cardinal airplant (*Tillandsia fasciculata*)
Fakahatchee grass (*Tripsacum dactyloides*)
shoestring fern (*Vittaria lineata*)

underlying limestone marl and sand geology facilitates a high degree of permeability between surface waters and groundwater.

3. vegetation - Vegetation communities in the Everglades basin vary but are dominated by sawgrass marshes. Sloughs and deeper "flag marshes" tend to support a greater variety of other emergent and floating plants besides sawgrass. Higher elevation "tree islands" support a significant share of the biodiversity in the Everglages. **Plant guides: 1a-1j.**

4. urban overlap - Thankfully, most of the central Everglades were spared from urban development. However, a number of today's south Florida cities are sited directly over what were once the same kinds of habitat. These include Loxahatchee and Wellington in Palm Beach County; Parkland, Coral Springs, and Weston in Broward County; and western portions of Hialeah, Kendall, and Homestead in Miami-Dade County.

01 red maple (*Acer rubrum*)
02 Everglades palm (*Acoelorrhaphe wrightii*)
03 giant leather fern (*Acrostichum danaeifolium*)
04 pond apple (*Annona glabra*)
05 strap fern (*Campyloneurum phyllitidis*)

06 cocoplum (*Chrysobalanus icaco var. pellocarp*
07 sawgrass (*Cladium jamaicense*)
08 stringlily (*Crinum americanum*)
09 dahoon holly (*Ilex cassine var. cassine*)
10 giant sword fern (*Nephrolepis biserrata*)

11 white waterlily (*Nymphaea odorata*)
12 royal fern (*Osmunda regalis var. spectabilis*)
13 Florida peperomia (*Peperomia obtusifolia*)
14 red bay (*Persea borbonia*)
15 goldfoot fern (*Phlebodium aureum*)

16 pickerelweed (*Pontederia cordata*)
17 royal palm (*Roystonea regia*)
18 arrowhead (*Sagittaria lancifolia* subsp. *lancifolia*)
19 coastalplain willow (*Salix caroliniana*)
20 pond cypress (*Taxodium ascendens*)

21 bald cypress (*Taxodium distichum*)
22 swamp fern (*Telmatoblechnum serrulatum*)
23 alligator flag (*Thalia geniculata*)
24 cardinal airplant (*Tillandsia fasciculata*)
25 Fakahatchee grass (*Tripsacum dactyloides*)

26 shoestring fern (*Vittaria lineata*)

a (*Acoelorrhaphe wrightii*) @ margins
sobalanus icaco var. pellocarpus) @ margins
borbonia)
ow (*Salix caroliniana*) @ margins
t (*Tillandsia fasciculata*)
ass (*Tripsacum dactyloides*)

Glades Guild
cocoplum (*Chrysobalanus icaco var. pellocarpus*) @ margins
sawgrass (*Cladium jamaicense*)
stringlily (*Crinum americanum*)
pickerelweed (*Pontederia cordata*)
arrowhead (*Sagittaria lancifolia* subsp. *lancifolia*)
pond cypress (*Taxodium ascendens*) as dwarf

02. tranverse glades

historic orientation

In pre-history, numerous rivers connected the Everglades basin with the Atlantic. As the global climate changed at the end of the last ice-age, many of these outlets lost their direct connection to the ocean, the remaining few today include the Middle River, New River, Little River, and Miami River. Remnants of other rivers that once emptied east from the Everglades remained as eastward "fingers" of wetland habitat protruding into the relative north-south "coastal ridges" of uplands habitat that were formed long before. These rivers and "transverse" protions of glades that penetrated the coastal ridges were a distinct "ecotone" where extremely diverse and unique ecosystems thrived in the spaces between fresh and salt and between lowlands and uplands.

modern orientation

In modern times, the transverse glades are an extinct ecosystem. The extent of this coast-adjacent, subregional ecotone has since been drained, filled, and developed by urban south Florida. The regional drainage network assured that any remaining natural areas of the transverse glades would be too dry to persist. However, with sea level rise threatening to upend the regional drainage system, these habitat types may yet reform, or at least provide adaptive inspiration.

attributes

1. soils - Similar to the Everglades proper, featuring shallow deposits of peat and muck overlaying a base geology of limestone and/or marl, however, these areas tend to be more "sandy" than the 'Glades, and some areas near to rivers may have historically exhibited some silt deposition.

2. water table - The transverse 'Glades were essentially drainage corridors for water over-topping the "rim" of the Everglades basin and running off to sea level, resulting in a broad "floodplain." Groundwater from the 'Glades would also flow out beneath the landscape, through the porous karst, and at such volumes that freshwater springs offshore were common in certain areas.

3. vegetation - The transverse glades were a diverse blending of habitats, or an "ecotone," ranging from freshwater "wet prairies" and swamps, to brackish mangrove marshes. Unique "freshwater tidal marhes," connected to and influenced by tides but having very low salinities on average, were also common.
Plant guides: 2a-2l.

4. urban overlap - Cities overlapping with the historic extent of the transverse glades tend to be in Broward and Miami-Dade Counties. Following the inland route of the rivers mentioned above roughly outlines some of these areas.

brackish mangrove marsh

freshwater tidal marsh

wet prairie glade in cypress swamp

03. uplands

historic orientation

Between the Everglades basin and coastal estuaries lies a north-south ridge of relative elevation composed of a series of limestone and fossil sand dune "relicts." These strips of higher ground, hardly discernable as ridges at all in some cases, formed millennia ago, long before the Everglades, when sea levels were much higher than they are today. Where ancient waves once washed over beaches far inland of today's coast, reefs and sand dunes grew and accumulated, eventually becoming stranded as sea levels dropped with the onset of the ice ages. The fossilized remains of these habitats define the south Florida "uplands" today.
In the recent past, upland habitats differed greatly between the north and south of the region. To the north, deep sand deposits supported pine flatwoods and scrub. To the south, the rocky substrate of fossilized limestone and tropical climate produced the highly diverse and unique "rockland" habitats found in Miami-Dade.

modern orientation

Historic upland habitats were among the most amenable to early settlement as they were the highest elevation areas and generally devoid of difficult wetlands. Transit corridors like the first railways and early iterations of US-1 followed the north-south upland ridges, and the early urban centers expanded outward from these areas. Today, these areas are some of the most developed in the region, supporting an outsized portion of the region's heavy industry.

01 marlberry (*Ardisia escallonioides*)
02 gumbo limbo (*Bursera simaruba*)
03 american beautyberry (*Callicarpa americana*)
04 satinleaf (*Chrysophyllum oliviforme*)
05 pigeon plum (*Coccoloba diversifolia*)

06 silver palm (*Coccothrinax argentata*)
07 redberry stopper (*Eugenia confusa*)
08 spanish stopper (*Eugenia foetida*)
09 strangler fig (*Ficus aurea*)
10 shortleaf fig (*Ficus citrifolia*)

11 black ironwood (*Krugiodendron ferreum*)
12 false tamarind (*Lysiloma latisiliquum*)
13 wax myrtle / bayberry (*Morella cerifera*)
14 muhly grass (*Muhlenbergia capillaris* var. *capillaris*)
15 myrsine / collicwood (*Myrsine cubana*)

16 sword fern (*Nephrolepis exaltata*)
17 south florida slash pine (*Pinus elliottii* var. *densa*)
18 resurrection fern (*Pleopeltis michauxiana*)
19 wild coffee (*Psyschotria nervosa*)
20 live oak (*Quercus virginiana*)

21 cabbage palm (*Sabal palmetto*)
22 miami palmetto (*Sabal x miamiensis*)
23 saw palmetto (*Serenoa repens*)
24 paradise tree (*Simarouba glauca*)
25 mahogany (*Swietenia mahagoni*)

26 thatch palm (*Thrinax radiata*)
27 florida gama grass (*Tripsacum floridanum*)
28 coontie (*Zamia integrifolia*)

Pine Rockland Guild
marlberry (*Ardisia escallonioides*)
american beautyberry (*Callicarpa americana*)
satinleaf (*Chrysophyllum oliviforme*)
silver palm (*Coccothrinax argentata*)
false tamarind (*Lysiloma latisiliquum*)
wax myrtle / bayberry (*Morella cerifera*)
muhly grass (*Muhlenbergia capillaris* var. *capillaris*)
myrsine / collicwood (*Myrsine cubana*)
south florida slash pine (*Pinus elliottii* var. *densa*)
cabbage palm (*Sabal palmetto*)
saw palmetto (*Serenoa repens*)
florida gama grass (*Tripsacum floridanum*)
coontie (*Zamia integrifolia*)

attributes

1. soil - Upland soils are distinct between the north and south. Deep gypsum sand deposits are common to the north, although limestone "hardpans" and clay deposits are also common. To the south, limestone and marlstone mixed with sand is common.

2. water table - In uplands areas farther north, deep sandy soils without a limestone hardpan or strong groundwater influence from the Everglades generally have a water table far removed from the surface. To the south, the water table can vary considerably but is usually much closer to the surface.

3. vegetation - Uplands were largely defined by expansive stands of fire-thinned slash pine (*Pinus ellіotii*) and saw palmetto (*Serenoa repens*) interspersed with dry prairies. Scrub habitats are also common in more northern areas. The hardwood and pine rocklands specific to the southern end of the region are distinct from the pine flatwoods and hardwood hammocks to the north, supporting biodiversity found nowhere else. **Plant guides: 3a-3d.**

4. urban overlap - Few south Florida cities only contain historic uplands. In Palm Beach County, large portions of Jupiter, Lake Worth, and Boynton Beach are uplands. In Broward, most cities north of Oakland Park and east of the Turnpike have uplands. Uplands in south Broward and Miami-Dade are highly variable.

pine flatwoods

dry prairie & hardwood hammock

04. coastal estuarine

historic orientation

South Florida's "estuarine" landscape includes lagoons and tidal creeks with brackish waters, common along Florida's extensive coastline. Just east, the "coastal ecotype" faces direct ocean exposure. Both zones, typical of subtropical regions, host a rich diversity of plants and animals, though many were once far more abundant. At the southern end, Biscayne Bay is a vast estuary shaped by freshwater from the Everglades, forming a unique ecotone where protected and exposed conditions mix. Historically, beaches and barrier islands shifted with storms, forming or closing inlets after major events.

modern orientation

Like uplands, elevated coastal areas were early sites of development, with waterways serving as key transit routes. Today, only scattered parks and preserves remain of these historic ecotypes. A few urban shorelines were left natural, but most habitats have been dredged, filled, and built over, making them exceedingly rare. This extensive development has led to critical erosion along many regional beaches.

attributes

1. soils - While sandy soils dominate Florida's coasts, silts, clays, shell hash, and other types also appear locally. All are shaped by complex physical and biological interactions in tidal environments.

2. water table - Groundwater near tidal lands is thin, saline due to saltwater intrusion, and closely tied to sea level. In elevated areas isolated from other freshwater sources, a freshwater lens may form from rainfall alone.

3. vegetation - South Florida estuaries are mainly mangrove forests, though less saline marshes once thrived too. Coastal beaches support diverse salt-tolerant upland plants, naturally zoned by salt exposure and ocean proximity.
Plant guides: 4a-4h.

Coastal South Florida beaches host a rich variety of salt-tolerant upland plants, naturally zoned by salt exposure and distance from the ocean. Plant guides: 5a-5f.

4. urban overlap - Many South Florida cities along tidal waterways were once estuarine ecotypes, while areas east of barrier island ridgelines are coastal. Large parts of some cities were built by dredging and filling wetlands, often forming "finger" canals and island neighborhoods.

Beach Dune Guild
cocoplum (*Chrysobalanus icaco*)
seagrape (*Coccoloba uvifera*)
beach croton (*Croton punctatus*)
blanketflower (*Gaillardia pulchella*)
beach sunflower (*Helianthus debilis subsp. debilis*)
sea lavender (*Heliotropium gnaphalodes*)
spiderlily (*Hymenocallis latifolia*)
railroad vine (*Ipomoea pes-caprae*)
beachelder (*Iva imbricata*)
bitter panicgrass (*Panicum amarum*)
shoreline purslane (*Sesuvium portulacastrum*)
saltmeadow cordgrass (*Spartina patens*)
sea oats (*Uniola paniculata*)

Beach and beach dunes are used for foraging and nesting by beach mice, shorebirds, and sea turtles, especially Loggerhead (Caretta caretta).

01 gumbo limbo (Bursera simaruba)
02 beach bean (Canavalia maritima)
03 cocoplum (Chrysobalanus icaco)
04 seagrape (Coccoloba uvifera)
05 silver palm (Coccothrinax argentata)

06 beach croton (Croton punctatus)
07 blanketflower (Gaillardia pulchella)
08 sevenyear apple (Genipa clusiifolia)
09 firebush (Hamelia patens)
10 beach sunflower (Helianthus debilis subsp. debilis)

11 sea lavender (Heliotropium gnaphalodes)
12 spiderlily (Hymenocallis latifolia)
13 railroad vine (Ipomoea pes-caprae)
14 beachelder (Iva imbricata)
15 wild sage (*Lantana involucrata*)

16 beach peanut (*Okenia hypogaea*)
17 erect pricklypear (*Opuntia stricta*)
18 bitter panicgrass (*Panicum amarum*)
19 cabbage palm (*Sabal palmetto*)
20 inkberry (*Scaevola plumieri*)

21 saw palmetto (*Serenoa repens*)
22 shoreline purslane (*Sesuvium portulacastrum*)
23 necklace pod (*Sophora tomentosa*)
24 saltmeadow cordgrass (*Spartina patens*)
25 bay cedar (*Suriana maritima*)

26 thatch palm (*Thrinax radiata*)
27 sea oats (*Uniola paniculata*)

tidal creek & mangrove forest

maritime forest

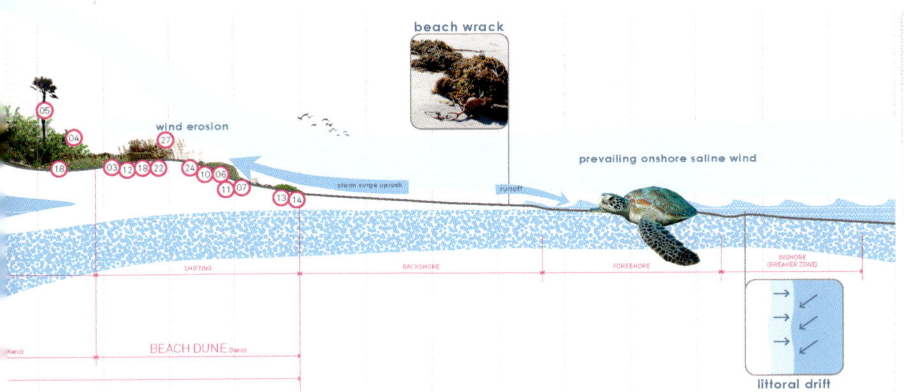

climate

South Florida's climate is subtropical to tropical and defined by a wet-dry seasonality, rather than the four seasons of more temperate regions. The wet season ranges from June to September with an average of about seven inches of rain per month while the dry season ranges from November to April and averages at less than three inches per month. Although it typically rains somewhere within the greater region every day, it only rains at any given location about fourteen to eighteen days per month on average, meaning that a majority of south Florida's ample rainfall occurs in relatively small bursts. Afternoon thunderstorms and tropical storms/hurricanes during the wet season account for roughly two-thirds of south Florida's total annual rainfall. While it is difficult to predict exactly how this system will shift with a changing climate, estimates point to a drier future for the region, with the climate shifting to one resembling the Florida Keys - dry on average, but also experiencing more frequent tropical storms and greater localized runoff rates, a combination that will make both landscape and infrastructure design increasingly challenging.

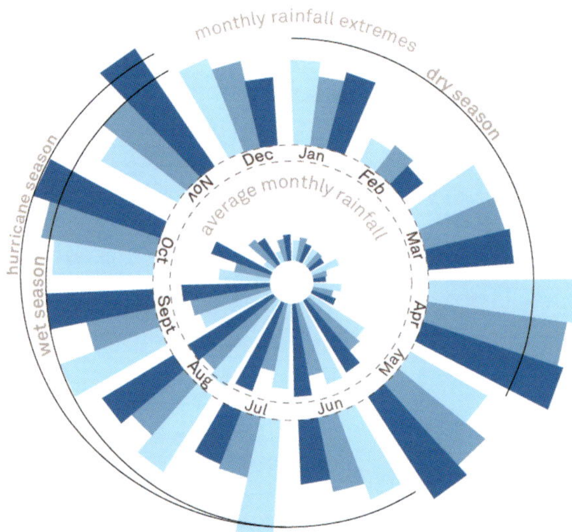

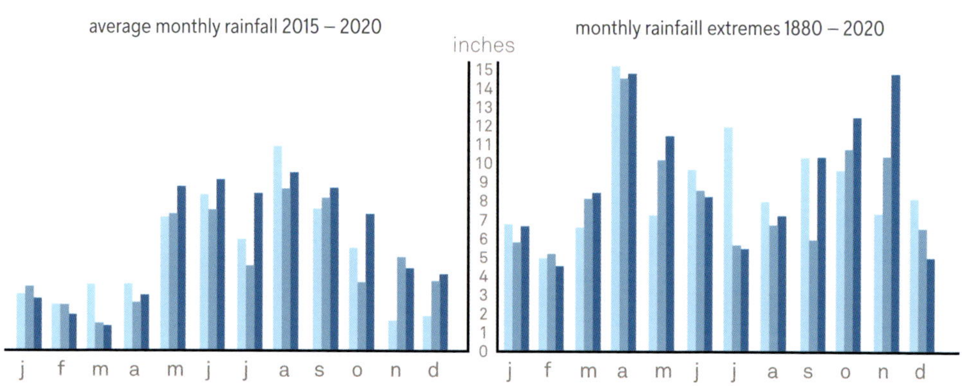

January is considered "peak" dry season, July "peak" wet season, while May and October are transition months and are less predictable. Despite these average patterns, relatively large volumes of rainfall can occur at any time of year, and for any given year, often by way of ocean-induced weather. For example, "nor'easter" storms will occasionally blow down from the north Atlantic during the dry season months.

January / beginning of dry season

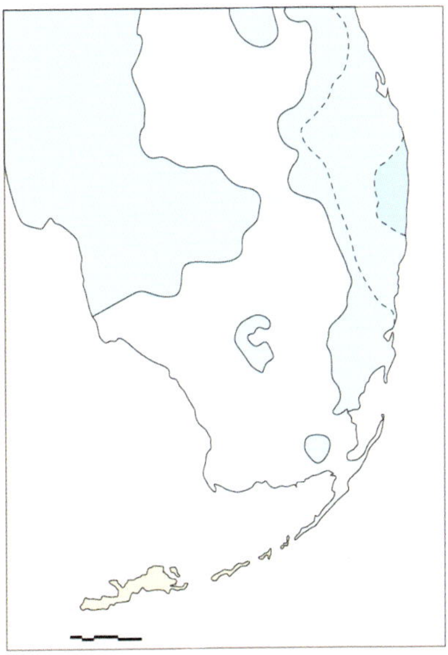

May / transition to wet season

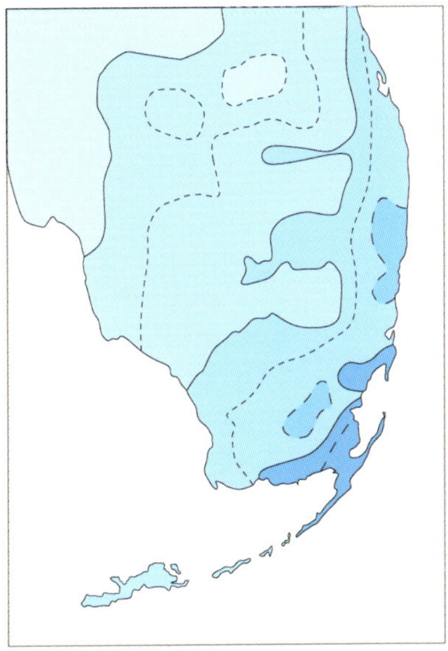

July / beginning of wet season

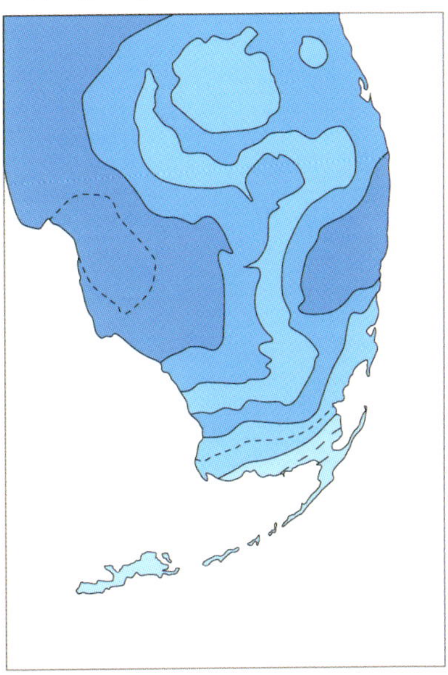

October / transition to dry season

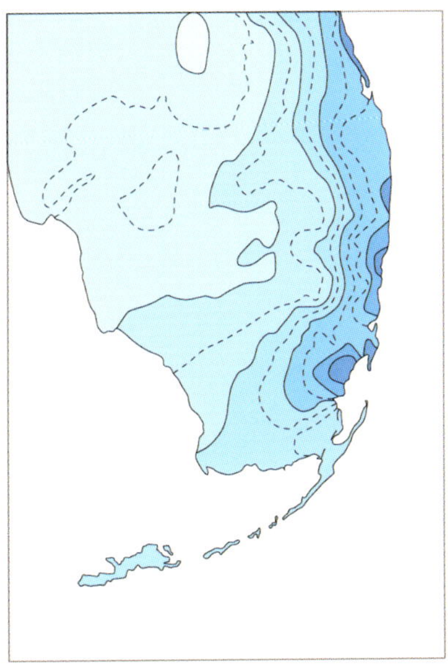

tidal cycles

Tides in southeast Florida follow a "semi-diurnal" cycle with two, roughly equal-sized high tides and two, roughly equal-sized low-tides each lunar day (twenty-four hours). In most years, the relative position of the Earth, moon, and sun cause sea levels to rise twenty-four inches above the normal range between the months of September and November, resulting in "King Tides." Various elevation benchmarks can be set according to the average heights of key points in the daily tidal cycle (e.g, low tides and high tides) and these metrics can have important implications to designs, especially on shorelines.

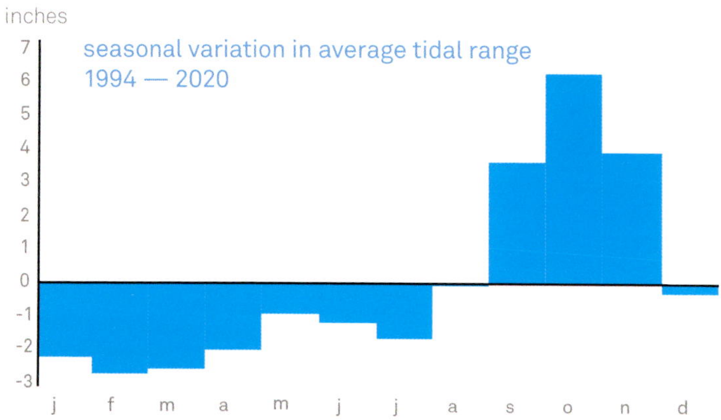

temperature

Wet season months are associated with the highest average and extreme temperatures, with the compounding influence of high relative humidity also at this time making these months in south Florida among the most uncomfortable in the nation. Some estimates predict climate change could cause the region to experience a 2.7°F increase in summer high temperatures within the next fifty years, which could result in an increase of temperatures above 95°F by as much as seventy-five to eighty days per year.

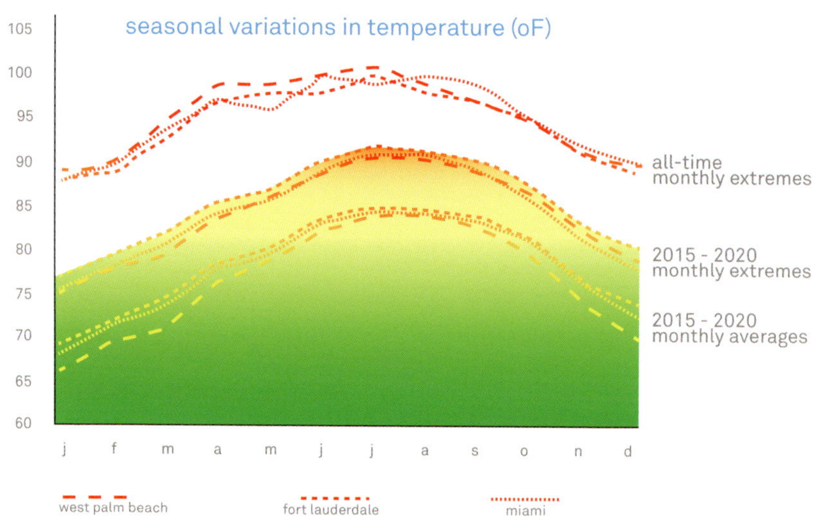

design storms

While it is difficult to predict storms, historic rainfall records can help to estimate the likely frequency, duration, and distribution for rainfall events of a certain magnitude. Such hypothetical events are called "design storms" and are critical to informing stormwater management and infrastructure design as a metric for estimating "peak flows."
Design storms are often referred to by their frequency, or "return rate," however, this nomenclature can be misleading, especially given the changing climate. For example, a design storm with a "100-year" return rate (often called a "100-year storm") is not a storm that occurs every one hundred years but, rather, a storm with a 1 percent chance of happening any year, and could occur multiple years in a row. It is also important to remember that rain and tides can combine. A three-day, twenty-five-year design storm is the recommended minimum, which is a three-day long event with a 4 percent chance per year.

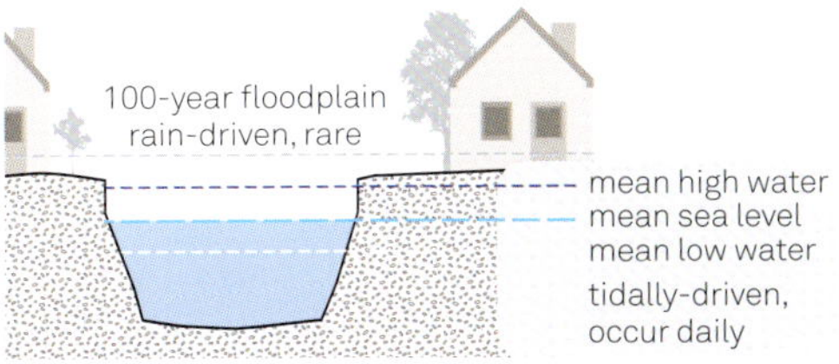

Design in south Florida must consider water elevations related to both tides and rain – generally, these compound most during September – November.

mild storm | 1-day, 5-year storm
1-day event; 33% chance/year

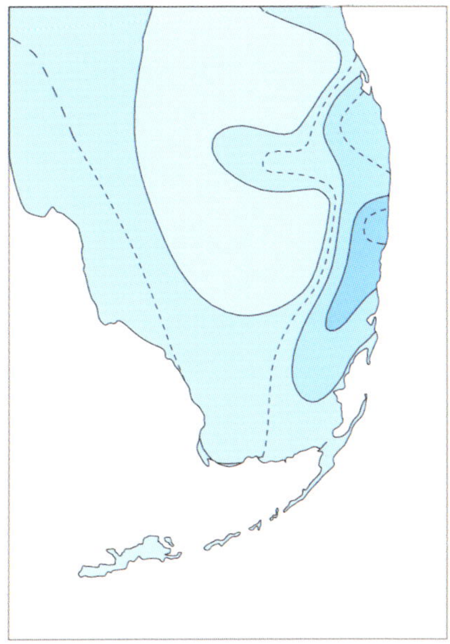

moderate storm | 3-day event; 4% chance/year
3-day event; 4% chance/year

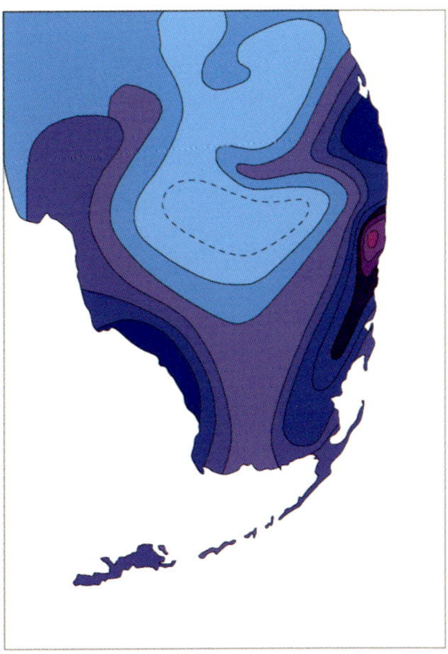

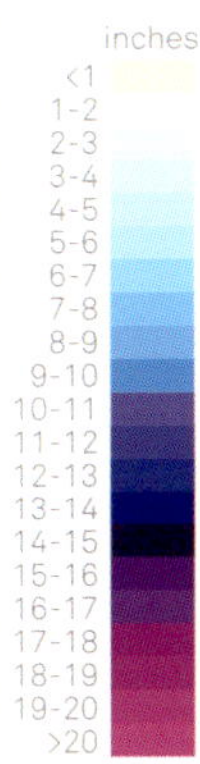

severe storm | 3-day, 100-year storm
3-day event; 1% chance/year

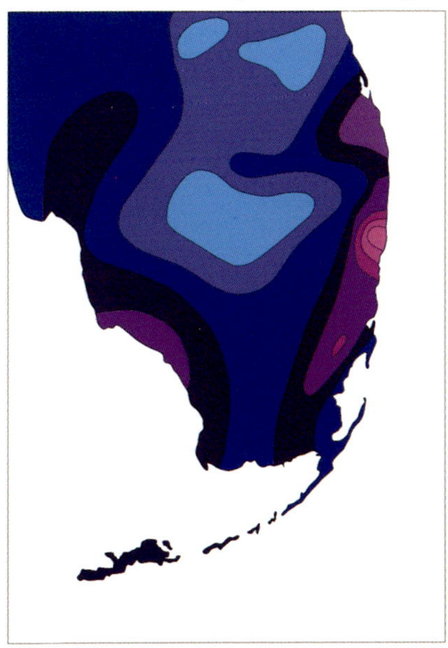

regional soils

The native soils of south Florida, particularly those within the greater Everglades basin (pictured in map), are considered "geologically immature," having only formed within the past few millennia as sea levels rose and fell. Understanding soils is critical to many aspects of adaptive design, but especially to green infrastructure, as the soils found in any given area will dictate the permeability of the landscape (how fast water can drain from the surface into soil) and which varieties of plants can be recommended.

While soil constituencies and distributions in urban areas today are likely to differ considerably from the historic soils featured here, having been replaced by and/or amended with fill material, aggregates, and human-generated debris, understanding soil history for a location of interest can provide invaluable insight to low-impact landscape design and planning.

Organic "muck" soils (top) and urban sand/gravel/ limestone "fills" (bottom) are both very common soiltypes to urban south Florida and are both challenging to work with, but will also require very different nature-based responses.

everglades basin

1 - everglades muck/peat - These soils are very poorly drained and mostly consist of fine organic material (decaying plant matter) often underlain by marl/limestone. These are generally mildly acidic, saturated with water, and lack oxygen in their natural state – support "hydric" habitats such as swamps and marshes.

2 - sandy soils - Soils to the north and along much of the coast throughout the region tend to be dominated by gypsum or calcareous sands mixed with loam. The quality of these soils varies, with some areas presenting deep sand deposits that drain rapidly and others with shallow deposits, high water tables, or are underlain by subsoil clay or limestone "hardpans" that prevent drainage – support "mesic" or "xeric" flatwoods and scrub.

3 - rockland soils - "Rockland" refers to areas where the soils are extremely thin, often featuring a layer of sand or sandy loam, underlain by deposits of marl and/ or lime rock that are frequently exposed at the surface. These poorly drained, alkaline soils are associated with the southeastern-most portion of the region - support an array of unique habitats found nowhere else on Earth.

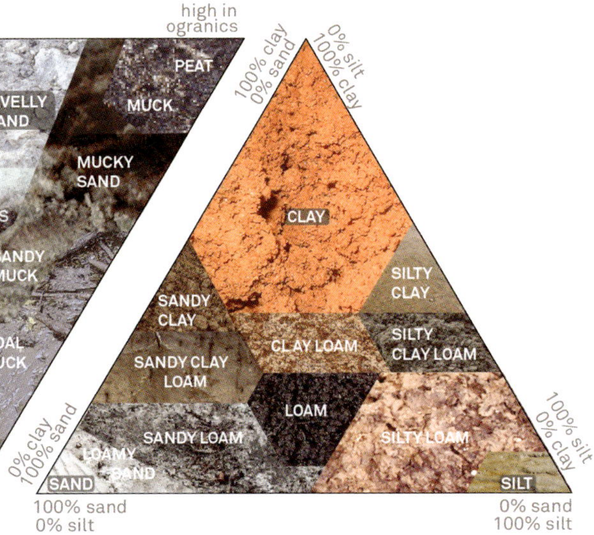

Many of the most common soil textures to south Florida are the "geologically immature" products of wetlands from the relatively recent past. These soils are difficult to define within the the classic soil texture pyramid but can be thought of as adjacent to it, instead aligning by criteria relevant to local wetlands.

The classic "soil triangle" demonstrates how soil texture can be defined as a spectrum of alignment with respect to the mixing of three prevailing soil constituents: sand, clay, and silt. "Loam" tends to have an even mixture of all three but also commonly includes some organic matter. "Sandy loam" is very common to south Florida.

soil drainage classes	description	example soil types	habitat soil moisture
very poorly drained hydrologic soil group D	water drains so slowly that standing water remains at or near the surface for most of the year unless artificially drained, soilis usually anoxic - ponding is typical	muck, peat, fine sand, silty-clay, wet marls, areas with subsoil clay/gley layers, areas with subsoil limestone "hardpans"	hydric
poorly drained hydrologic soil groups A-D	water drains slowly such that standing water remains at or near the surface for much of the year but is not permanent and drains somewhat at dry periods - ponding is common	mucky sand, silty loam, fine sand, wet rockland, dry marls, urban fills, shallow sand or loam deposits, areas with subsoil clay/gley layers	
well drained hydrologic soil groups A-D	water drains from surface readily but not rapidly, saturated soil is common at depth but not anoxic (lack oxygen) - ponding is uncommon	sand, loam, sandy loams, dry rocklands, sandy calcareous soils	mesic
very well drained hydrologic soil group A	water drains from surface very rapidly and saturated soils are rarely present even at depth, often defined by coarse-textured and/or "shallow" soils - ponding is rare	sand, gravel, gravelly sands, shell hash, dry marls/rocklands, deep fine sand/sandy loam deposits	xeric

historic plant communities

As south Florida experienced one of the first of its many major development booms in the 1940s, ecologist John Henry Davis set out to produce the first comprehensive map of vegetation communities in the region. Thanks to this and similar efforts at that time, today we have an invaluable snapshot of the natural greater Everglades from a period in history when systematic drainage of the basin was well underway but before the landscape had been completely cleared, leveled, and paved. While understanding climate patterns and soils is critical to developing resilient green infrastructure, nothing is quite as instructive to nature-based solutions as native plant communities.

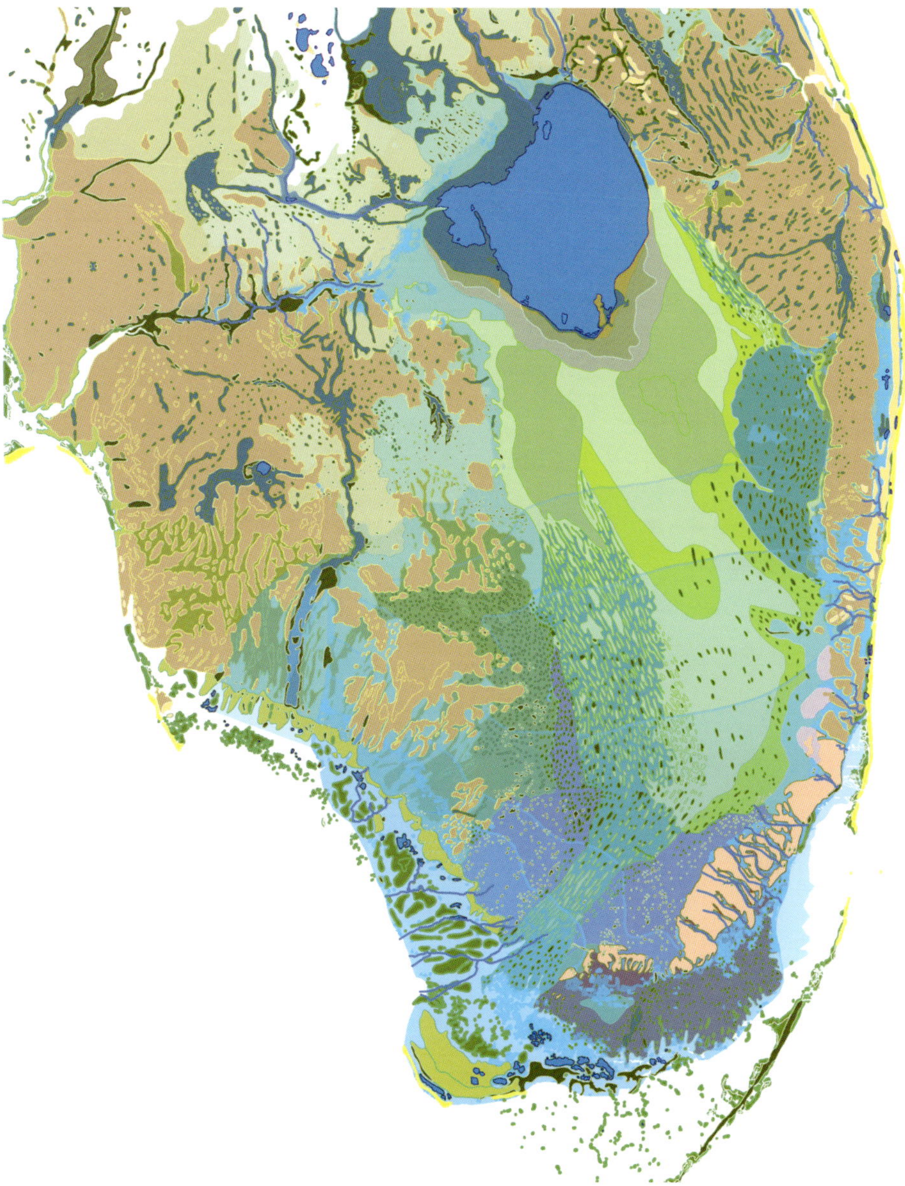

coastal-estuarine

By the late 1940s, most coastal areas in south Florida had already been developed to some extent. Still, portions of natural coastal habitat remained, including beach dunes with full plant community zonations and mangrove swamps alongside "salt prairies." Coastal freshwater inputs were greater then.

coastal riverine floodplains

South Florida's coastal rivers likely experienced marked seasonal fluctuations in water levels pre-Everglades drainage and channalization, featuring wide, marshy floodplain areas along their banks, like those seen in the image at right of the Miami River. Trillions of gallons of wet season water historically exited the eastern flank of the Everglades basin through channals known as "transverse sections of Everglades" or "the transverse glades." So much water historically flowed over and beneath this karst/rockland south Florida landscape that freshwater springs and marshes commonly out to the coast and even offshore.

map legend

- coastal dunes
- pine flatwoods & scrub
- saw palmetto scrub & dry prairie
- pine rocklands
- Miami pine forest
- hardwood forest
- cypress swamp
- freshwater marshes
- sloughs, ponds, rivers, & lakes
- dense sawgrass
- patchy-dense sawgrass
- sawgrass-wax myrtle scrub
- ridge & slough landscape
- tree islands & sawgrass marsh
- inland wet prairies
- coastal wet prairies
- Everglades marsh prairie
- southern coastal marshes
- salt prairie
- mangrove forests & swamps
- fringing mangrove islands

wet prairies & the transverse glades

Farther inland, the transverse glades also existed as "fingers" of wet prairie habitat penetrating upland pine and hardwood islands or "hammocks." These seasonally inundated grasslands surrounded by forest were called "glades ." Today, these low-lying areas have since been developed but are still prone to flooding and sea level rise issues.

land of fire & water

The occassional landscape "disturbances" of wildfires in the dry seasons and floods/hurricanes in the wet seasons defined the historic habitat structure and complexity of south Florida, resulting in "ecotypic" plant communities with species highly adapted to distinct sets of environmental conditions.

the evolving south florida water story

Industrial efforts to "drain the Everglades" began in earnest as early as the late 1800s and continued for decades, only succeeding after millions of dollars in systematic federal investment were made available in the aftermath of several deadly hurricanes. This culminated in the "Central and Southern Florida Project," which is still considered one of the world's largest and most complex water control systems, and which allowed the rapid development of the coasts that followed and continues to this day.

But by the 1990s, managers began to realize that wholesale drainage of the Everglades was not without consequences. Development of the interior for sugar-cane, suburban sprawl on the coasts, and construction of roads/levees bisecting what remained of the Ever-glades flow has taken a collective toll on the region's watershed, having far-reaching impacts on ecosystems and water quality.

Today, billions in federal investment are being spent to undo much of what was done with the original Project. The South Florida Water Management District (SFW-MD) and others have the unenviable task of balancing the often conflicting needs of reinstating the historic flow to the Everglades, thereby restoring much of its ecological function, while simultaneously bolstering drinking water reserves and providing flood control for the rapidly growing coastal populations.

As climate change progresses, the coastal cities have become increasingly reliant on the Everglades to recharge aquifers, however, intermittent drought-years and flood years, as well as the complexity of the system itself, make this very challenging indeed. Presently, there are several large-scale projects planned to promote the regional sustainability of the watershed, including giant surface reservoirs, "Aquifer Storage and Recovery" wells, widened canals, and new Stormwater Treatment Areas.

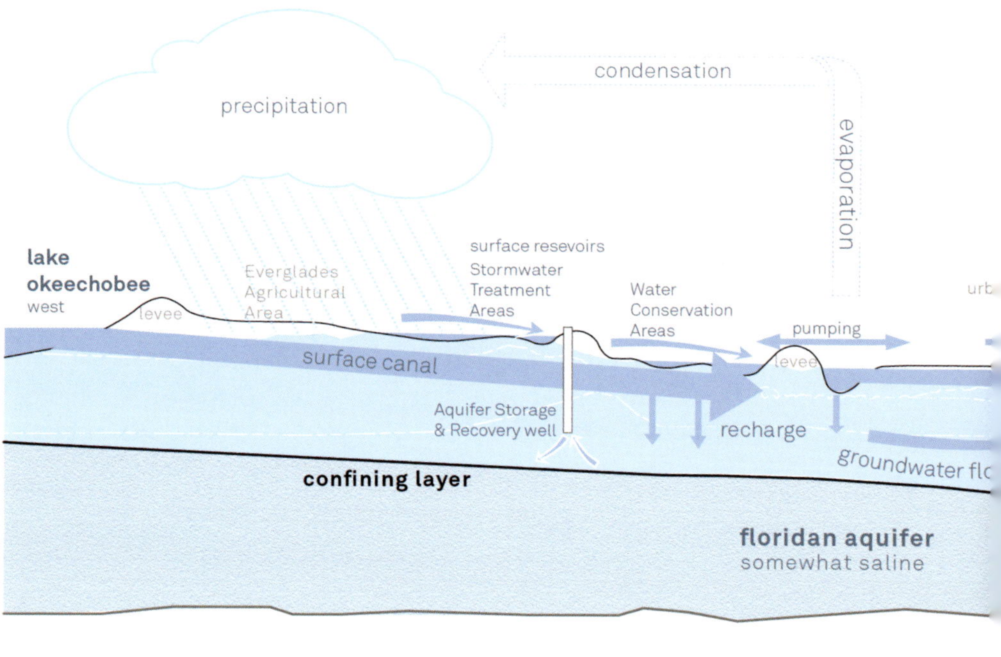

the historic watershed

Wet season excess would spill out from Lake Okeechobee as sheetflow, through the Everglades basin, and drain to tide, either east through the "transverse glades," or south to Florida Bay. Trillions of gallons also flowed out through the porous limestone geology.

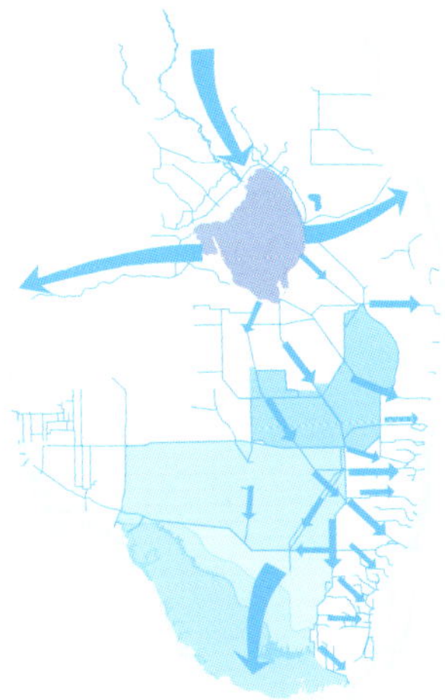

the modern watershed

Lake Okeechobee is encircled by a massive levee with excess water being discharged to estuaries on the East and West Coasts. Water is channeled through large canals, some of it treated for pollutants and recharged to the aquifer along the way within remnant tracts of the Everglades known as "Stormwater Treatment Areas" and "Water Conservation Areas," respectively. Large pumps and subsidiary canals farther help to store and move excess runoff in urban areas. Dams along major canals near the coast, known as "Salinity Control Structures," maintain a regional head pressure that promotes aquifer recharge and discourages saltwater intrusion. The Everglades basin itself is at a slightly higher elevation than much of today's urban coast.

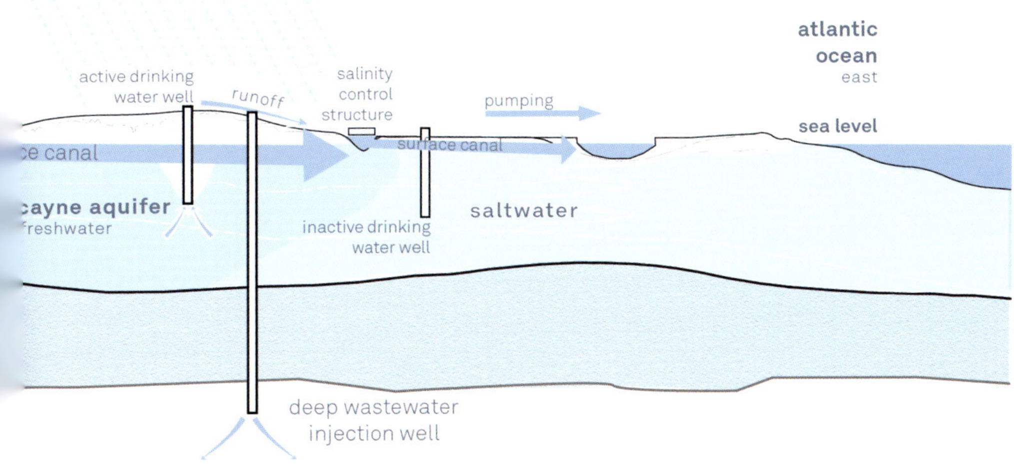

infra–
structure

"the infrastructure in place today was built for a climate that no **longer exists**"

Jeffrey Huber

infrastructural menu

legend

00. relevant scale(s)
01 - buildings only
02 - buildings to blocks
03 - parcels only
04 - parcels/shorelines
05 - parcels to neighborhoods
06 - blocks to neighborhoods
07 - street/shore to blocks
08 - street/shore to neighborhoods
09 - sub-regional to regional
10 - coast region only
M - modular

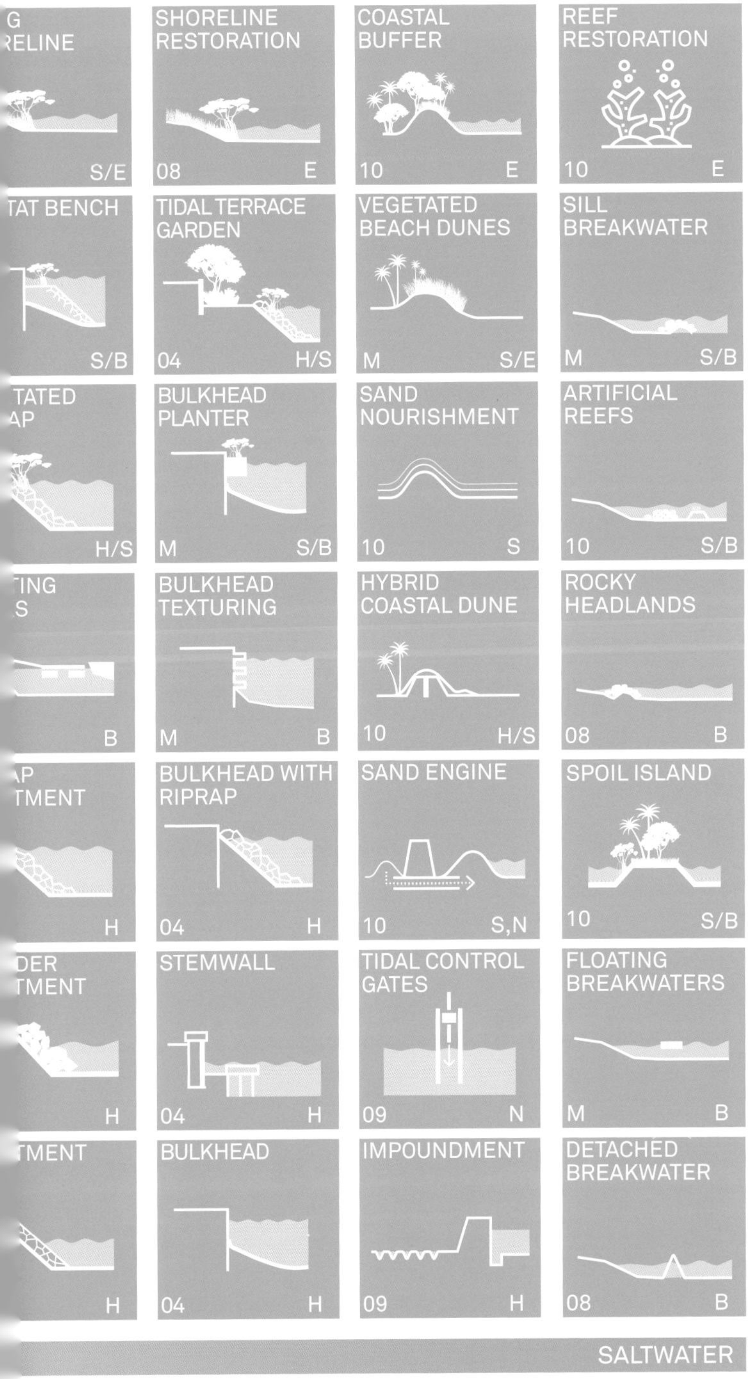

X. infrastructural focus
E - ecological
D - detention
R - retention
C - conveyance
I - infiltration/exfiltration
R/E - bioretention
S - soft stabilization
H - hard stabilization
H/S - hybrid stabilization
S/E - nature-based stabilization
B - breakwater
S/B - hybrid breakwater
N - network enhancement

floodplain management

Urban flood control infrastructure functions as a network of individual elements, ideally connected together across scales and political boundaries through strategic policy and design to create cohesive systems of management. Generally, stormwater and shorelines are distinct but, as sea levels rise, designs will experience increasing overlap as stormwater receiving areas lose capacity to a tidally elevated water table and as increased compound flooding incites more shoreline failures. Gravity-driven drainage facilities will be challenged as conventional approaches to pollution control reliant on pipes and stabilization reliant on armoring will provide increasingly expensive and less cost-effective levels of service with each passing decade. Every aspect of built landscapes will need to be reassessed in order to design a livable and resilient future.

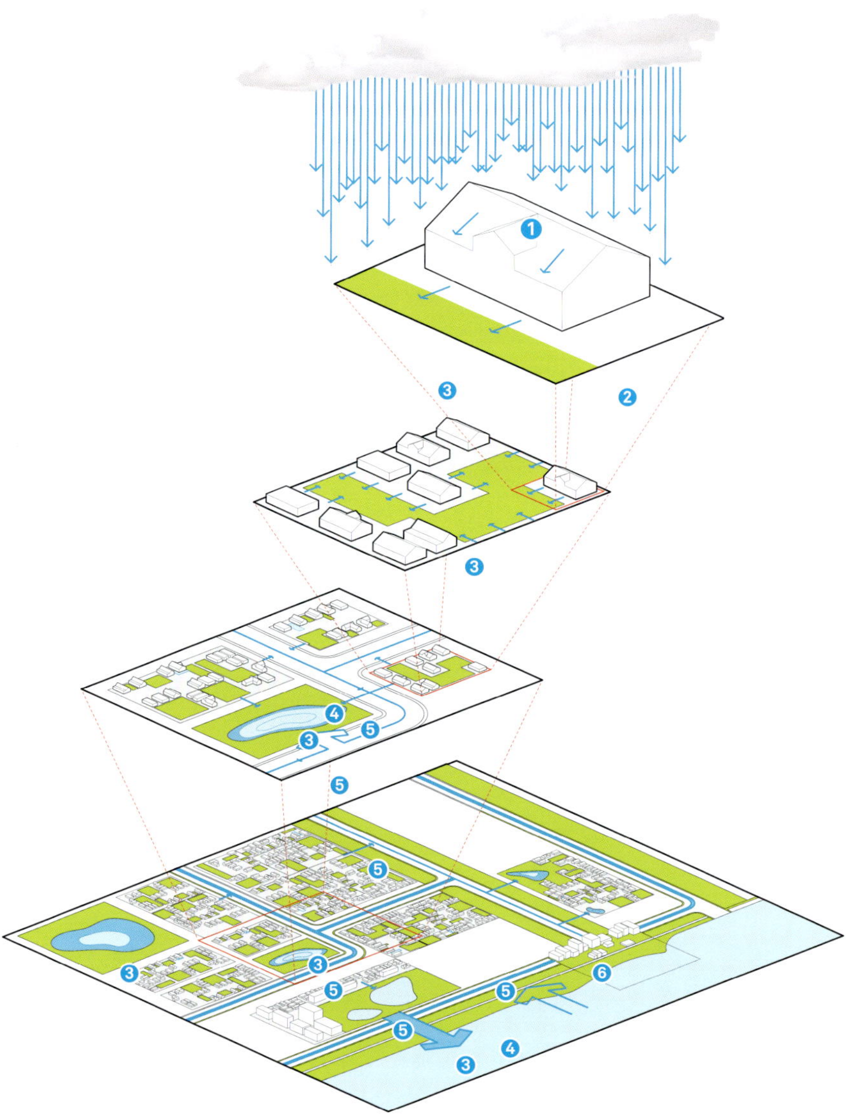

1 - building catchments
Building rooftops represent a sizable share of the impervious surface in urban areas - this is often where urban runoff issues begin.

2 - paved catchments
Streets and other paved surfaces accumulate stormwater runoff and convey it downstream.

3 - receiving areas
Runoff generated by urban catchments is discharged to stormwater treatment areas and/or nearby waterways.

4 - canal conveyance
Most of urban south Florida relies on extensive networks of surface canals to safely convey both rain and tidal floodwaters.

5 - water control structures
Working in tandem with canal components is an equally extensive network of culverts, gates, and pumps used to control flows.

6 - shorelines
Urban shorelines in south Florida are largely armored, thus maximizing land area, but also provide less of a buffer against flooding.

structural vs. non-structural

Management strategies concerning both stormwater and shorelines can be grouped into two, broad-scale approaches: structural and non-structural. Strucutral approaches include the infrastructural "features" themselves (e.g, swales, pumps, seawalls, etc.) as well as key structural improvements and the organization of multiple features into a single network. Non-structural approaches include nature-based and urban design solutions that can reduce runoff volume, mitigate peak discharge, facilitate groundwater recharge while simultaneously reducing flood risk for local residents and improving quality of life. Both approaches are equally valuable, but it is imperative that non-structural approaches are always considered first during design as they may negate the need for structural measures, saving on costs and environmental impact.

non-structural design elements

stormwater

disconnect impervious areas
Redesigning existing neighborhoods by increasing their total pervious area reduces runoff velocity and increases infiltration, helping to mitigate both stormwater volume and peak discharge downstream.

cluster development
Encouraging more clustered development and preserving open spaces are urban design solutions that can influence stormwater runoff generation, reduce volume, and mitigate peak discharge rates.

densify development
Encouraging higher density development with high-rise buildings, and discouraging low-density development, can directly reduce runoff volumes by reducing the total area of impervious surfaces.

redesign streets
Removing or reducing certain aspects of streets, such as curbs, reducing the number of lanes with "street diets," and/or reducing the number of streets/their total amount of surface area can greatly reduce runoff.

redesign buildings & common open spaces
Designing buildings with smaller footprints or elevating foundations provide opportunities for increasing pervious areas. Continuous corridors design of shared open spaces similarly encourages infiltration.

improve existing networks & maintenance
Improving the function of basic structural components in an existing network, such as storm drains or storm ponds, can greatly improve the performance of the network, mitigating potential issues.

ordinances, credits, education & policy
Regulating certain urban activities and educating urban residents about flood risks is arguably one of the most impactful, if difficult, non-structural approaches available. Relevant policies can facilitate the implementation of both structural and non-structural measures through systematic incentives, disincentives, and public communication on key management issues.

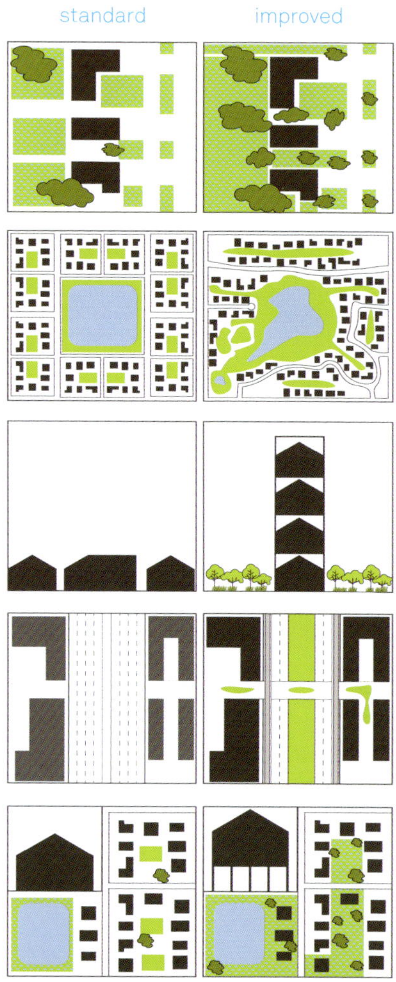

shorelines

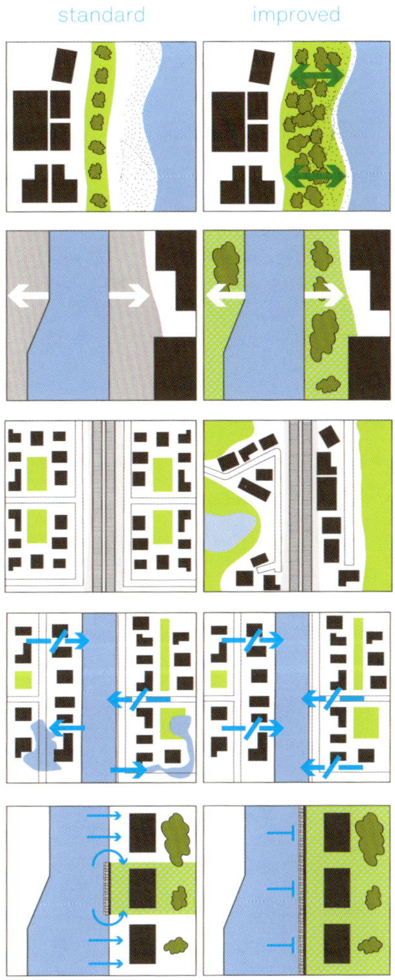

expand aquatic buffers & setbacks

Increasing the distance between built elements (i.e, building foundations) and shorelines can greatly reduce the flooding risk to those elements by providing space for floodwaters to retreat and dissipate.

design coastal easements as "blueways"

Protecting existing open spaces separating built elements from waterways can reduce the likelihood of new, at-risk development – designing such corridors as greenways can farther support adaptive flood management.

orient development along transit routes

Encouraging the clustering and densifying of new development along major transit routes can simultaneously reduce the total amont of development at-risk while also reducing the area that needs structural protections.

integrate tidal control networks at scale

Where there are existing tidal control structures (e.g, tidal check valves) additional measures should be taken so they function as a cohesive whole and effectively protect the greatest scale of area they can by design.

integrate shorelines by elevation

Even if one property does everything right to elevate their shoreline for protection against sea level rise, if the immediately adjacent are not properly integrated, all may flood just as badly if as if no action had been taken.

improve existing networks & maintenance

Improving the function of basic structural components in an existing network, such as improving drainage behind seawalls, can greatly enhance the longevity of shoreline armoring and mitigate failures.

ordinances, credits, education & policy

Regulating certain urban activities and educating urban residents about flood risks is arguably one of the most impactful, if difficult, non-structural approaches available. Relevant policies can facilitate the implementation of both structural and non-structural measures through systematic incentives, disincentives, and public communication on key management issues.

structural design elements

grey stormwater components

flow control

The collection, diversion, and slowing of stormwater runoff using structural features, landscapes, and/or mechanical devices.

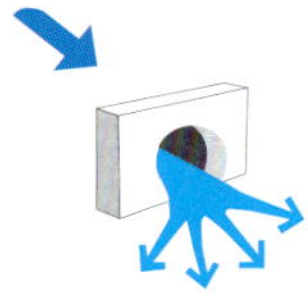

examples

-surface filters
-landscape berms
-culverts

conveyance

The efficient and managed movement of surface waters from points of catchment to points of discharge.

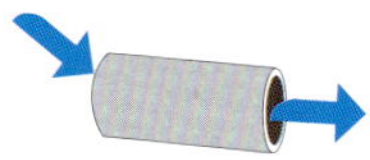

-canals
-pumping stations
-exfiltration drains

detention

The temporary storage of stormwater within ponds, cisterns, underground vaults, or landscape features, attentuates flow rates and encourages sedimentation.

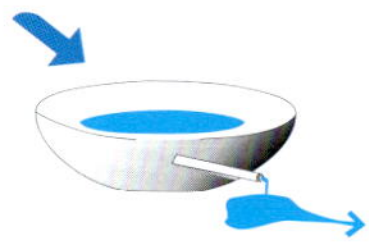

-detention basins
-underground vaults
-stormwater towers
-rainwater harvesting

retention & infiltration

The permanent, on-site storage of stormwater using landscape features that encourage evaporation and/or infiltration.

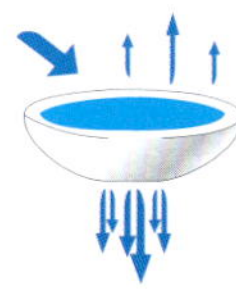

-retention swales
-retention basins
-storm ponds
-infiltration drains

green stormwater components

bioretention

The flow of runoff through planted landscape depressions that encourage infiltration and plant uptake of water, nutrients, and pollutants.

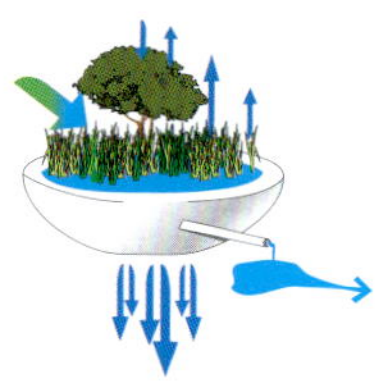

-bioswales
-bioretention basins
-bioretention planters

wetland treatment

The permanent storage of water within and above landscapes specially designed and planted to recieve urban runoff discharge and to bioremediate urban pollution through diverse wetland ecosystems.

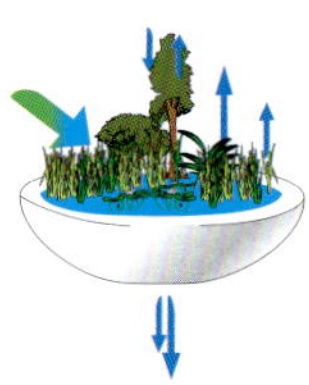

-constructed wetlands
-enhanced storm ponds

impervious surface conversion

The purposeful conversion of impervious surfaces into fully and/or semi pervious surfaces, either through the partial or complete removal of the impervious material or through the covering of the impervious surface with one or more layers of pervious materials – often coupled with extensive plantings meant to improve water retention, bioremediation, evapotranspiration, and/or other environmental co-benefits.

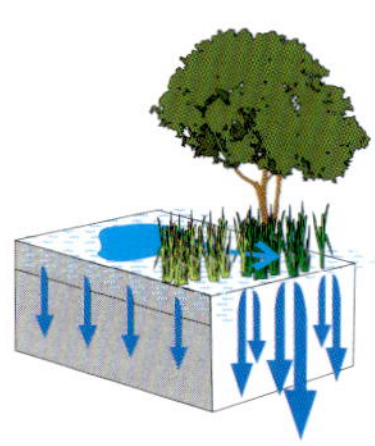

-pervious pavements
-blue-green roofs
-stream daylighting
-impervious surface removals

grey shoreline components

tidal control

The diversion, slowing, and/or blocking of the bi-directional flows associated with the daily changes in water levels and currents that occur in coastal and estuarine areas.

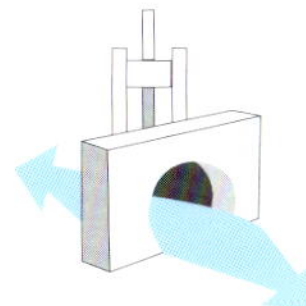

examples

- -canals
- -tidal check valves
- -tidal control gates
- -pumping stations
- -impoundments

shoreline armoring

Covering shorelines with armored facings of hardened materials to retain inland soils and to protect shorelines against erosion from daily average waves and storm surges.

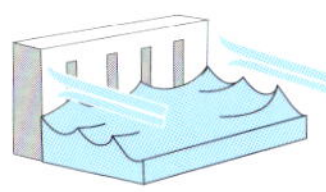

- -bulkheads
- -revetments
- -levees
- -floodwalls
- -stemwalls

breakwaters

Hardened features sited within the water and parralel to shore, designed to dissipate, reflect, and refract incoming wave energy before it reaches shorelines, reducing erosion while helping to accumulate and retain sediments within leeward areas.

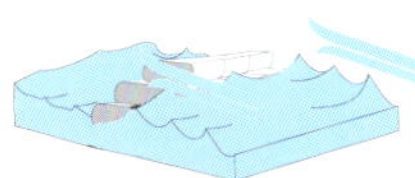

- -detatched breakwaters
- -rocky headlands
- -floating docks
- -bulkhead texturing

green shoreline components

soft stabilization

Stabilization of shoreline sediments and inland areas through the artificial input of natural sediments, dense plantings of specialty vegetation, the siting of minor, naturalistic structures, or some combination thereof.

- -living shorelines
- -aquatic buffers
- -sand nourishments
- -geotextile stabilizers
- -vegetated beach dunes

hybrid stabilization

Shorelines that utilize some combination of armoring, vegetated techniques, and/or breakwaters to leverage the benifits of multiple approaches, retaining shorelines against erosion while providing co-benefits through dense plantings.

- -vegetated ripraps
- -tidal terrace gardens
- -hybrid coastal dunes

nature-based breakwaters

Hardended structural features, sited within and underwater, that reduce wave energies before shore but that also primarily focus on enhancing key ecosystem components (e.g, reefs) through the use of breakwater design.

- -bulkhead planters
- -habitat benches
- -sill breakwaters
- -artificial reefs
- -spoil island breakwaters

tidal wetlands

The storage of tidewaters within specially designed and planted landscapes that can both recieve and discharge the bi-directional flows of tidal currents while improving bioremediation and/or providing other environmental co-benefits.

- -tidal gardens
- -constructed tidal wetlands

stormwater

The term "stormwater" is generally used to refer to runoff volumes generated by rain (made disambiguous here from other types of flooding with the more generic term "floodwater"). The structural features required to adequately handle a given site or area's stormwater will depend on a variety of factors but the most critical will always concern the given area's hydology – how water moves over and through the landscape – and the maximum volume of rain that area can be expected to receive in any given year. Many of these considerations are regionally accounted for by "ecotype."

characterizing site hydrology

Water moves through natural landscapes by a combination of three main mechanisms: 1) "infiltration" – the direct, downward movement and percolation of water through soils, 2) direct interception by vegetation, and 3) "evapotranspiration" – where water is released to the air as vapor through the metabolic activity of plants. Where soils and plants are replaced with impervious surfaces (i.e, urban areas) these natural mechanisms no longer function, resulting in excess runoff. "Urban stream syndrome" is a term sometimes used to refer to the high volumes of runoff that can result from a lack of care to the design of upstream/downstream integrations in urban areas, producing impromtu "streams" of runoff in urban streets and open spaces, spreading pollution and causing other problems.

Where topography and elevation changes are more pronounced, contouring and variations in landscape also influence site hydrology. In certain urban contexts where there are nearby roads or parking lots at higher elevations than a site of interest, for example, it will be critical to consider the likely routes runoff could take into the site. Additionally, the route of runoff out of a site should be considered, not just to prevent undue harm to neighboring areas, but to mitigate the potential for offsite volumes "backing-up," for example, when drainage sewers are overloaded with tidal flooding.

More often than not, site hydrology in urban south Florida can simply be determined by the percent of impervious surface cover there is at any given site. The greater the impervious area, the greater the resultant runoff volume that can be expected.
Where pervious surfaces are present, the next, critical consideration will be the relative permeability of the underlying soils and how quickly ponding water can drain through them. Land-use data are often used as a proxy to estimate these varied considerations.

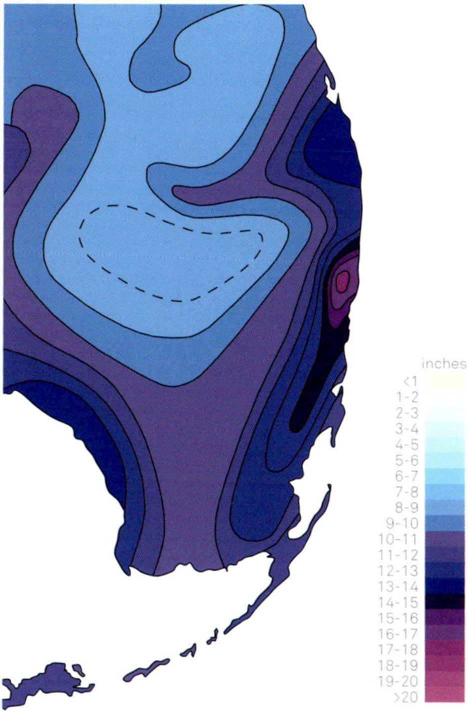

selecting design storms & peak flows

Once site hydrology has been characterized, the next step in determining which structural stormwater features are appropriate for a site is to select a theoretical maximum volume of rainwater that could reasonably be expected to fall on that area during a single storm event. The theoretical maximum volume a feature and/or network is designed to handle is called its "peak flow", and the hypothetical storm events that produce peak flows are called "design storms."

The SFWMD recommends using at least a three-day, twenty-five-year design storm (shown in map to left), which can produce over eighteen inches of rainfall in some south Florida areas. This means that a stormwater feature and/or network must be designed to handle at least eighteen inches of rainfall within any three-day period that has a 10 percent chance of happening in any year. Volumes derived from design storms represent the upper limit and maximum amount of volume stormwater features/networks must be able to recieve, but designing to handle more is recommended.

storm frequency	storm magnitude	annual probability	recurrence interval
very rare	*severe storm*	*0.2%*	*500 yr.*
rare	*major storm*	*1%*	*100 yr.*
		2%	
		4%	*50 yr.*
freqeunt	*minor storm*	*10%*	*25 yr.*

design storms & climate change

As the global climate changes, the historical rainfall patterns that underpin design storms may become less relavent. In the future, the entire design storm convention itself may give way to an alternative more adaptable to climate change. Regardless of conventions used, and while it is impossible to know exactly how conditions will change, we can be fairly certain that our region will shift toward a drier climate on average while also experiencing larger and more frequent storm events. This means that a more resilient design approach would be to utilize at least a three-day, one hundred-year storm. Many flood insurance entities and local municipalities have already adopted one hundred-year storms as an improved standard. While designing for larger storms will increase costs associated with structural stormwater management, it will help to ensure that flooding risks are mitigated while also potentially contributing to reductions in flood insurance premiums. Ultimately, stormwater feature design is a balance between risk reduction, cost, and regulatory mandates, with each of these potentially varying by site.

pollutants & treatment volumes

The Clean Water Act of 1968, mandated by the EPA and locally enforced by the FDEP, requires certain land-uses that impact water quality to limit the total volume of pollutants they release into water bodies via runoff. The total volume of any harmful pollutant allowed into a given watershed and/or water body via stormwater is referred to as the "Total Maximum Daily Load," and this quantity is continually reassessed and updated by the FDEP for each regulated pollutant and water body, respectively. Since most of the many urban pollutants, ranging from heavy metals to nutrients to sediments, are associated with runoff from impervious surfaces and other human land uses, the FDEP has streamlined the regulation of these daily loads to simply mandating the treatment of runoff volumes. In this way, any project or develoment that creates a significant amount of impervious area will likely be required to treat a corresponding volume of its runoff using one or more approved features. Each feature, in turn, has a pre-determined "Required Treatment Volume," and this volume is often the most stringent regulatory requirement for stormwater features in place.

"facilities" & online/offline networks

Stormwater features function best when networked together into cohesive systems, and how this is done influences designs. In this manual, multiple features networked as a single system are referred to as "facilities." Elsewhere, and with respect to pollutants and treatment volumes, connected features are often called "treatment trains." In that context, these have important design and regulatory considerations distinct from single features. For the purposes of this work, and concerning stormwater specifically, "facility," "network," and "treatment train" are roughly synonymous. "Flow-through" systems, where the total volume that enters one feature moves directly into the next, are called "online" facilities. Designs that have some features retain all or most of the "first-flush" of rain (a specified volume of water that first enters a facility during a rain event), and only overflows to the greater network when that volume has been exceeded, that set of features recieving the first-flush is called an "offline" facility. Both online and offline facilities have important uses in stormwater management but require distinct design considerations. Bioretention features can be used in either online or offline facilities, but the overall design and total number of flow control and pre-treatment components required to integrate them will differ by each. Generally, bioretention features are more often used as components in offline facilities as this can make their network integration simpler and because these features are often diffusely spread across landscapes.

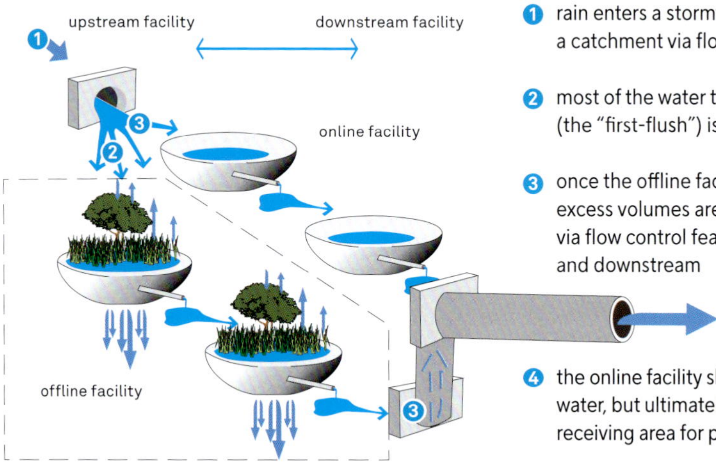

1. rain enters a stormwater network from a catchment via flow control features
2. most of the water that first enters (the "first-flush") is sent to an offline facility
3. once the offline facility reaches capacity, excess volumes are sent to an online facility via flow control features sited both upstream and downstream
4. the online facility slows and spreads the stormwater, but ultimately conveys it to a waterway or receiving area for permanent "discharge" (disposal)

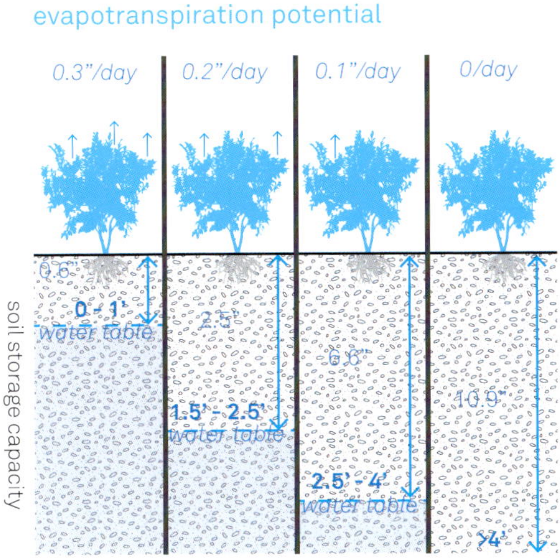

managing water with landscapes

Most landscape stormwater facilities and features rely on the ability of underlying soils to store excess surface waters (i.e, retention). A soil's storage capacity is dependent on the rate that water can infiltrate through it and the depth to the underlying water table below from the soil's surface. For facilities and features that include plants (i.e, bioretention) the evapotranspiration rate of plants is also largely determined by the relative depth to the water table. Although specific criteria can vary among sites (e.g, soil types), the combination of soil storage capacity (i.e, depth to water table x rate of infiltration) and the potential rate of evapotranspiration can both be roughly estimated by simply determining the average depth to the water table for any upland landscape of interest.

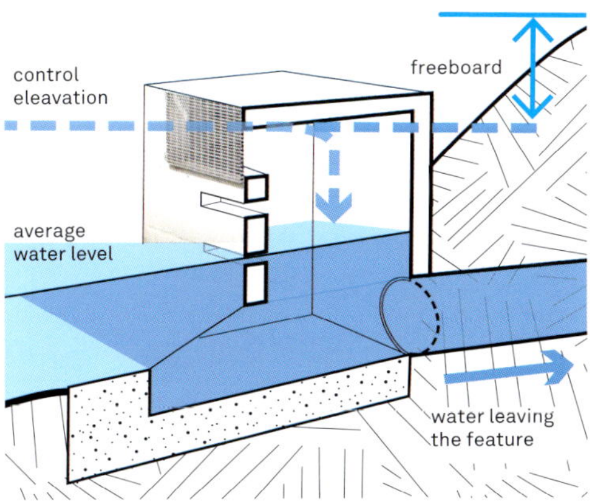

freeboard & control elevations

Many stormwater features either temporarily (i.e, detention) or permanently (i.e, retention) store some volume of water on-site. For landscape features that do so, storage volumes are critical to design and are determined by bank elevations. The difference in vertical distance between an upper design water level and the actual, upland crest elevation of a landscape feature is referred to as its "freeboard." While the uppermost water level will differ among designs, it is often directly correlated to the "control elevation" designed for any given feature. Control elevations also vary by design type, but are generally defined for most landscape features through the use of key flow control features, such as inflow culverts and flow splitter boxes. In practice, the vast majority of stormwater feature designs are dictated by relavent regulations. Required treatment volumes for pollutant mitigation often define feature control elevations while the minimum required freeboard is often set by relavent municipal ordinances, often with respect to elevations determined using a design storm (usually one hundred-year storms, or the "100-year floodplain").

photo credit: UF

flow control

Flow control of runoff is the critical first task in stormwater management. Slowing and spreading runoff flow is critical to decreasing its speed and to determinining the timing and direction of its discharge. The delay of peak flows to reduce downstream flooding is called "attenuation," accomplished with detention. Flow control is also used to reduce erosion on slopes, direct flows through facility connections, and provide valuable pre-treatment by promoting sedimentation and the separation of pollutants and debris.

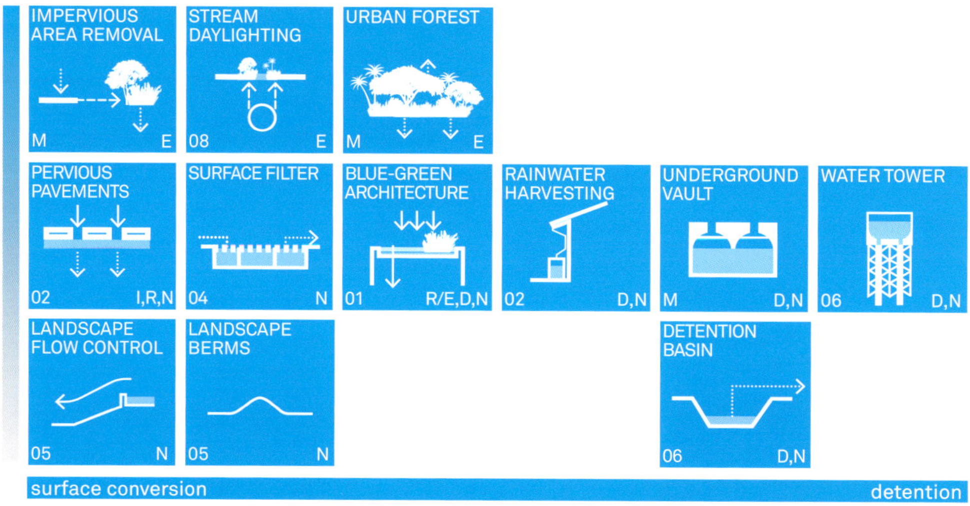

filter strips & level spreaders

Turfgrass lined slopes of 1 to 3 percent grade and/or linear concrete channels sited adjacent to roads, small parking lots, or other impervious areas can be designed and used to slow runoff by promoting an even sheetflow while also providing some initial filtration/sedimentation of runoff. These are useful for connecting landscape features to impervious catchments while adding some upstream pre-treatment capacity. Not suitable for sites adjacent to very large (>80 ft. linear distance) impervious catchments.

photo credit: UF

Flow control is diverse but generally falls into one of three categories: landscapes, detention, and in-line features. Landscape features vary from gutters and check dams to trenches and berms. These are useful for collecting and distributing runoff evenly to facilities while providing pre-treatment. Directing runoff through landscapes, bioretention planters, and blue-green roofs can provide similar benefits. Designs that make creative use of landscapes should be farther explored as flood issues multiply. In-line designs insert into conveyance routes and range in scale from buildings to entire networks. Detention provides meaningful amounts of attenuation, reducing peak flows.

underground vaults

Traditional detention basins are not always feasible in urban settings. These features can be sited underground but will require different design considerations. Unlike exfiltration vaults, detention vaults are closed to ground and do not allow infiltration into soils. For this reason designs must consider hydraulic bouyancy in addition to overhead loading. Unlike detention basins, sedimentation is best provided by upstream pre-treatment features. Pumping may be required.

summary

problem areas addressed	runoff, erosion (pollution)
applicable scales - facilities	varies
infrastructural goals/ outcomes	flow attenuation, erosion control, pre-treatment, network integrations
ecological pairings	varies
architectural setbacks	varies
upstream	flow control
downstream	bioretention, retention, exfiltration, conveyance

cost
attenuation
erosion control
pre-treatment
integration

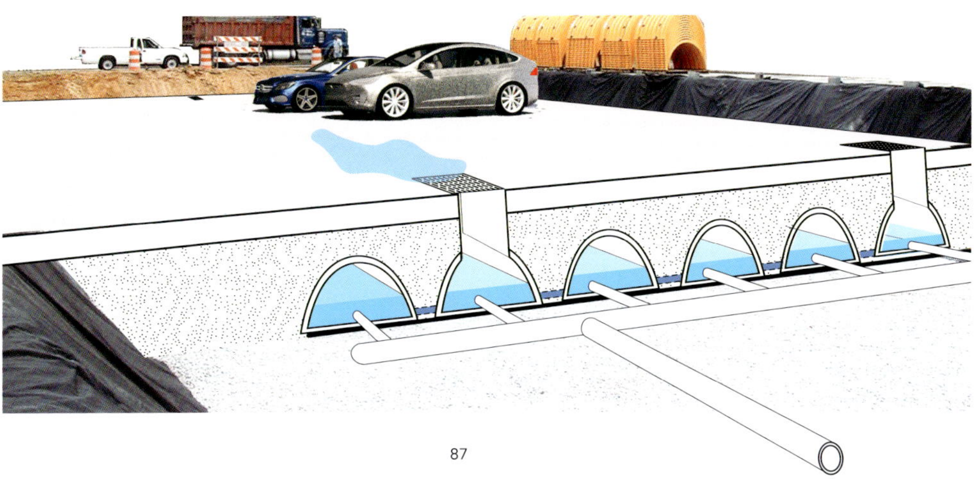

After stormwater flows are controlled within a network, conveyance facilities (e.g, sewer pipes) move water to a point of discharge, often a waterway, for permanent disposal. This conventional emphasis on disposal and the transit of "wastewater" has helped to keep urban areas dry but has also caused and excacerbated a wide array of environmental problems. While rising sea levels will necessitate the increased use of certain conveyance features, others will need to be radically altered and/or replaced.

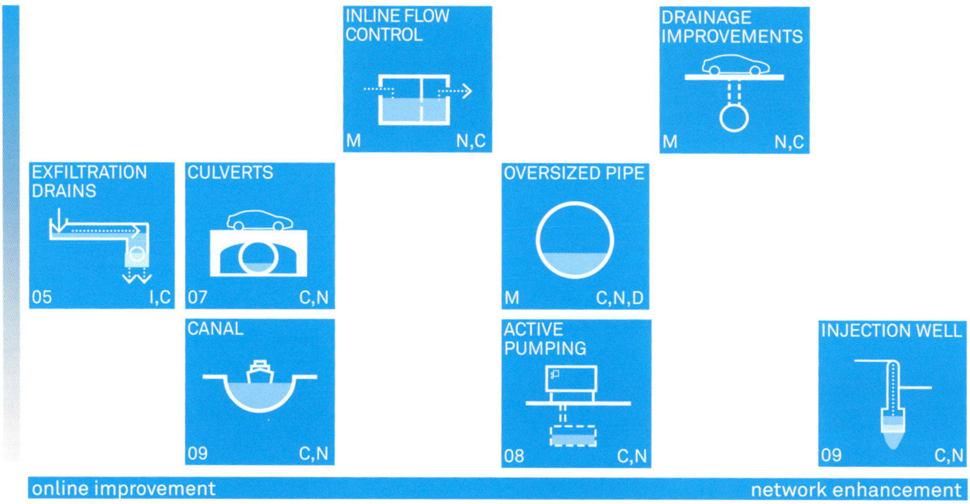

active pumping

Pumping effeciently achieves a wide array of flood volume reduction goals but at great cost as the operation, maintenance, and up-front price of these features can be high. For certain sites and network designs they are required, but this is often a result of poor non-structural management. Still, pumping is the only means for effectively dealing with groundwater flooding and is essential to many facility designs.

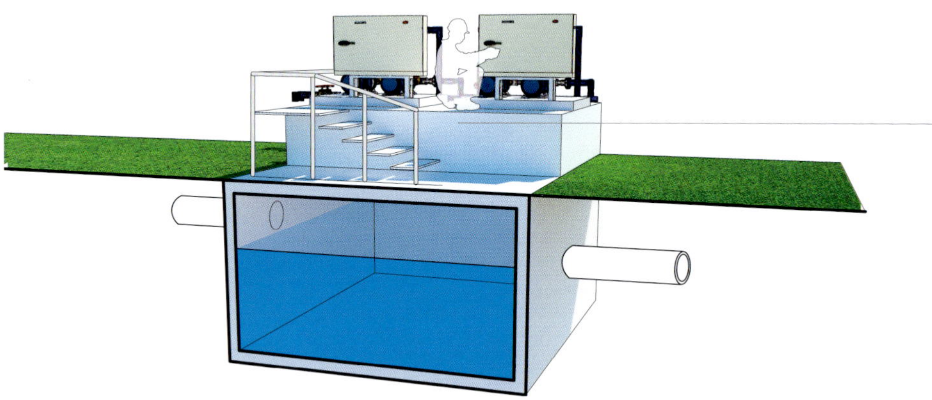

Urban stormwater conveyance systems may need to be redesigned and expanded soon as current capacity is not likely to address the emerging issues associated with sea level rise. In low-lying areas, exfiltration trenches and storm sewer pipes may already be inundated daily by salty groundwater, reducing the performance and longevity of these aging features. While improved non-structural management and urban design should always precede expensive capital improvement projects, when and where improvements are needed, managers and designers should look to increase peak flow capacities and promote more seamless integrations with emerging management strategies, such as urban bioretention features and wetlands.

oversized pipe

Replacing existing stormwater sewer lines with oversized pipes is costly but can eliminate large pressure drops and high velocities associated with smaller pipes during peak flow events. Large pipes can also act as linear detention features, temporarily storing excess water within the pipe itself until peak flows and/or high tides subside. Space, both overhead and underground, as well as installation costs are the main limiting factors.

summary

problem areas addressed	all flood types
applicable scales - facilities	block or greater - online facilities only
infrastructural goals/ outcomes	flow redirection, flow attenuation, network performance, network integrations
ecological pairings	-
architectural setbacks	varies
upstream	flow control, detention, retention, bioretention
downstream	varies

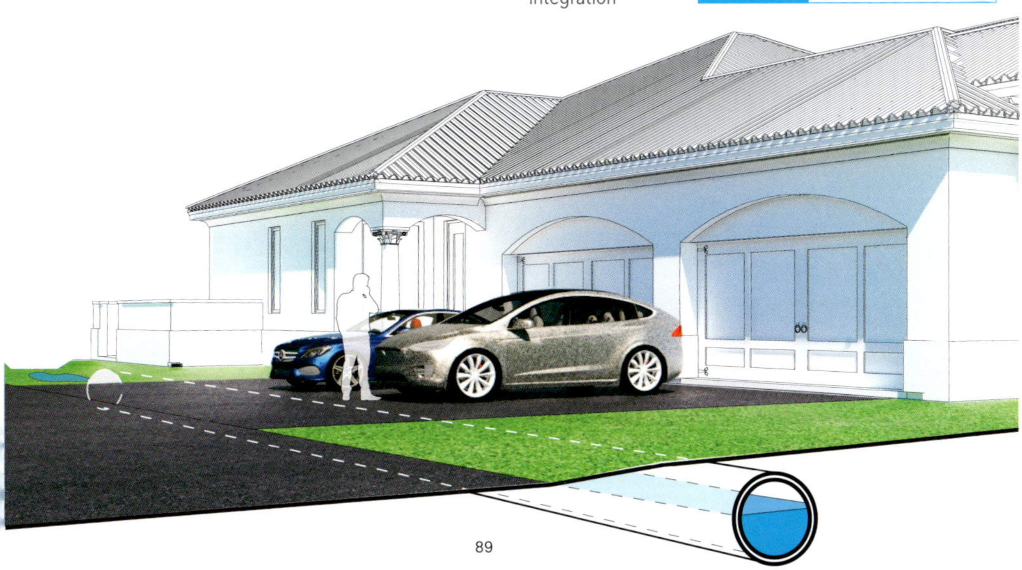

retention & infiltration

"Retention" and "detention" are related concepts that can be easily confused. Retention features provide many of the benefits that detention does but are also designed to permanently store some amount of stormwater on-site. This is generally accomplished with landscape depressions that encourage direct infiltration into soils. "Wet" designs (e.g, ponds) also encourage water to evaporate and/or incorporate growing plants to maximize this effect while providing added co-benefits.

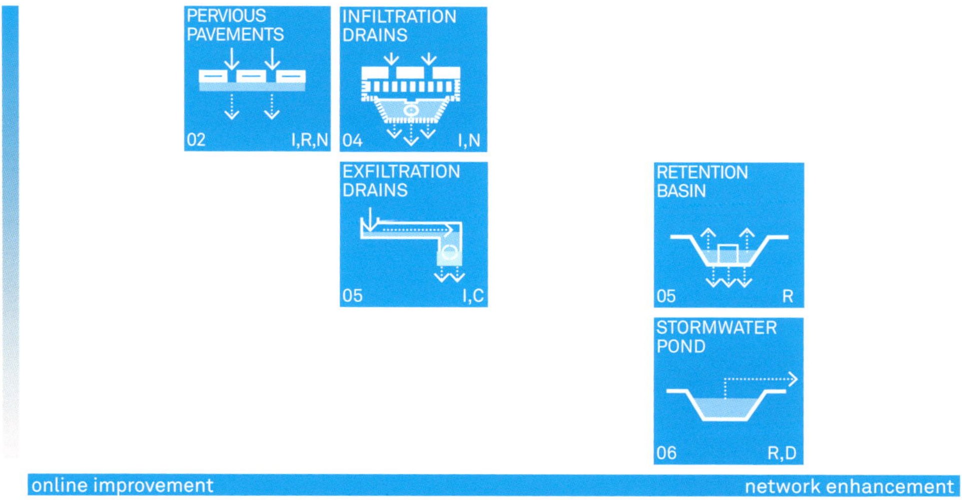

pervious pavement

Pervious paving systems attempt to balance the benefits of both pervious and impervious surfaces. Designs best suited to south Florida include an expanded "reservoir" layer of gravel or sand that maximizes retention storage and infiltration rates. Only suitable for low-traffic, low-density area where native soil infiltration is good. Requires routine maintenance.

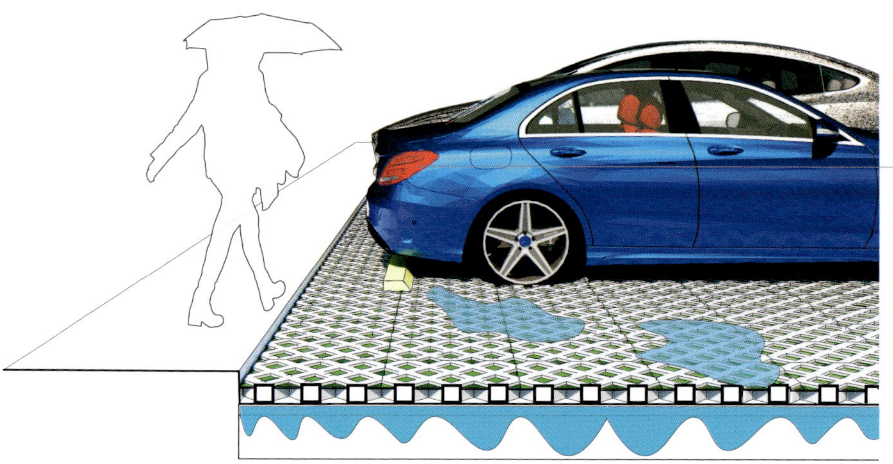

Many retention and infiltration features will become increasingly challenged as a rising water table reduces storage capacities regionally and more frequent flooding causes clogging locally, both of which can greatly decrease facility performance. Therefore, it is highly recommended that facilities incorporating retention also include one or more of the following design aspects: 1) added pre-treatment features upstream, 2) additional freeboard elevation, and/or 3) emergency online overflow routes. While designs like "improved underdrains" and "wet exfiltration tenches" can enhance facility performance in difficult soils, longer-term planning should consider designing retention features that function more like flow-through detention facilities for safety.

infiltration/exfiltration drains

Underground trenches filled with permeable material, often aggregates and perforated piping, are commonly used to improve on-site retention. Infiltration and exfiltration only differ by the mode in which water is delivered to the trench – exfiltration conveys water to a trench from another location through pipes while infiltration drains water to a trench directly from the surface. When infiltration drains are coupled with other features they are called "underdrains," and these are useful for improving drainage rates in difficult soils.

summary

problem areas addressed	runoff, tidal flooding, heat islands, (pollution)
applicable scales - facilities	block or greater - online or offline (varies)
infrastructural goals/ outcomes	on-site storage, water treatment, flow attenuation, flow control
ecological pairings	-
architectural setbacks	30 ft or more
upstream	flow control, detention, conveyance
downstream	conveyance

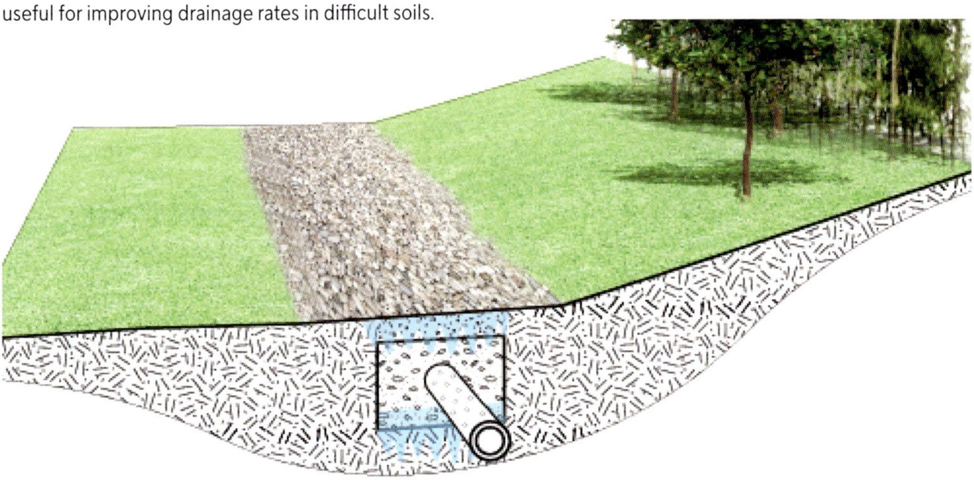

bioretention

When retention designs incorporate dense plantings to provide evapotranspiration, enhance bioremediation, and/or other co-benefits, it is called "bioretention" and requires unique considerations. Because the performance of such features can be highly variable they are often designed as "flow-through" components (i.e, detention) and/or arrayed as offline storage elements within a greater network. The term "rain garden" is synonymous with "bioretention basin," both referring to shallow landscape depressions, but the former is generally only used to refer to smaller-scale features.

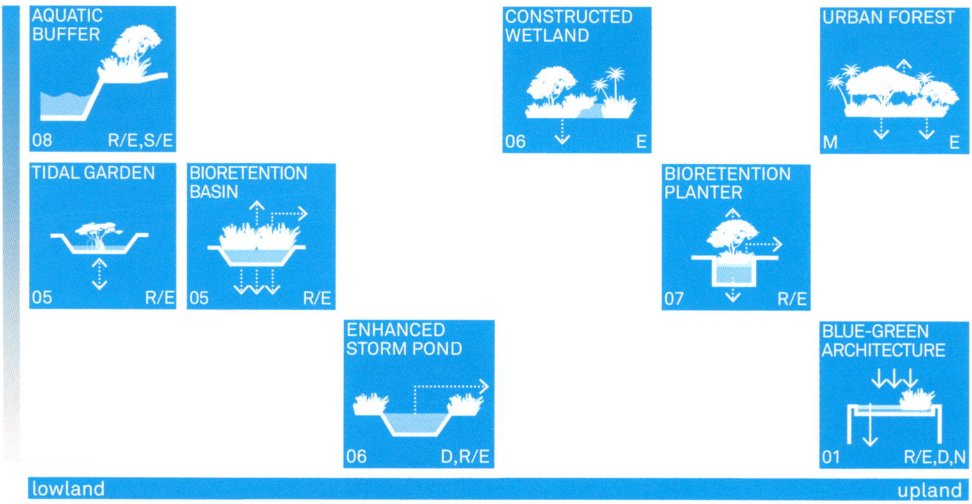

bioretention basin

Both rain gardens and bioswales are examples of bioretention basins and have shared design considerations. These shallow landscape depressions use slopes of 1:3 or shallower to slow runoff, generally from a single, nearby catchment area, while plants and soils treat and store a specified volume. Specialty soils are commonly used to enhance treatment and/or permeability as are "underdrains" that enhance infiltration rates into underlying soils. Soils, runoff distributions, plant selections, and maintenance are critical design aspects to facility performance.

Bioretention features encompass most of the same goals/outcomes that retention-infiltration features do but with a different order to their priority. The emphasis on plants in bioretention is to enhance treatment with bioremediation, evapotranspiration, or to provide other co-benefits (e.g, mitigating heat). As cascading urban-climate problems increasingly affect low-lying south Florida, bioretention provides a compelling option for urban areas experiencing these chronic problems but which also have little available landscape area to implement solutions. However, standardizing performance of these facilities can be challenging and is extremely dependent on proper design and maintenance. See pages for more on bioretention design.

bioretention planter

Bioretention can also be achieved at the micro scale through the use of specialized planters. Design of these varies considerably, which can be beneficial for creating neworks of modular "cells" of interconnected components in tight urban areas, but also problematic where standardized design outcomes are desirable. Planter designs can be either made-in-place or prefabricated, and either open-floor designs that encourage soil infiltration or closed-floor designs that function as micro-detention wetlands.

summary

problem areas addressed	runoff, tidal flooding, pollution, heat islands
applicable scales - facilities	lot and greater - mostly offline (varies)
infrastructural goals/ outcomes	water treatment, flow attenuation, flow control, on-site storage
ecological pairings	guides- fresh: 1a,1a,1a,1a,1a, brackish: 1a,1a,1a,1a,
architectural setbacks	palettes- fresh: 1a,1a,1a,1a,1a, brackish: 1a,1a,1a,1a,
upstream	15 ft or more (varies)
downstream	flow control, detention

canals & the regional network

integrating with today's canal network

Drainage canals in south Florida are ubiquitous and play a vital role in the region's floodplain management. At the heart of this extensive system are several large, dam-like structures sited at key locations along major canals, separating tidally influenced areas from non-tidal waterways farther inland. These dams are known as "salinity control structures," a title referencing the critical function they serve in preserving the region's fresh groundwater supply. While a variety of local "drainage districts" operate and manage many of the smaller, local canals, the SFWMD is responsible for the vast majority as well as for the overall function of the system. When private and local municipal interests seek to integrate with canals in any way, whether for stormwater drainage or shoreline development, it is imperative that the relavent controlling agency and their corresponding regulations for canal right-of-ways are understood and observed. For SFWMD - controlled canals, design considerations will vary most depending on whether the canal of interest is east or west of a salinity control structure.

Generally, regulations concerning right-of-ways are more strict along canals west of the control structures than they are along tidally influenced canals because these inland canals provide a critical conveyance function, recieving most of the runoff from western urban areas and conveying it east, by way of gravity past the salinity control structures, or by actively pumping it past the western boundary levee and into the remnant Everglades. Because the canals west of the control structures need to maximize storage, flow control, and conveyance, and because the control structures themselves are vulnerable to clogging by debris, the District maintains strict rules concerning landscapes along these canals.

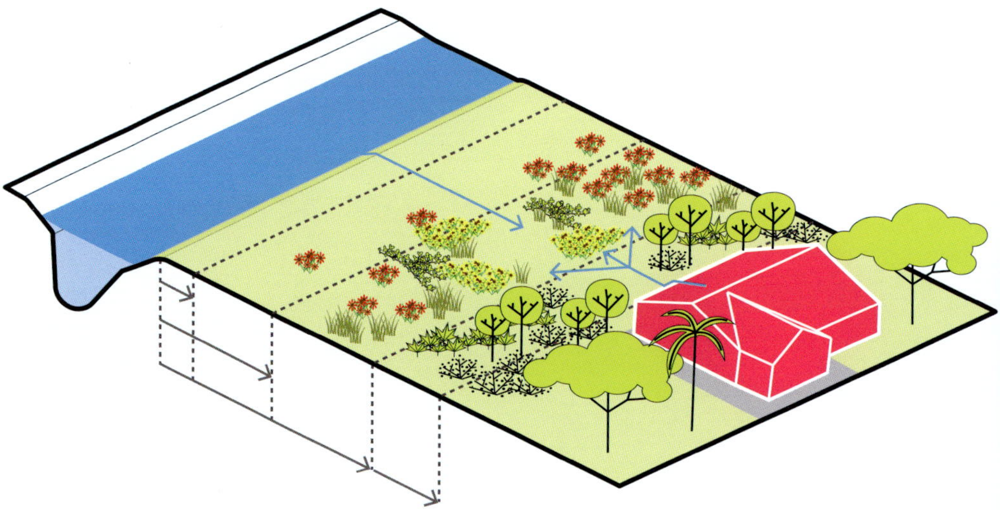

District's list of acceptable landscaping plants categorized by the canal right-of-way zones.

the future of the canal network

The SFWMD, along with a variety of federal, state, and local partners, has begun an extensive, multi-phase process to assess the future of the region's canal infrastructure given the threats posed by sea level rise and a changing climate. While the District is still in the process of identifying "priority basins" and the areas/facilities that are at greatest risk across the region, they have already made several preliminary findings with widespread relavence to future planning and design across the region.

One of the most impactful of these initial findings is that the level of flood protection provided by many of the regionally important canals and pumps is presently inadequate to accomodate the higher groundwater tables, increased tidal elevations, and enhanced storm intensities and frequencies predicted to occur over the coming decades. Given the network's current design, the compounding nature of these increasing flood pressures will likely overload some of these eventually, which in turn is likely to result in more frequent and more intense flooding issues propagating upstream into urban catchments and communities.

all in the same boat

The SFWMD and its local partners have proposed a series of large-scale improvements to counteract these impacts, ranging from expanding canals and installing larger pumps to improving predicitive management technologies to creating new surface storage reservoirs. But in addition to these large-scale facilities, the District and local partners also recognize the importance and potential value of diffuse, nature-based facilities and green infrastructure networks to contribute to regional flood resiliency. However, for these smaller adaptations to be effective at a regional scale, nearly every aspect of the urban environment will need to be reimagined as a place to live with, on, and over water, and every stakeholder, both public and private, will need to contribute where they can and as they can.

architectural networks

storing at the top

The potential for roofs and other architecture to collect and store stormwater in the urban environment is theoretically quite high since architectural surfaces are plentiful in cities. Stopping and/or slowing rain where it falls on buildings can benefit all other networks as rooftops collectively represent the highest point of the urban watershed in south Florida. This potential of rooftop stormwater facilities is an invitation to architects, landscape architects, and designers to reimagine the relatively underutilized margins of built features as multi-functional adaptation spaces, that not only contribute to runoff reduction, but also mitigate heat islands, create uniquely aesthetic recreational features, and improve building insulation, reducing energy consumption and costs associated with internal cooling. However, the obvious challenge with storing rainwater on roofs is that water is heavy, weighing ~10 lbs./ga. While the possibilities are many, in practice, opportunities are often few as retrofitting existing buildings is challenging and expensive while designing new buildings to accomodate appreciable volumes of water can become easily overlooked as most engineered structures represent a complex balance between form, function, and cost. Adding to these existing disincentives are uncertainties associated with design, maintenance, and optimization of outcomes. Not every building need catch all of its runoff to make better use of marginal spaces like rooftops. A variety of other options, and their various combinations, are also available to designers and provide equally valuable benefits compared to conventional roof assemblies. Farthermore, not every building need use the roof to catch and store stormwater as a variety of other architectural surfaces may be used just as effectively.

building facility strategies

cool roofs

Simply designing roofs to have a high solar reflectance can translate to direct heat reduction and energy savings. Insulating roofs with specially designed white paint or thermoplastic can provide cooling benefits similar to green roofs but at much lower initial costs. However, these materials tend not to last as long as green roofs and require complete replacement with time, increasing their long-term cost and life-cycle impact while also not providing any of the various co-benefits associated with green roofs1.

blue roofs

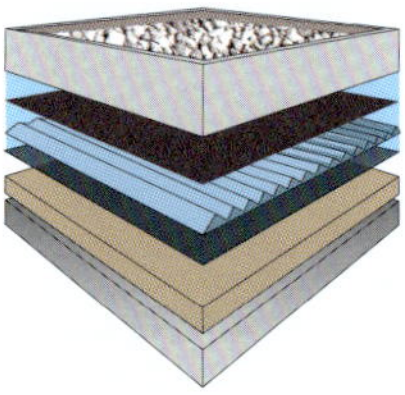

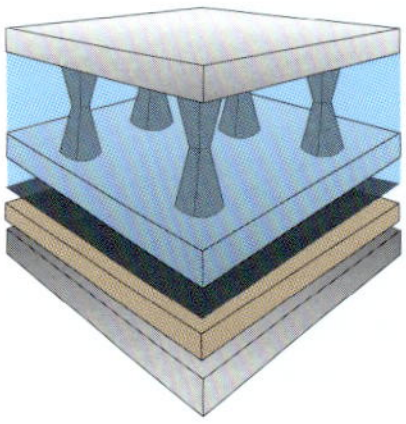

Rainwater can be temporarily stored in shallow basins or modular trays with "rooftop detention" or "blue roofs." These features can attenuate runoff by as much as 34 percent on average and as much as 60 percent for peak flows, reduce local air temperatures and significantly insulate buildings while protecting roof materials from UV radiation. Not having to worry about the health of plants can free designs to incorporate other beneficial uses, like solar panels, but "blue-green" roof designs are also possible.

extensive green roofs

Green roof designs that are not concerned with supporting recreational uses of the roof area and which opt to only grow plants and catch rain are called "extensive green roofs." These are generally easier and cheaper to design, install, and maintain than their intensive counterparts, largely because they feature a single, relatively thin (<6 in.) layer of planting media and a selection of low-lying, hardy plants. These types of roofs can reduce building electricity consumption associated with cooling by as much as 2.2 kWHh/meter2 and retain between 40 and 80 percent of the annual volume of rainfall hitting the roof.

intensive green roofs

Where recreational use of the roof area is desired, and frequent human visitation is expected, designs can become far more elaborate and challenging, but also more rewarding. Nothing is quite as impressive as a lush rooftop garden, and building roofs offer a rare opportunity to gain scenic vantages and refreshing breezes in the otherwise flat south Florida landscape. Since aesthetic considerations are center focus for these designs, it is recommended that blue roof and/or rainwater harvesting elements be directly incorporated to help achieve predictable infrastrucutural outcomes.

other rainwater architecture

While urban rooftops remain underutilized, a variety of other architectural surfaces are even less well realized. Large urban parking garages, for example, present enormous potential, not only as a rainwater catchments, but also as focal points for reducing urban heat islands. Vegetating surfaces on these structures may also be somewhat easier to design due to minimal competing interests and a structural integrity already intended to sustain considerable loads. Smaller, purpose-built architecture in open common spaces is another promising area. Structures designed to act as shade and rain umbrellas for outdoor seating, for example, could easily be designed to capture rainwater as part of a diffuse detention/retention network. These structures could also grow certain species of vining plants, farther adding to their heat and runoff mitigation value, as well as aesthetics.

rainwater harvesting

landscaping with stormwater

Rainwater harvesting can be considered a form of stormwater detention – temporarily storing peak flow volumes for discharge later, as either irrigation or for some other non-potable use. While harvested rain can be used as drinking water with proper filtration and management, this is not recommended in urban settings as rainwater can contain a variety of toxins collected from the air and roof materials. But rainwater harvesting for landscape irrigation presents a synergistic climate adaptation solution that could simultaneously improve regional stormwater management through detention while also supporting regional drinking water reserves by reducing total use. Optimal rainwater harvesting at scale could provide significant cost savings competitive with both reclaimed wastewater reuse and industrial desalinization as a method for enhancing the long-term sustainability of water resources. Regardless of the scale being considered, whether a single-family home or a multi-story high-rise, the essential components and design considerations for any rainwater harvesting system are the same, requiring careful consideration of the catchment area (i.e, the roof size and material), methods for treating the "first-flush" of water coming off of the roof during storm events, and matching storage means and capacities with the timing and volumes desired of end uses.

1 catchment area
For irrigating landscapes, asphalt shingles, new metal roofs, and green roofs are the best catchment materials as they provide water that will not harm plants. Cedar and some tile shingles contain toxic materials that are harmful to plants and soil fungi and may leach into rainwater. Approximately 600 ga. of water can be collected for every inch of rain that falls onto every 1000 ft of roof area.

2 pre-treatment filters
Water coming off of the roof will need to be filtered of larger debris like fallen leaves. This can be accomplished by simple screen fittings mounted into gutters or by specialty scupper boxes utilizing multiple porosities of screen. Larger buildings may want to use more elaborate filtration devices that slow, filter, and treat water in a single step with in-line elements inserted into downspouts, such as vortex filters. No matter the design or scale of these, regular clean-out maintenance will be required.

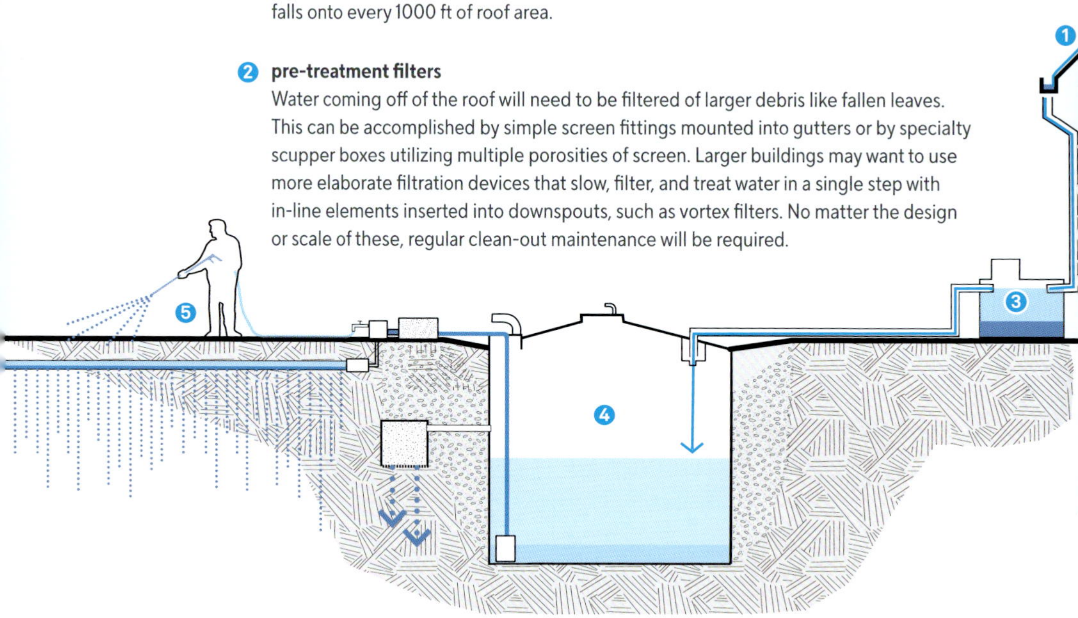

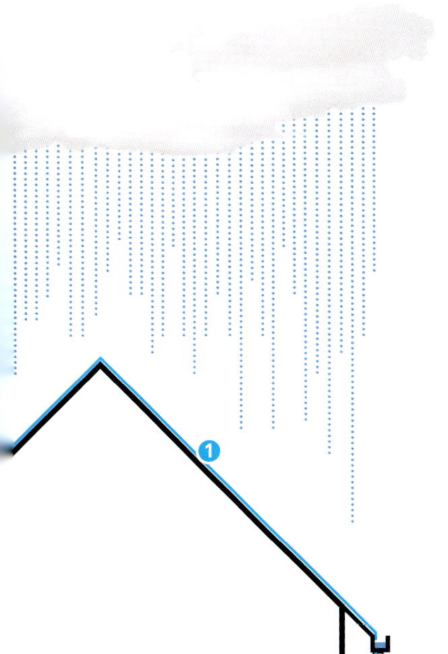

❸ first-flush chambers

Besides larger debris, the initial volume of rainwater coming off of roofs contains a variety of smaller particulates, toxins, and bacteria that can be harmful to the greater system. Diverting at least the first 10 percent of the first quarter inch of rain volume to a first-flush chamber is recommended. These chambers are normally passive designs and utilize gravity to divert initial volumes to a separate chamber. Design of the chamber itself should consider the ease of clean out and maintenance.

❹ storage

Appropriate storage vessels can include a great variety of materials, but all should generally be UV resistant, non-toxic, and relatively opaque so as to discourage algal growth. For single-family homes, 35 and 55 ga. food-grade drums are a popular choice; consider using multiples of these connected together to enhance capacity. Emergency outflow points and pressure relief openings are important to many designs but great care should be taken to prevent the potential ingress of mosquitos and small animals through these apetures. Where containers are fully or partially buried, the vessel must be designed to be bouyant to the upward pressure of groundwater. Small ponds can also be used in a similar fashion to cisterns but will require different design considerations.

❺ end use

Pumps will be useful to most forms of end use and include types that can be placed directly inside of storage cisterns or externally. If the intended end use is irrigation, plan to maximize storage capacity for the dry season by utilizing the largest cisterns possible. Non-potable indoor reuse applications are possible but will require far more elaborate treatment and filtration devices/systems.

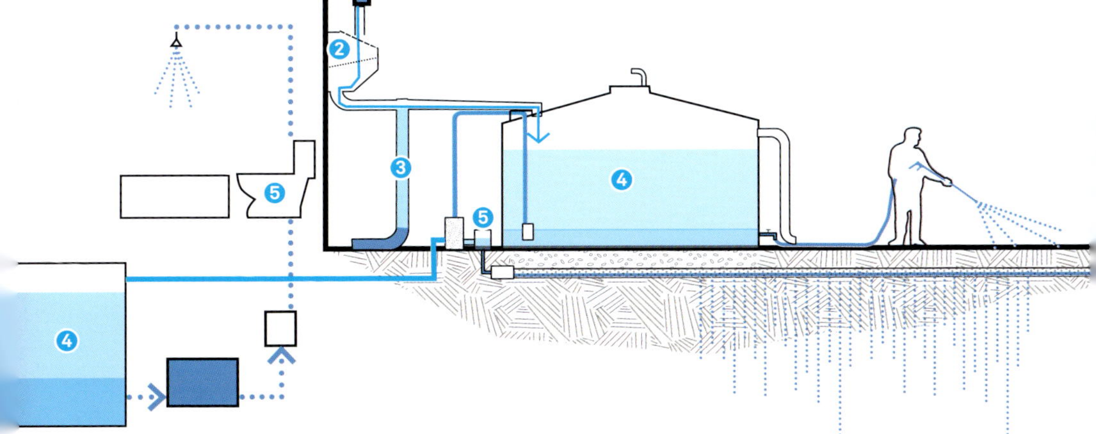

blue-green buildings in FL

combining strategies with design

Blue-green building technologies and the large-scale implementation of building-level rainwater harvesting remains relatively under-developed in urban south Florida. This is likely at least partly due to uncertainties associated with design aspects such as appropriate plant selections and their design, but also to uncertainty regarding their maintenance and expected long-term performance. While these may not assuage every concern nor answer all possible questions, looking to existing designs that have been tried in the region can be instructive for how creative design can be used to overcome many of these uncertainties. A common pattern that seems to be successful among south Florida designs, in particular, is a networked combination of intensive and/or extensive green roofs, rainwater harvesting, and bioretention planters.

Coconut Creek Seminole Casino

This design utilizes a series of filtration boxes, or "biofilters," sited on the wall of a parking garage structure to slow and pretreat runoff from the garage before it enters a series of at-grade cisterns and a wet bioretention planter with native plants. Excess volumes are discharged to a nearby bioswale and/or stormwater pond.

Frost Science Museum

Featuring an intensive green roof design, museum guests are encouraged to walk through a rooftop garden of native coastal plants, arrayed in a series of poured-in-place concrete planters. Excess stormwater captured by these and from the roof generally is filtered and conveyed to a networked series of below-grade cisterns, sited on the lowest level of the nearby parking garage.

Florida's Showcase Green Envirohome

Integrating green roofs with rainwater harvesting is also possible for single-family homes. This experimental extensive green roof in Indiatlantic successfully integrates a series of specialty planters on a pitched roof with a system of connected rainwater barrels and an extensively planted, Florida-Friendly Landscape. This facility is able to mitigate almost all of the site's runoff during hurricane events while the roof planters provide meaningful energy savings. A variety of native coastal plants are utilized.

Escambia Municipal Complex

Although not in south Florida, this extensive green roof design located in Pensacola showcases a variety of plant species and their configurations that are equally well-suited for the south Florida context. The roof's relatively tall parapets help to protect plants and soil from wind scour, as does the strategic placement of taller grasses along corner edges and siting lower-lying groundcovers in exposed, central areas.

photo credit: UF

photo credit: UF

photo credit: UF

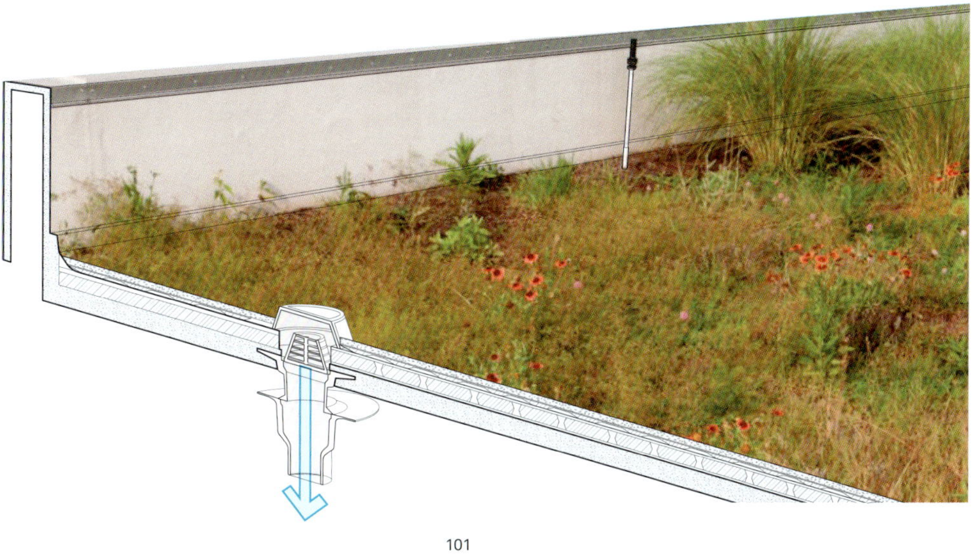

bioretention & street networks

Once rainwater flows off buildings and architecture it enters lots and, more often than not in urban settings, streets. Small right-of-way spaces in urban areas represent a potentially large amount of area for capturing and storing stormwater when considered collectively. Medians and pervious landscaping areas that separate sidewalks and roads, for example, are often designed and maintained at costs similar to green infrastructure but provide few benefits beyond pervious area and aesthetics. With some relatively simple adjustments in elevation, soils, plant selection, and curb structure, these areas can be reconfigured to become micro-wetland features that provide some combination of filtration, retention, bioremediation, and/or heat mitigation within either online or offline facilities, all without being any more difficult to maintain than conventional landscaping. Design and maintenance of these features is highly dependent on site context and optimizing run-off distributions.

infiltration & basin features

Bioretention designs that rely on direct infiltration into underlying soils and/or gently sloping sides need to be sited at least thirty feet away from buildings and other foundations to reduce the potential for erosion. Retention and infiltration features can also impact sensitive groundwater and will need to be sited at least fifty feet away from active drinking wells. They are best suited for upland areas in long-term planning but may be utilized in lower-lying areas when coupled with an underdrain. Standing water should ideally be present in these features for no longer than twenty-four hours after storm events to discourage mosquito reproduction.

detention & wetland features

Bioretention designs may also be "wet" and include some volume of permanently standing water where there is sufficient design and maintenance consideration for mitigating the proliferation of mosquitos. These designs may become increasingly valuable at smaller, street-side scales as sea level rise progresses and urban areas become flooded regularly, never able to fully drain water from the underlying soils. The concept of such "micro-urban wetlands" is wholly under-explored and is worth farther study and consideration as a potentially important facility for a wetter urban future.

photo credit: UF

Infiltrating bioretention planters with curb inlets, internal check dams, and ample freeboard at Innovation Square in Gainesville

"Wet" bioretention planters/ponds, closed off to underlying soils, can be sited directly adjacent to building foundations.

photo credit: UF

An access port for an underground feature. Small maintenance design considerations like this are critical to the long-term performance of subterranean stormwater features.

Exfiltration trenches and underdrains beneath bioretention features in wetter areas should have a "reservoir" layer with at least as much aggregate spaced around the central, perforated pipe as the pipe is wide as well as have regular access ports for maintenance.

neighborhood networks

rainwater co-ops

A central issue holding back decentralized rainwater harvesting at-scale is properly incentivizing, standardizing, and actualizing at-home systems across a meaningful breadth of the urban landscape. One potential solution to this problem may be for municipalities, businesses, and private homeowners to work together through semi-decentralized, "communal" rainwater harvesting systems. In such a system, individual homeowners would pay a one-time fee to "hook up" to a community rainwater harvesting network, similar to how homes using on-site septic systems can connect to centralized sewer now. Local municipalities, along with capital and technical support from the private sector, could provide all of the necessary equipment, maintenance, and design expertise for the system's filtration, storage, maintenance, and delivery to end-uses, while homeowners would simply pay a fee. In this way, multiple roofs in a neighborhood could become a single, well managed facility, contributing to a central filtration and cistern system, owned and operated by a single, professional entity, but benefiting all. Such a system could realize up to a 1.5 percent increase in volumetric reliability for reuse applications like irrigation in a Florida climate, making the year-round use of harvested rainwater more realistic and the stormwater management impact of rainwater harvesting more effective. However, such a system would also require communal consensus and support, not to mention a political will and backing.

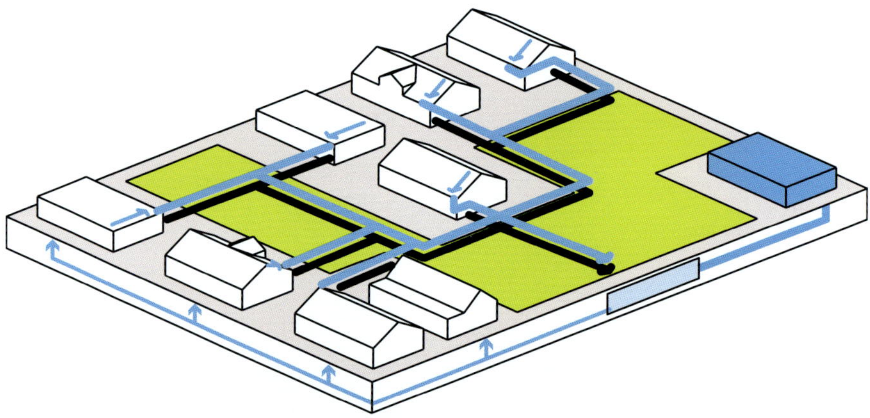

management & networking

Another issue with successfully managing and operating diffuse networks of urban stormwater features is effectively predicting and managing peak flows to and from various components while optimizing outcomes for respective elements. This problem can occur at all scales of organization, from managing the metered discharge of water from a single blue roof to managing the entire regional canal network. While standardizing feature design, implementation, and maintenance can help in these regards, the complexity of this task continues to challenge managers and will only become more challenging as the climate changes and extreme rainfall events become more unpredictble State-of-the-art digital sensing and computing technology offers some possible relief to these problems. Real-time management of stormwater systems have now progressed to the point of creating entire "digital clones" of buildings and systems, and well-designed computer algorithms can now predit unfolding changes that would greatly help to integrate and optimize complex urban stormwater management systems.

neighborhood treatment wetlands

A few, isolated pockets of urban south Florida today have already developed innovative, multifunctional landscapes for treating wastewater at the community scale. Facilities like Green Cay and Wakadahatchee Wetlands in Palm Beach County, or Snake Warrior Island Natural Area in Miami-Dade, have enhanced acres of previously underutilized spaces and converted them into neighborhood treatment wetlands that provide wastewater storage/treatment as well as high quality urban green space in the middle of otherwise heavily developed areas.

These larger, wetland bioretention facilities may have increasing importance to urban stormwater management in south Florida as rising sea levels elevate the regional water table, making infiltration more difficult, and as more frequent flooding farther degrades already poor urban water quality. This sort of forward-thinking informed the development of the River Oaks stormwater preserve in Fort Lauderdale, which reimagined 9.1 acres of undeveloped land between I-95 and the New River as a wetland park, designed to cleanse urban stormwater, recharge the local aquifer, recover native habitat, provide public recreational space, and enhance neighborhood livability overall. The proximity of this wetland to the New River farther situates it to potential re-designs as an emergency storm surge reservoir, receiving and mitigating excess tidal volumes from the river in addition to urban runoff.

While these moderately large-scale projects are expensive and only possible with sustained public investments, smaller-scale treatment wetland options appropriate to more confined urban spaces have similar potential but remain largely unexplored. Floating wetlands expand enhancement options for existing water bodies without requiring earthworks, while semi-contained, aboveground systems, such as the flow-through treatment wetland utilized by the Corkscrew Swamp Sanctuary visitor's center (bottom right), could help redefine urban relationships with wastewater generally.

Green Cay Wetlands

Snake Warrior Island Natural Area

River Oaks Stormwater Preserve

integrating facilities

culverts & network integrations

The humble and ubiquitous culvert provides an invaluable urban water management service, safely collecting and diverting surface waters under, around, and through areas that must remain dry, such as roads, while also integrating networks. As accelerating sea level rise forces south Florida to live increasingly close to water, the diverse roles of culverts, from mitigating erosion and promoting sedimentation, to reducing peak flows and instituting control elevations, are likely to warrant closer scrutiny.

Culverts have two main design functions: 1) inflows, generally used to recieve excess water overflowing from retention/detention features, thereby defining a control elevation, and 2) outflows, which are often used as storm drain discharge points. As sea levels rise, the design of outflow culverts, in particular, will need to be reconsidered as receiving wayways begin to "back-up" into drainage networks. Future culverts may need to be designed to manage bi-directional flows, acting as both inflow and outflow, providing flow control and preventing erosion equally in either direction. Tidal check valves and tidal gates are related components, but the simple utility of well designed culverts integrated with landscape features should be preferred wherever feasible for its design simplicity.

basic outflows

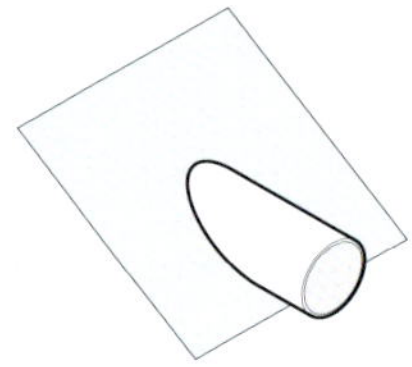

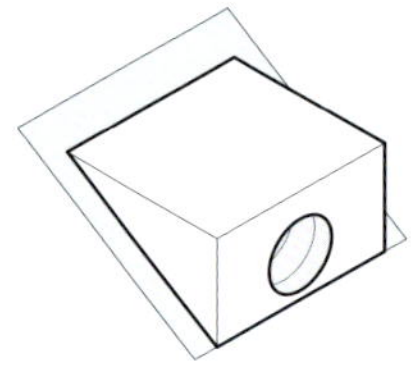

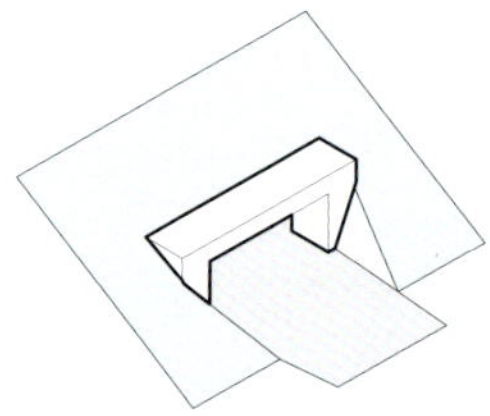

energy diffusing outflows

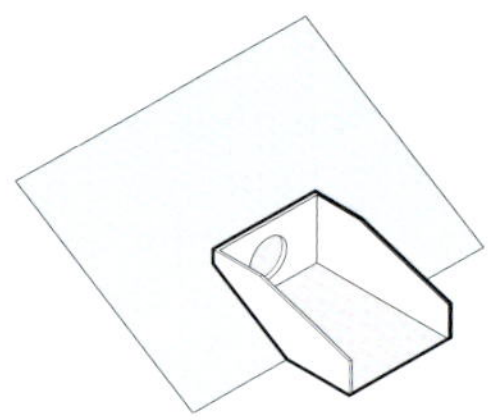

energy diffusing inflows & outflows

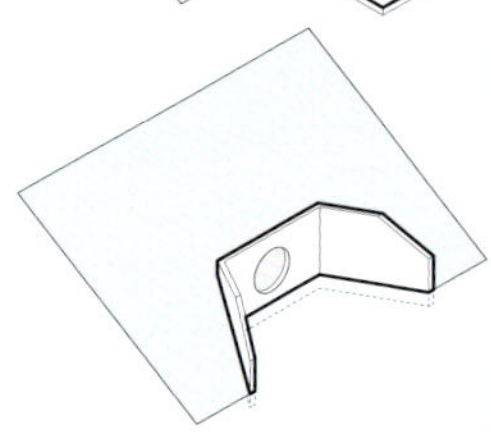

energy diffusing inflows & outflows with forebay

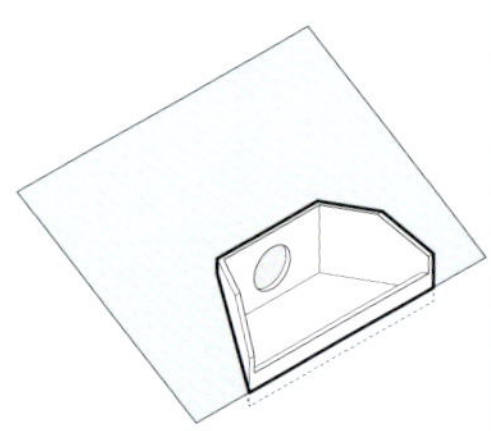

maintenance & offline integrations

As more bioretention features are integrated into existing urban drainage networks, there will be an accompanying need to incorporate enhanced maintenance routines into designs, to better maintain performance and longevity. Cities produce huge amounts of trash that clog facilities, degrading both environments and performance. Including in-line pre-treatments like "baffle boxes" (pictured below and at left and in figure below) upstream of features can both streamline maintenance and improve performance.

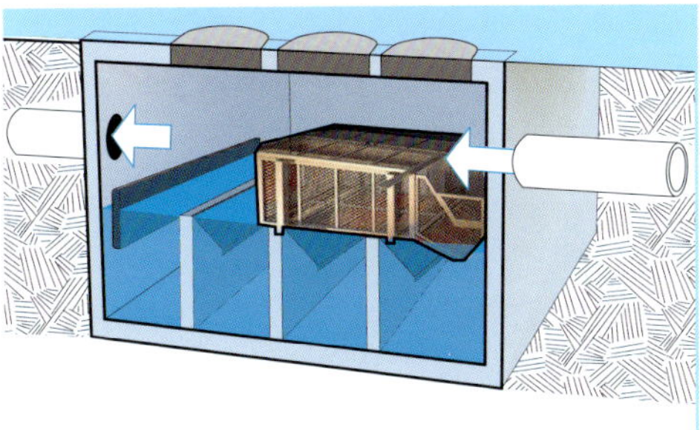

Another important in-line feature to nature-based facility designs are "flow splitter boxes" (pictured below). These relatively simple devices create a self-contained control elevation upstream of offline features, as opposed to inflow culverts, which do so downstream. When an offline bioretention feature reaches maximum capacity, the excess peak flows back-up, through the route they came into the feature, and flow over an internal weir or check-dam structure within the flow splitter box, where they are then directed to an online facility or storm sewer network. Besides the relative simplicity of their design, flow splitter boxes are invaluable tools to nature-based infrastructure networks because they allow for newly constructed bioretention features to be safely and effectively integrated with exisiting networks as offline components, reducing overall design considerations and costs for entire facilities.

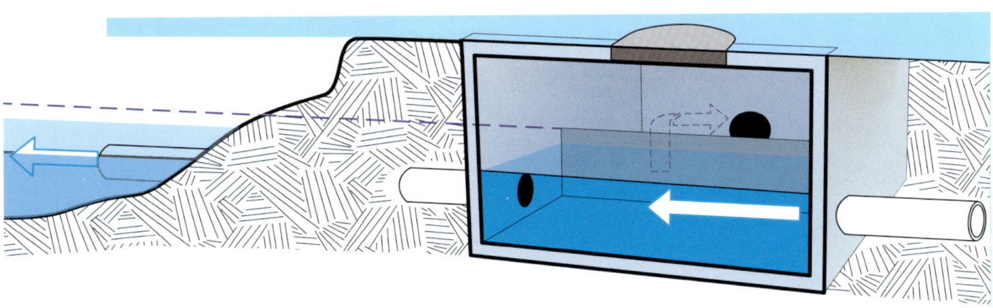

shorelines

The term "shoreline" refers to the overlapping boundary between any contiguous and permanent water body and adjacent upland area. This term is made disambiguous here from "coastline" in that the latter is strictly used to refer to shorelines that are immediately adjacent to the open ocean and which are highly exposed to marine conditions. The design of shoreline facilities is heavily dependent on the degree of exposure – to winds, waves, and/or currents – at any given site. Often inland land uses, as well as many nearshore topographical and biological features, can also have a strong influence on design considerations but, generally speaking, shoreline designs will vary most depending on whether the site is on an exposed waterway, protected waterway, or isolated water body. "Waterway" is made disambiguous here from "water body" by being a type of water body with discernable and predictable flow patterns (i.e, riverine or tidal flows). For example, a pond is simply a "water body," while a river is also a "waterway."

erosion, stabilization, & energy

Shoreline management has very different considerations, goals, and outcomes from stormwater management. While mitigating erosion along the slopes of landscape features or at points of outflow, for example, are important subsidiary considerations to many stormwater designs, shoreline infrastructure is entirely concerned with these kinds of "stabilization" design issues.

The main, overarching objective of shoreline infrastructure is to mitigate and/or resist the continual rearrangement of shoreline sediments that flowing waterways naturally conduct, thereby preserving the shoreline's overall shape and protecting upland areas.

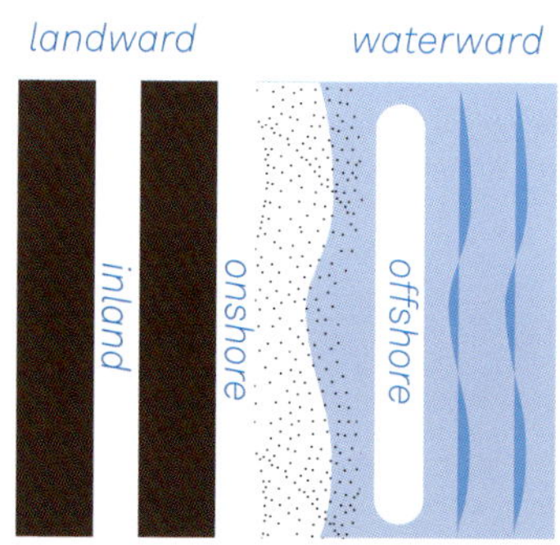

Individual shoreline features don't array into a facility quite like stormwater features do. Instead of "upstream" and "downstream," shoreline facilties orient in terms of "waterward" (or "seaward") and "landward" (or "leeward"). Multiple features are oriented into a unified facility based on the prevailing direction of winds, waves, and erosion forces.

As sea levels rise, and storms become increasingly frequent and intense, all of low-lying south Florida's shorelines will be challenged in a variety of essential ways. Many of the built shorelines in the region are now more than fifty years old, meaning that they are reaching the end of their intended life expectancies. The need to re-imagine shoreline designs, and to retrofit them for an increasingly turbulent future, has never been more urgent nor apparent.

characterizing site hydrology

South Florida has hundreds of miles of shoreline, much of it exposed to daily tidal exchanges and, occasionally, to the extreme waves and currents of storm events. Determining which shoreline features can be recommended for any given site is principally a matter of defining the amount of energy, or "exposure," the site experiences on average. The degree of exposure for any given site can be even farther simplified, in most cases, by assessing its relative proximity to the ocean and exposure to associated marine currents, waves, and winds.

exposed coasts

The coastline itself, lying directly adjacent to the Atlantic Ocean, is the most exposed shoreline in the region and requires highly specific design considerations. Within the framework of this manual, these are the shorelines of the "coastal" ecotype, but can include some areas farther west of the barrier islands that are oriented to regularly experience oceanic conditions via inlets, for example.

protected tidal waterways

Waterways that experience marked, daily tides but are inland of the coastal barrier islands and largely insulated from the effects of oceanic weather are considered "protected" tidal waterways. Shorelines in these areas are of the "estuarine" ecotype. Conditions here are less intense on average than exposed coasts and so have a greater degree of design flexibility but must still consider the intense, punctuated erosion events associated with tidal storm surges.

inland waterways & water bodies

Waterways and isolated water bodies far from the coast, where tidal influences are either subtle or completely absent, are found in the "glades" and "transverse glades" ecotypes. While these areas generally experience the least amount of exposure, many of these shorelines are also along regionally important drainage canals and so, in some cases, require specialized design considerations.

design waves & shorelines

Similar to the "design storms" of stormwater management, coastal managers also use hypothetical scenarios to estimate the maximum amount of stress a given shoreline design should be able to withstand. The "design wave" represents the single greatest, energetic event that a shoreline is designed to resist, since wave/current energies are often the most impactful aspect of such events on shorelines. Like design storms, these scenarios are based on historical records (i.e, past hurricanes), but other important factors include site water levels throughout the year as well as the given shoreline's form and composition, both onshore and offshore. Also like design storms, design waves represent hypothetical events and so can be concieved of as probabilities. The USACE recommends using a design wave that has at least a 50 percent chance of occuring during the feature's life-time as a minimum design standard. A more robust design would plan for storm energies that are even less likely, but such risk-averse outlooks can also increase construction costs and cause designers to create features that are more armored (and, therefore, have a higher environmental impact) than they may need. Like any aspect of the built environment, shorelines are a fine balance between form, function, and costs. Shoreline designers should attempt to let a given site's existing characters inspire design and strive to support as many of the natural aspects present as possible.

determining water levels

One of the first and most critical site criteria to determine for any shoreline are the relavent water levels impacting the shore. The height or elevation of a water body's surface at any given time changes in predictible ways throughout the year and, in some cases, throughout the day. Waterways in coastal areas are tidally influenced, experiencing both daily and seasonal variations in water level that are determined by the astronomical interactions of the Earth, moon, and sun. These changes in water level are highly regular and predictible but also present a certain degree of added design complexity. Water bodies fartherthest from the coast and nearest to the Everglades have water levels that are more pluvially influenced, changing seasonally based on the abundance (or lack) of rain falling over the surrounding region. While less predictible than tides, estimating maximum, minimum, and mean water levels in these areas is still possible and recommended, but more similar in design considerations to the "freeboard" concept of stormwater management. In many areas half way between the Everglades and coast, both water level mechanisms are strongly influential and must be considered by designs both separately and as compounding forces.

freshwater elevations

Water bodies and waterways that are pluvially influenced have a yearly maximum and yearly minimum water level associated with the wet and dry seasons, respectively. Site observations should ideally span multilpe seasons to account for interannual variation in regional rain inputs. The presence/absence of certain soils, plants, and plant communities can also help to determine water extents or at least identify poorly draining areas.

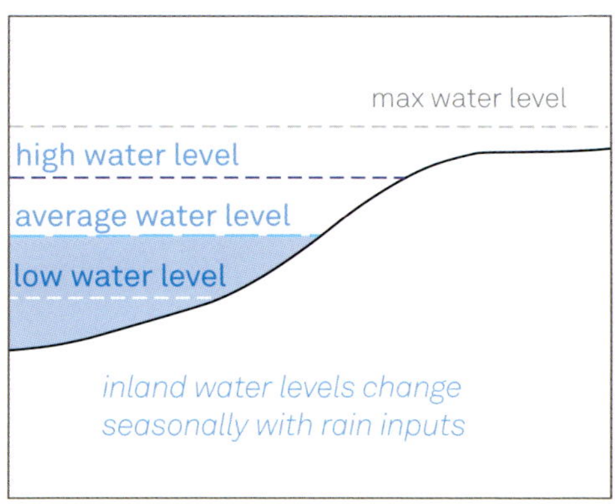

tidal elevations & datums

Where waterways are tidally influenced, water elevations are described by a convention that takes various averages of key phases in the daily tidal cycle (e.g, low tide and high tide). These averages are known as "tidal datums" and are a unique method for measuring elevation anywhere with respect to a "0" elevation that is a hypothetically static water level. These average are derived from locally relavent observations that are carefully developed by NOAA for the southeast Florida region from data collected at the tide station on Virginia Key, near Maimi. However, the resultant datums are equally relavent to anywhere on the southeastern Florida coast, as tidal patterns are similar across the region. While the two high tides and two low tides our region experiences every twenty-four hours are roughly equivalent they are rarely exactly the same, with one of the events often being higher or lower than the other, respectively. This means that there are two types averages – one where all observations are used, and another where only the most extreme values (i.e, highest or lowest) are used. In this way, the "mean higher high water" datum refers specifically to an average of only the highest of the two daily high tides, while "mean high water" averages all high tides. On any given day, these are reported as "+/-ft.," deviating from a "0" value of the average itself. For the purposes of shoreline design, Mean High Water (MHHW) and Mean Lower Low Water (MLLW) are the most important as these define upper and lower boundaries to the typical water level conditions that can be expected, however, other datums are also used.

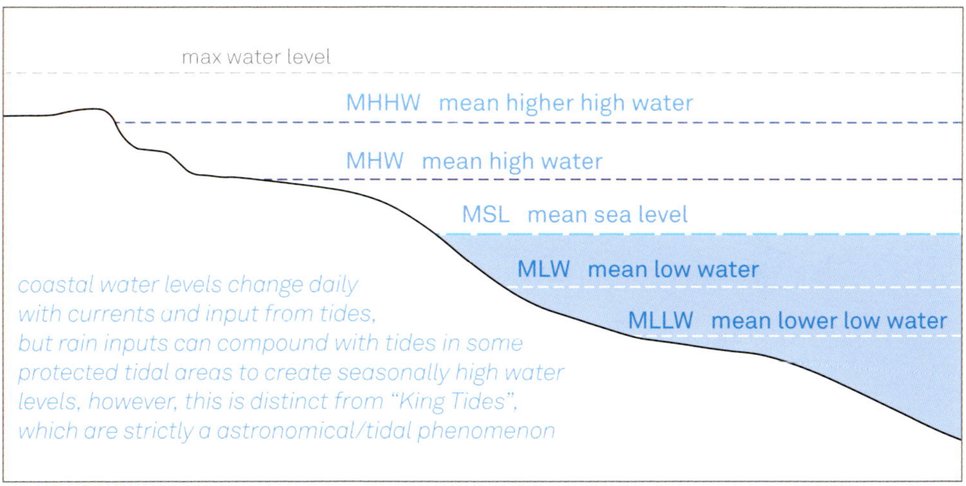

When building shoreline features, engineers and marine contractors will utilize exact elevation benchmarks and tidal datum measurements. However, for the more generic purposes of design, the apparent maximum and minimum extent of typical tides is often sufficient and can be readily determined by tracking certain features along shorelines. These directly observed datums are referred to as "Max Tide" and "Min Tide," respectively. Similar to freshwater shorelines, it is ideal for designers to observe tidal shorelines of interest over several seasons to help account for any interannual variability, especially following storm events. However, if the ability for site observation is limited, the most useful time of year to observe shorelines in south Florida with respect to design is between September and November, when astronomical conditions incite "King Tides," hurricane season is most active, and when regional rain inputs from inland areas are at their greatest.

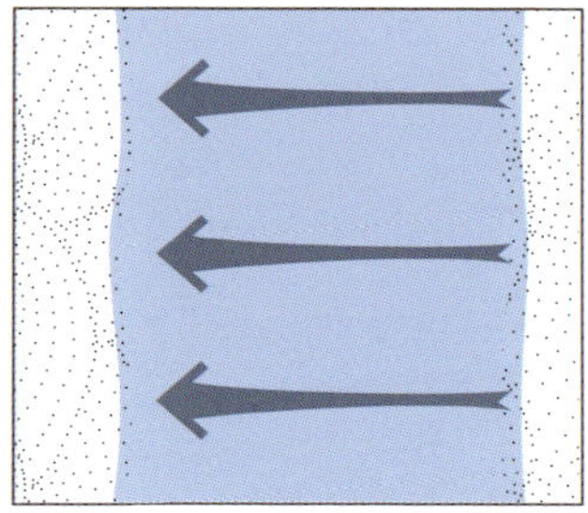

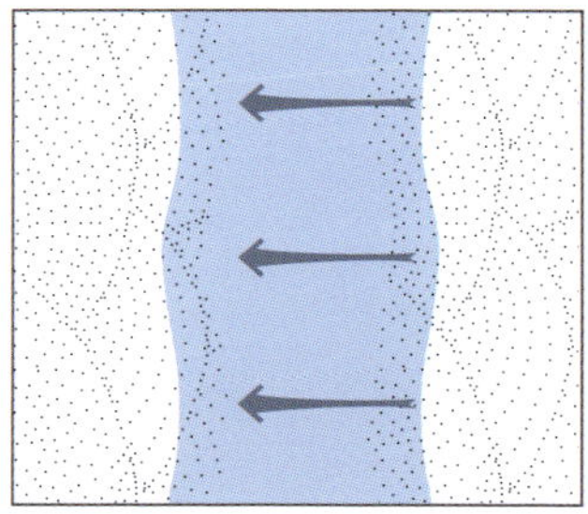

consider fetch & wind-wave energy

Many waves and coastal currents are intially generated by wind passing over the water's surface. Where wind speed and direction over water are fairly consistent, and not interrupted by obstructions like land, the ability for wind to generate rough seas increases through a phenomenon called "fetch." The wider a body of water is, the greater the fetch length. This means that, when there are windy conditions, there is likely more wave energy impacting shorelines along wider water bodies than along narrower ones. This is obviously part of the reason for the special status of exposed coasts, but fetch can also have an influence on protected water bodies, if they are wide enough. Even relatively isolated, inland lakes of sufficient size can experience intense waves with sufficient wind. Although orientation to prevailing winds influences fetch, designs should generally assume that wider water bodies will experience stronger wave energy on average than narrower ones.

consider boat wakes & wave "echos"

In addition to wind - generated waves, a considerable amount of wave energy can also result from passing boat traffic. This is especially true for urban south Florida, where large numbers of people and a thriving marine tourism industry often coincide with narrow waterways. Even in "no wake zones," sustained boat traffic can still add a considerable amount of wave energy to adjacent shorelines, causing erosion that might not have been expected otherwise. Additionally, for natural shorelines facing armored ones on opposing shores, an "echo" effect may result, where the energy of waves and wakes impacting the armored shoreline reflects back in the direction it came from to the other side. Shorelines in these situations will have to consider both the waves generated by passing boats themselves and the waves being reflected toward them by opposing armored shorelines. In an opposite fashion to fetch, the echo effect is amplified in narrower waterways with wider ones tending to diffuse wave echos before they can reach the opposing shoreline.

note shoreline type, slope, & use

Shoreline designers will never be starting from a blank slate. Each site will always have a range of existing characteristics directly influencing designs. The character of the shoreline itself is obviously critical to assess. Note aspects such as type: Is the shoreline armored or natural? Is the slope shallow or steep? Sediments rocky or sandy? Note how existing shorelines features interact across property lines: Do neighbors have different shoreline types? Are their banks at different elevations? Note land uses inland of the shoreline: How far away are buildings or roads from the beginning of the shoreline slope? Are there natural upland habitats present? It is generally recommended that building foundations be set back at least forty feet. from the beginning of the nearest shoreline slope to mitigate the potential for erosion. Finally, it is important to consider any desired uses of the shoreline, such as docks and boat access.

survey nearby submerged areas

Some shoreline designs require the siting of built elements within a waterway, but any project seeking to site structural features underwater may need special permitting. Generally, permit exemptions are granted for projects that do not go out beyond the MLLW line and impact less than 500 feet of continuous shoreline. Conversely, it should be generally assumed that designs with structure beyond MLLW and/or impacting more than 500 feet of shoreline will require more permitting, if they are allowed at all. A related consideration is the proximity of planned shoreline structural elements to existing submerged habitats, particularly seagrasses and coral reef, as these are especially vulnerable to any sedimentation caused during construction. Projects seeking a lower impact should prioritize designs that expand shorelines inland, wherever feasible, or that use soft/hybrid approaches that intentionally facilitate the expansion and/or migration of these valuable habitats.

soft stabilization

Natural shorelines, shoreline features that utilize naturalistic sediments like sand, and/or shore facilities that depend on littoral plant communities to stabilize inland areas represent viable, infrastructural solutions in many settings. This kind of "soft stabilization" optimizes and enhances the stabilization benefits provided by key aspects of natural environments. While these can be more resilient and adaptive to change, they are also more vulnerable to high wave energies and require more time and space to implement.

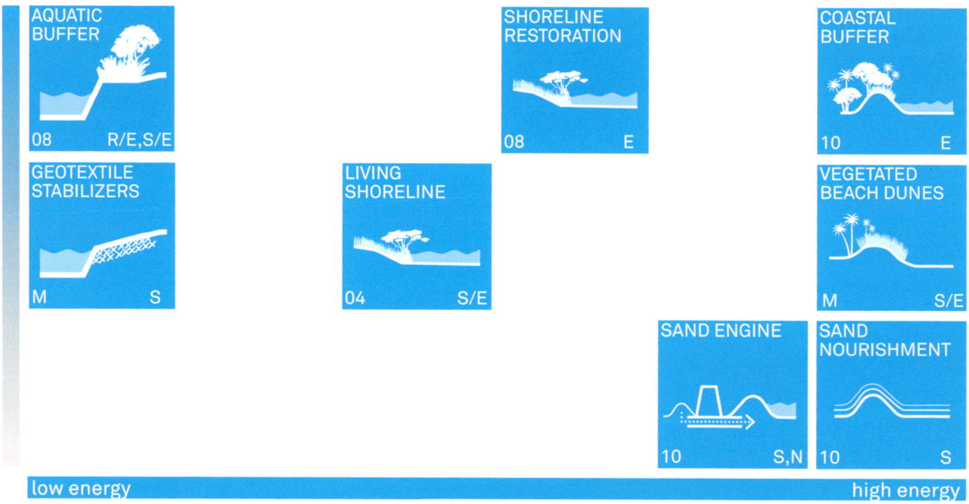

living shoreline

Natural or intentionally planted shorelines with plants growing up to or beyond high water and shallow slopes (1:12 or less). Dense groupings of littoral vegetation stabilize sediments. When fully mature, mangrove living shorelines can reduce wave energy up to 50 percent and adapt to rising seas but require more space and many years of growth to achieve full benefits.

Soft stabilization encompases two main design approaches: those that utilize native plant communities and those that rely on artificial sediment inputs. Generally, the most robust approaches utilize both. In south Florida today, the latter strategy is almost entirely represented by coastal "sand nourishments," which are common but also for larger scales only. Strategies using plants are comparatively rare today and include efforts such as vegetated beach dunes and estuarine shoreline restorations. Since these strategies utilize growing elements they have the potential to adapt to rising seas. Geotextiles (as in photo at top right) and "coir logs" are soft, artificial stabilizers only used in low-energy settings.

aquatic buffer

Similar to living shorelines but refers to shore parrallel plantings inland of the high water line at least fifty feet wide. Applies to fresh and saltwater. Primarily used to slow, spread, and treat runoff from upland areas but can also provide some stabilization benefits. Best when paired with living shorelines.

summary

problem areas addressed	erosion, (pollution), (heat islands)
applicable scales - facilities	lot, block, street (shore) - onshore, inland
infrastructural goals/outcomes	sediment stabiliztion, adaptive resilience, pollution treatment, upland soil support
ecological pairings	guides- resh: 1a,1a,1a,1a,1a, salt: 1a,1a,1a,1a,
	palettes- fresh: 1a,1a,1a,1a,1a, salt: 1a,1a,1a,1a,
architectural setbacks	at least 40 ft from beginning of slope bank
landward	hard stabilization
waterward	breakwaters

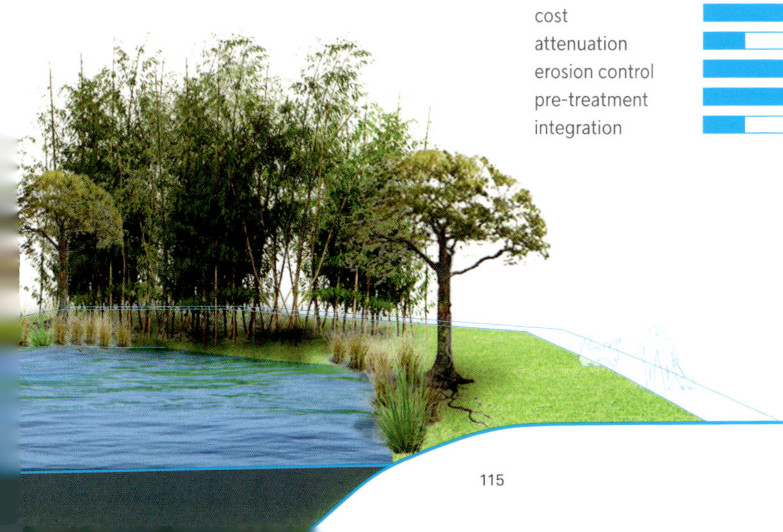

hard stabilization

Armoring is the most common stabilization strategy utilized in urban south Florida today and includes such ubiquitous features as seawalls, revetments, floodwalls, and levees. These "hard" strategies seek to stabilize and support inland sediments and landscapes with built features made of durable material – usually concrete, rocks, sheetpile, and/or treated timber. These "hard stabilization" features provide high-value protection immediately after construction but are more costly overall, in both price and impact.

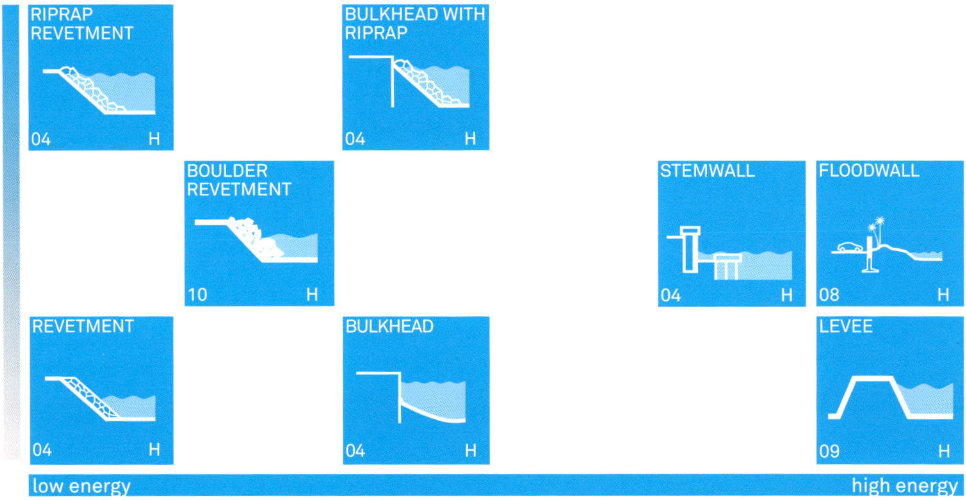

bulkhead

Although called "seawalls," the armored, vertical walls common to south Florida estuaries are more accurately described as "bulkheads," since they are only designed to resist moderate wave-energy settings, whereas true seawalls are designed for exposed coastal conditions. Bulkheads simply replace a shoreline with a wall meant to retain inland soils. A variety of retrofit options are available to enhance the longevity and performance of existing bulkheads and to mitigate their potential failure.

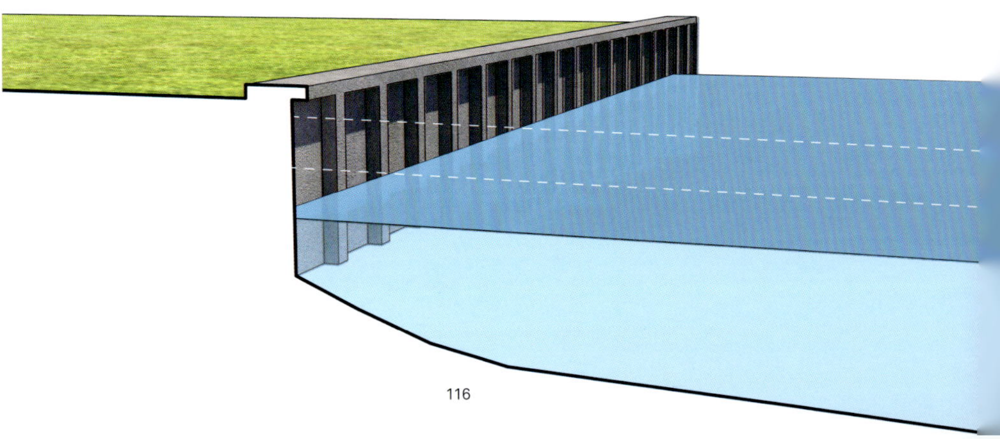

Armored shorelines are easily the most common strategy utilized along protected tidal waterways in south Florida. This is partly due to the relative ease of their design, installation, and integration with boat facilities. But is also due, in part, to the historical reality that much of urban south Florida was originally built over the "reclaimed land" of in-filled coastal wetlands – armored features like seawalls were the most cost-effective strategy for maximizing enough buidable land area to support this development pattern. Today, these strategies have the most institutional support of any strategy but are also vulnerable to rising sea levels, as they are highly dependent on a static, maximum water level, and provide little to no environmental co-benefits.

riprap revetment

Revetments are sloped armor facings that provide stabilization of sediments by covering shorelines and provide protection/support by using massive armoring materials. "Riprap" refers to revetments that specifically use a stacked series of stones as the armor layer. A filter layer, generally composed of a geotextile mesh, is placed beneath these rocks to prevent the erosion of finer sediments. While the sloped aspect requires more space, these features can last marginally longer than a basic bulkhead and the use of limestone rocks for riprap provides some environmental benefits to marine life.

summary

problem areas addressed	erosion, storm surge, (tidal flooding)
applicable scales - facilities	lot, block, street (shore) - onshore, inland
infrastructural goals/outcomes	sediment stabiliztion, inland soil support, wave/surge protection, operational longevity
ecological pairings	-
architectural setbacks	at least 40 ft.
landward	tidal flow control
waterward	soft stabilization, breakwaters

breakwaters

In highly-exposed settings, whether from fetch or boat activity, one effective option for mitigating erosion can be to site strategic structural elements offshore that redirect waves from vulnerable areas and/or foster sediment deposition landward. Since these features are sited underwater, their design and implementation is inherently more complex than other shoreline strategies and so are only recommended where their benefits are deemed necessary or can be easily achieved using existing site elements.

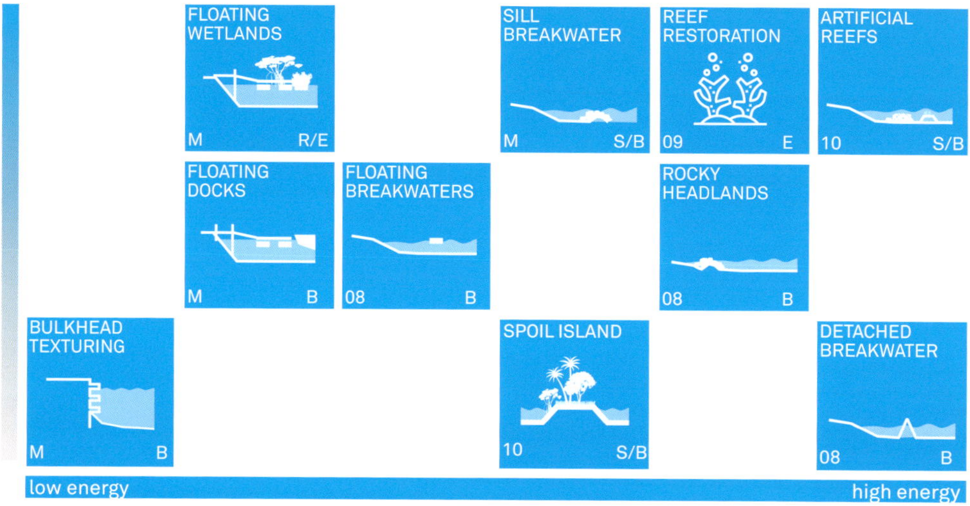

floating docks

Floating docks can be designed and sited to provide very small-scale breakwater benefits to some estuarine shorelines and may be especially useful for designs that wish to incorporate shoreline vegetation but also experience a lot of boat wake. Floating docks can be designed to adapt to some amount of sea level rise but also require careful consideration of storm conditions.

Example of seawall texturing showing contributor Dr. Keith Van de Riet's Mangrove Reef Wall System.

All breakwaters diffuse wave energy through a similar combination of methods, but designs tend to be either above or below water, with considerations differing dramatically between these. Currently, only a few south Florida settings utilize breakwaters, these being fairly exposed sites. The southeast Florida reef tract naturally provides breakwater benefits to much of the coast, as can oyster reefs, seagrass meadows, and even sand eroded from beach nourishments. While breakwaters are more difficult to permit and complex to design, they can also provide a variety of shoreline enhancement benefits not possible by any other means. Below are two uniquely small-scale designs accessible to property-owners.

seawall texturing

Covering the seaward walls of existing seawall with textured "habitat panels," designed to look and function like mangrove roots, can help to reduce the impact of wave energy on the seawall, improving it's longevity, while also providing enhanced wildlife habitat. Cheaper and easier to install than other breakwaters but provides fewer protection benefits.

summary

problem areas addressed	erosion, (storm surge)
applicable scales - facilities	varies - onshore, offshore
infrastructural goals/outcomes	wave-energy diffusion, wave/surge protection, sediment deposition, facility enhancement
ecological pairings	-
architectural setbacks	-
landward	tidal flow control, soft, hard, or hybrid stabilization
waterward	-

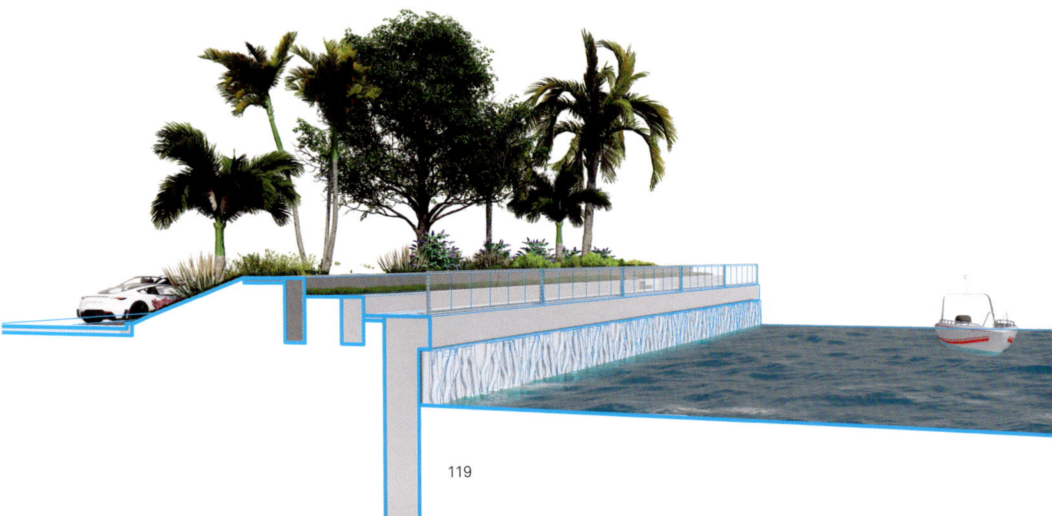

tidal flow control

While shoreline management in south Florida has traditionally centered on stabilization, sea level rise is slowly adjusting outlooks as the increasing frequency of "nuisance" tidal flooding entering inland urban areas under average conditions, not just during storms, is pushing managers to consider new designs. To mitigate the effects of overtopping tides on shorelines, design considerations are becoming increasingly similar to stormwater facilities, having to optimize flows, drainage, conveyance, attenuation, and storage.

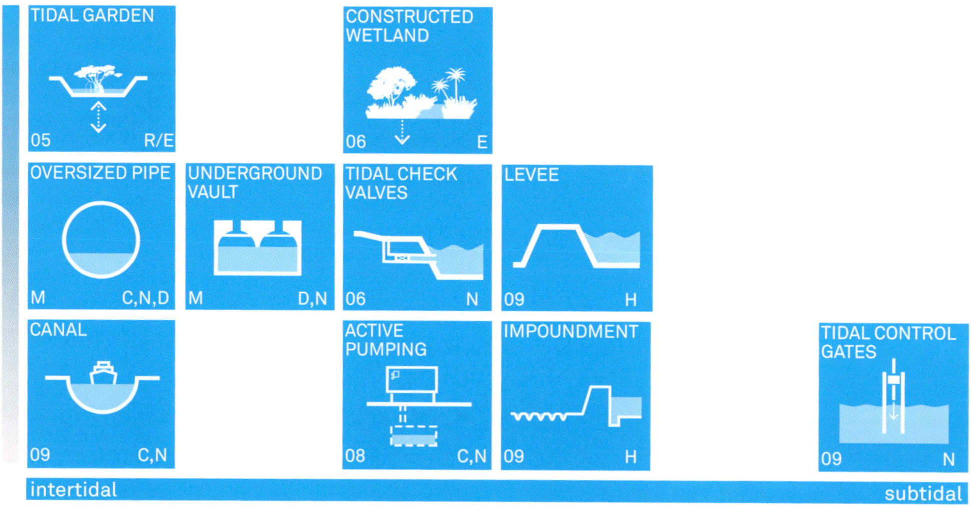

canal

The original south Florida tidal control method was to simply dredge material from low areas and pile the spoil onto higher areas. The resultant "fingers" formation of canals and islands proved adequate to handle most tidal flows and volumes under normal conditions. But as sea levels rise, these estuarine urban configurations will be increasingly challenged by overtopping and bulkhead shoreline failures. While little area remains to expand tidal canals, managers of the future may eventually seek to add new ones. Any future tidal canal designs should consider mitigating sedimentation, using hybrid stabilization methods, and integrating more seamlessly with urban architecture.

"duck" valves

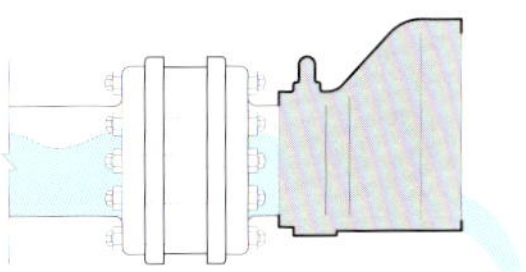

-compressed apeture
-increased backpressure
 increases flow rate
-promotes consistent inland
storage
-mounts to front of storm
drain outfall
-low maintenance, but
 can be difficult to site

swing valves

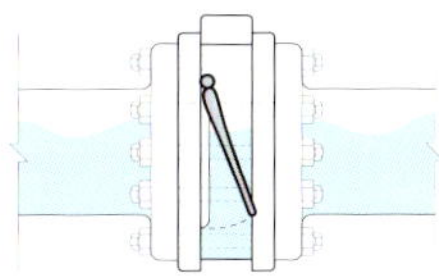

-hinged, 1-way disc
-opens when back-
 pressure > forward
-promotes consistent
 inland drainage flow
-handles solids well
-interal to sewer line,
 avoid installing
 backwards

Within shorter-term planning horizons, shoreline facilities can look to installing "check valves" that optimize the integration of existing storm drain networks with tides. Design variants of these (common examples above) have unique pros and cons related to both the mechanism used and site-specific criteria. For longer-term planning, and for areas already experiencing frequent "sunny-day" flooding, managers and residents alike are increasingly looking to active pumping to convey floodwaters elsewhere. But with few places for the water to ultimately go, a better mindset might be to look to the evolution of low-impact stormwater management and seek to utilize carefully managed, multi-functional landscapes, like "tidal gardens."

tidal check valves

Rising seas are increasingly causing high tides to flow upward through storm drain outfalls. This has created many issues inland of shoreline facilities that most were not designed to handle. A short-term solution is to install one-way check valves along storm drain routes, allowing stormwater to drain when tides are low but blocking high tides. These features work best when designs consider a given site at the neighborhood scale and are highly dependent on proper installation procedures.

summary

problem areas addressed	tidal flooding, (storm surge)
applicable scales - facilities	varies - inland, onshore, offshore
infrastructural goals/outcomes	flow control, flow attenuation, volume storage, stormwater integration
ecological pairings	-
architectural setbacks	-
landward	varies
waterward	varies

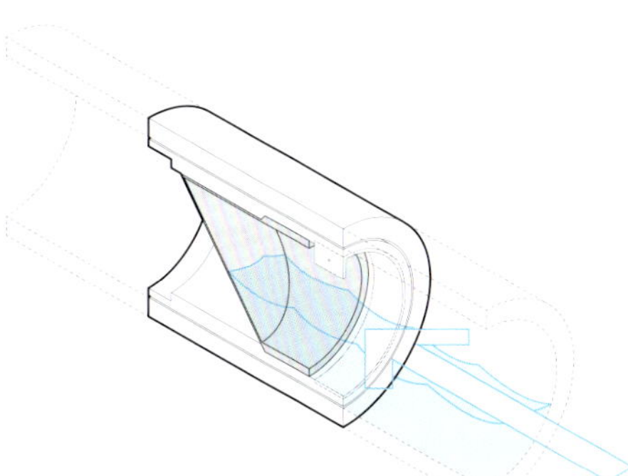

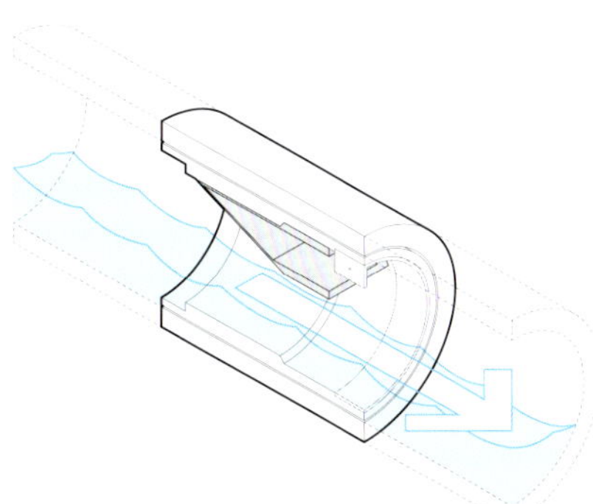

seawall failure & enhancement

As the incidence of tidal flooding increases, and the age of many bulkhead features reach or surpass their intended lifespan, incidents of failure are also becoming more commonplace. Causes for seawall failure include poor or infrequent maintenance, overloaded weights in upland areas, shallow foundations sited too close, increased water flows/volumes through nearby soils, shifts in depth or erosion of supporting seaward sediments, and corrosion of wall materials by saltwater.

Signs of compromised seawalls include cracks in seaward panels, eroded depressions and sinkholes along inland landscapes, water bubbling up through dry land, and leaning/bowing of the wall itself. A variety of seawall failures, their causes, and recommended actions for correction are presented here. Understanding how seawall failures overlap with site conditions can help to guide new designs and encourage more resilient enhancements and retrofits.

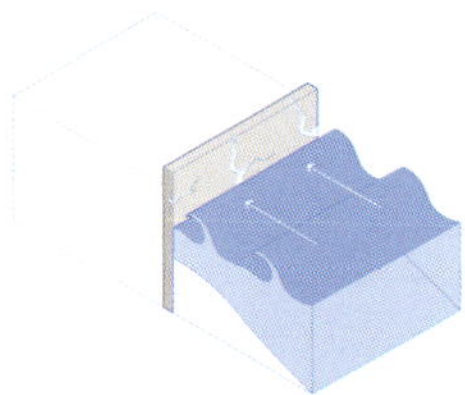

waterline, cap, & tie-back failures

Age and corrosion or parts in older seawalls often causes failure at the cap (top), the mean water line, or tie-back system (if applicable), manifesting as rust, cracks, and/or crumbling. Sealants, new reinforcment elements, and/or adding seaward features (e.g, riprap) can help prolong lifespans, but complete replacement may be recommended.

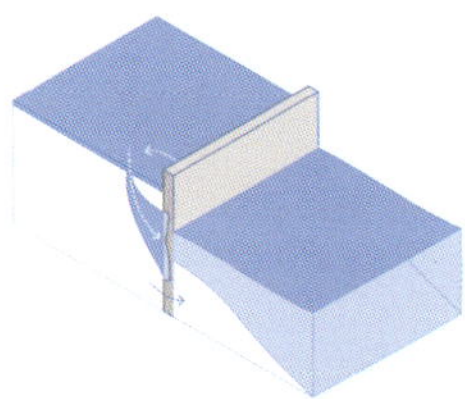

inland erosion & pressure

Where excess groundwater pressure and/or flows occur in soils inland of seawalls, local erosion and backpressure can cause seawalls to fail. Regular maintenance and/or enhancement of "weepholes," as well as the inclusion/enhancement of "apron" underdrains inland of the wall, can prevent this.

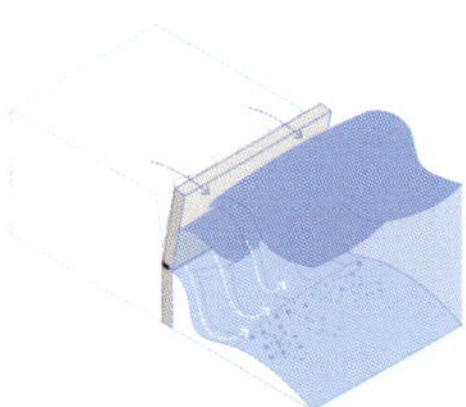

toe scour

If average wave-current energies increase and/or overall water depths increase, erosion of the seaward sediments anchoring and supporting the bottom of the wall, or "toe," can erode, causing the wall to fall forward. Hard enhancments, such as riprap revetments or "habitat benches," can help.

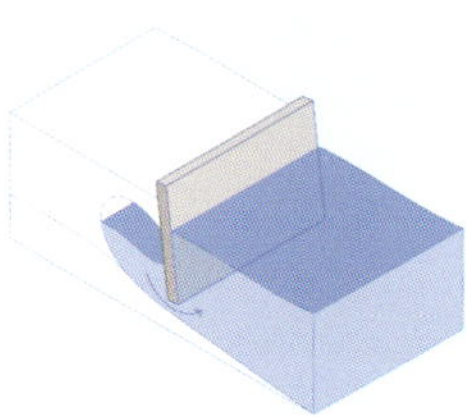

undercutting

If the anchoring system of a seawall is designed too shallow and/or if toe scour compounds with inland erosion sufficiently, seawalls can slide forward. Designs should seek to extend the anchoring depth of seawalls sufficiently to prevent this and consider the elevated sea levels of the future.

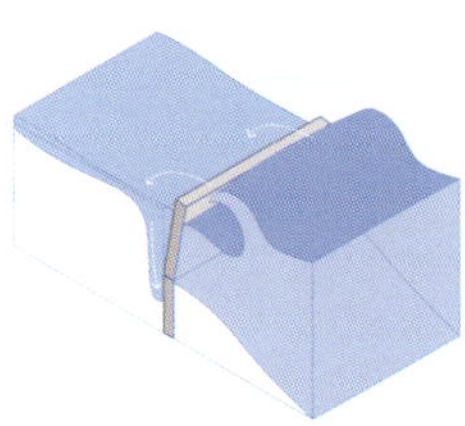

regular overtopping

If normal tides/waves regularly exceed seawall design elevations, inland erosion can swiftly accelerate and become difficult to manage by standard means. Elevating the wall's total height is the best possible course – hybrid shoreline strategies are recommended.

1 aprons & underdrains
a shallow gravel trench or full underdrain along landward edge reduces inland erosion and improves drainage

2 toe armoring
adding rocks or other structure along the seaward bottom edge reduces scour

3 weepholes
drainage holes on the face of seawalls need occasional cleaning
- replacement inserts are available and can improve drainage rates, maintenance, and some designs even include internal check valves to prevent tidal backflows
- underdrains can be integrated with weepholes as a drain system

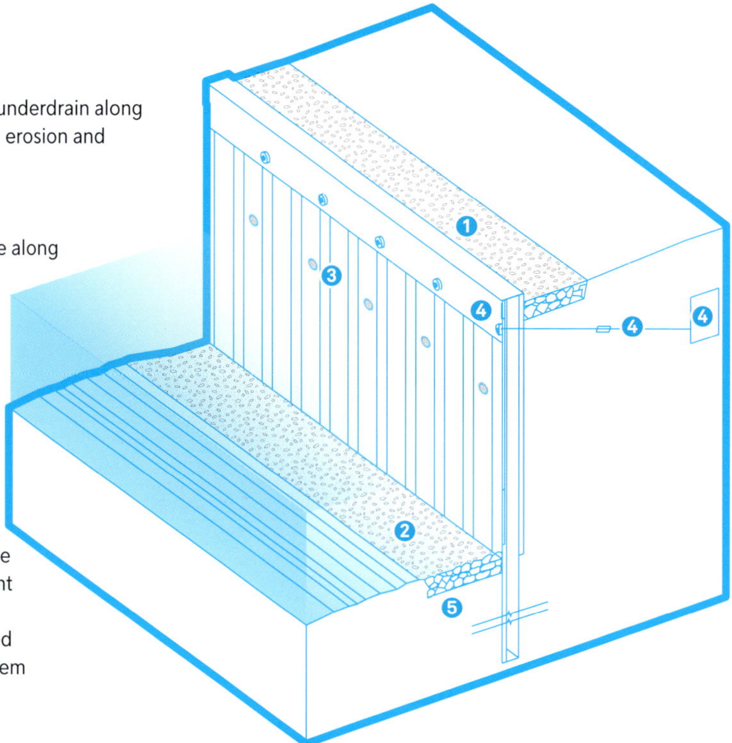

4 tie-back reinforcement systems
seawalls can be bolstered with tie-back systems that connect a concrete weight bar, buried inland, to the cap and supporting bars along the seaward edge via rods, providing additional support for walls without – walls with an aging tie-back system may need to consider replacment due to rusted rod metal

5 toe berms & the anchoring system
penetration depth of the wall itself is critical – adding hieght to the seaward bottom with a berm of sediment (or riprap) can provide similar benefits

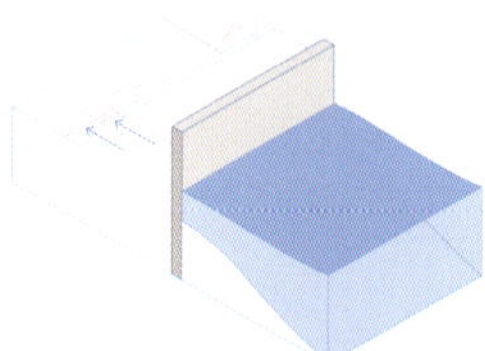

backsliding

If extensive erosion or removal of soils inland of seawalls is great enough, backsliding can occur and may cause walls to fail. Consider this potential when conducting major earthworks immediately inland of seawalls and take necessary precautions to retain seawall integrity.

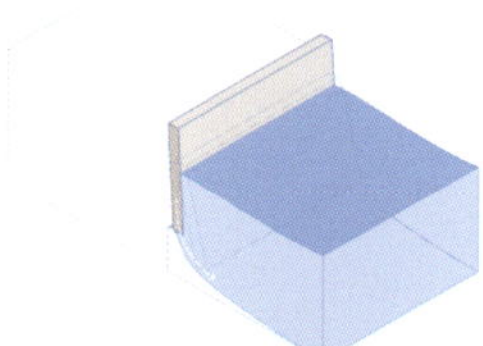

slope recession

If the slope offshore and beyond of a seawall's toe area becomes eroded, dredged too close, or otherwise made steeper, the global stability of underlying sediments supporting the wall's anchoring system can become compromised and cause failure. Good design/planning prevents this.

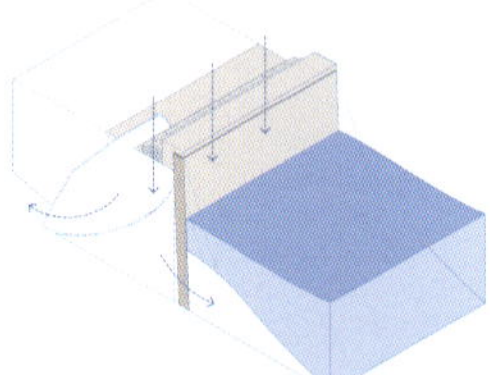

subsurface collapse

If too much weight is added above inland soils adjacent to seawalls it can result in soil instability inland and cause seawall failure. Maintain greater setbacks for shallow building foundations and vehicle traffic – avoid piling sandbags above seawalls as a means for temporary fortification.

hybrid shorelines

hybrid approaches

As described in the previous pages, shoreline stabilizations generally fall under one of two approaches: "soft" and "hard." However, a third option also exists that attempts to combine the benefits of both while achieving some balance or compromise regarding their respective drawbacks. Such "hybrid" approaches have long been identified as promising alternatives but have been slow to be widely adopted. From an engineering perspective, this may be due to uncertainties regarding their ultimate design outcomes, upkeep, and performance. From a socio-ecological perspective, this may be due to uncertainties regarding their actual benefits to nearshore ecosystems and urban well-being. Since hybrid features represent a compromise, these uncertainties might be better conceived of as a spectrum of potential outcomes related to design intent. Generally, the best hybrid features either maximize horizontal buffering space for coastal plant communities and multifunctional uses, or maximize enhancments to existing armor.

combining features into facilities

Hybrid shorelines present a range of options regarding design with respect to seaward or landward orientations, and the layering of multiple features. Traditionally, it has been more cost effective to use as few elements as possible when stabilizing shorelines, but with the varied and compounding threats posed by a changing climate, this calculus is beginning to shift. Elevated sea levels and increasing storm intensities present unique challenges that single-feature shorelines will likely struggle to manage, particularly concerning increases in both overtopping and erosion potential. Nearly all hybrid shoreline designs leverage the combined use of multiple feature types to improve overall performance. One of the most essential examples of this is the addition of a supporting riprap feature along the seaward face of a seawall and a "french drain" (i.e, underdrain) along the landward edge to improve drainage. However, while this is an example of feature integration into a facility, hybrid designs differ in that they incorporate nature. Combining a detatched breakwater with a living shoreline is an example of a hybrid approach (as depicted below). The breakwaters intercept boat wakes and regular wave action, effectively stabilizing the shoreline in the short term and providing some sediment accrual while also protecting young plants from erosion, enhancing their establishment and, ultimately, long-term stabilization outcomes. While breakwaters are a powerful tool, they can also be challenging to design and implement. As sea level rise and climate change progress, a variety of hybrid approaches will need to be assembled and implemented to provide the best protection available while preserving valuable and imperiled nearshore ecosystems.

stemwall stair planter

enhancing estuarine seawalls

Space and funds-limited hybrid designs that wish to maximize more engineering-oriented outcomes should focus on improving the longevity and performance of any existing armor. For urban shorelines with an aging seawall, likely the most cost-effective hybrid improvement is to combine an intertidal planter, habitat bench, or riprap feature seaward of the existing wall, and a "stemwall" inland of it. The seaward planter/bench/riprap provides long-term support and protects the toe area from erosion, while the stemwall adds elevation to the shoreline's overall height, compensating for sea level rise but also using less material than a full seawall. Since this facility retains the existing seawall, it can represent a cost-savings as high as 75 percent when compared with complete replacement by traditional means. Adding bioretention planters and/or underdrains, both between seawall and stemwall, as well as landward of the stemwall, is recommended to improve drainage and reduce the potential for inland erosion/pressure while adding co-benefits, such as cooling through shade (where shade trees are used).

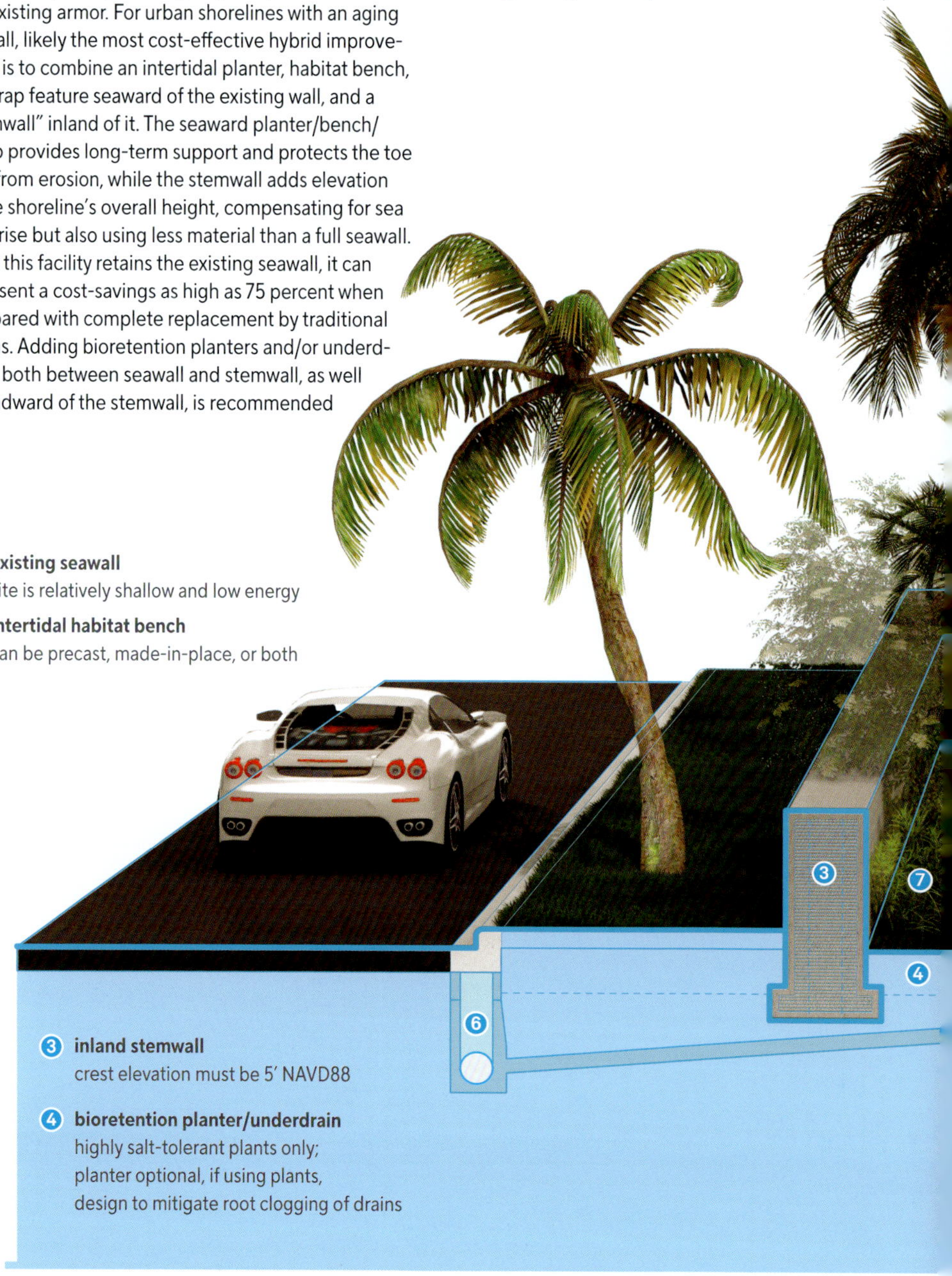

1 existing seawall
site is relatively shallow and low energy

2 intertidal habitat bench
can be precast, made-in-place, or both

3 inland stemwall
crest elevation must be 5' NAVD88

4 bioretention planter/underdrain
highly salt-tolerant plants only;
planter optional, if using plants,
design to mitigate root clogging of drains

summary

problem areas addressed	tidal flooding, erosion, storm surge, (heat)
recommended scales - sites	lots, streets - space constrained sites
infrastructural goals/outcomes	mitigate erosion, elevate shoreline, reduce adaptive costs, reduce impact guides - 2a,2b,2c, palettes -
useful ecology components	life-cycle to 2050, elevate stemwall crest to 5 ft. NAVD88
SLR planning considerations	life cycle beyond 2050, elevate stemwall crest to 8 ft. NAVD88 - consider including active pumping inland

5 **intertidal plantings**
red mangroves are recommended

6 **storm drain integration**
consider downstream connections; may need to add active pumping

tidal terrace gardens

armor-supported estuary migrations

Rising sea levels will squeeze already degraded intertidal ecosystems against heavily armored urban shorelines, inhibiting the natural ability of these growing features to migrate and adapt to rising seas. The continued loss of these valuable ecosystems will farther degrade key ecosystem services and exacerbate related urban quality of life issues. Rather than utilizing breakwaters, which can be intrinsically harmful to many of these same habitats (i.e, seagrasses and reefs), projects interested in optimizing ecological and recreational co-benefits, and that have a site with room and funds to spare, can design hybrid facilities that support migrations. Shorelines with existing riprap (or walls that add a seaward riprap of equal height) can regrade some of the landscape area inland, incorporating it into the overall shoreline design. At first, a "vegetated riprap" will likely form naturally as mangroves recruit to the old shoreline. A low-lying stemwall with evenly spaced slits/gaps, sited directly above and behind the original shoreline, can be designed to act as a sill breakwater under future conditions, recruiting and protecting mangroves to its lee while promoting beneficial sediment deposition. A dry-wet tidal fringe ecotone can be designed and maintained as an successional ecosystem keeping the planted terrace area vegetated while sea levels transition. A riprap/stemwall terrace along the newly defined upland bank provides a resilient elevation and stabilization for inland areas. Since this design is relatively wide, elements such as solid-raised building foundations may be sited adjacent. Elevated boardwalk platforms/docks and salt tolerant shade tree planters enhance heat mitigation, promote inland drainage, and add to aesthetics.

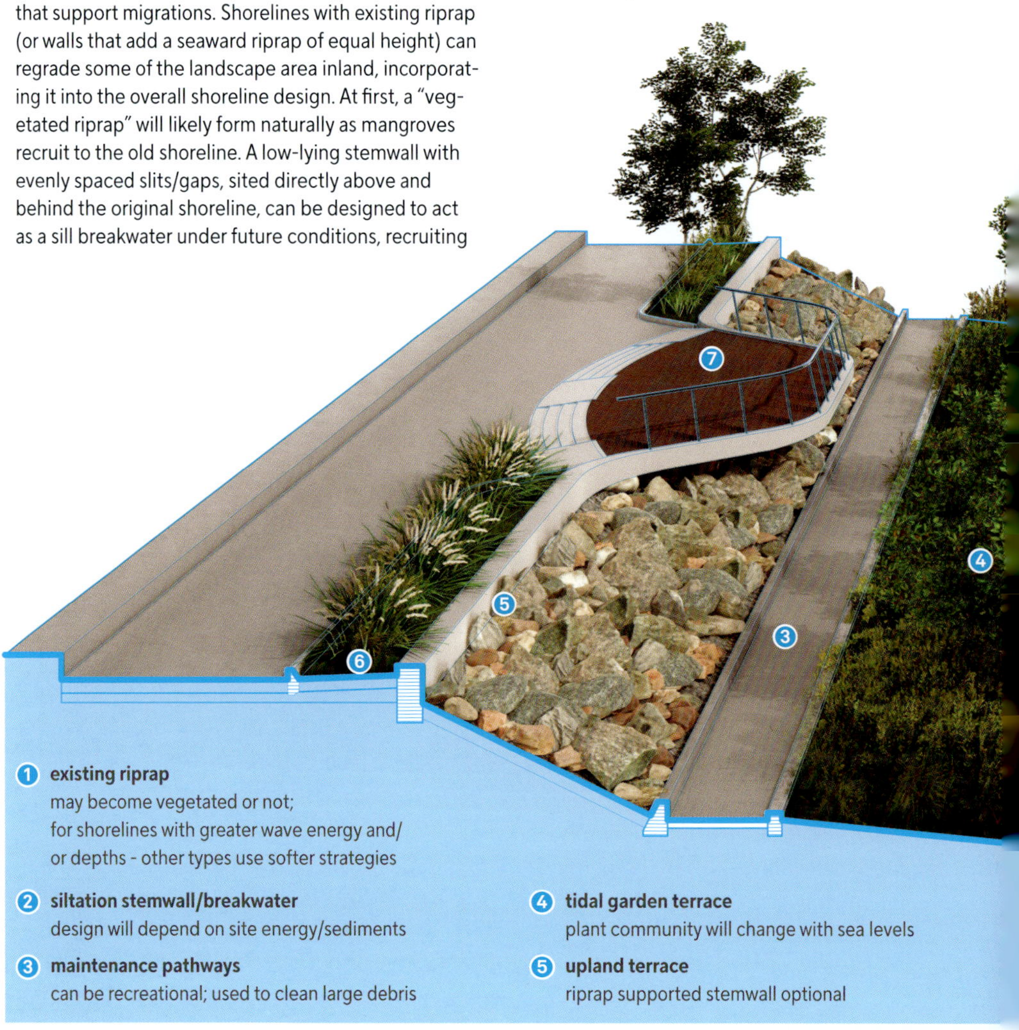

1. **existing riprap**
   may become vegetated or not;
   for shorelines with greater wave energy and/or depths - other types use softer strategies
2. **siltation stemwall/breakwater**
   design will depend on site energy/sediments
3. **maintenance pathways**
   can be recreational; used to clean large debris
4. **tidal garden terrace**
   plant community will change with sea levels
5. **upland terrace**
   riprap supported stemwall optional

summary

problem areas addressed	tidal flooding, erosion, surge, heat, pollution
recommended scales - sites	blocks, neighborhoods - ample space sites
infrastructural goals/outcomes	mitigate erosion, elevate shoreline, ecological co-benefits, recreation co-benefits guides - 2a,2b,2c,2d palettes -
useful ecology components	life-cycle to 2050 elevate inland terrace to 5 ft. NAVD88
SLR planning considerations	life-cycle beyond 2050 elevate inland terrace to 8 ft. NAVD88

biorention planter
salt-tolerant plants only

recreational boardwalks/docks
consult with locals for design details

tidal impoundment & sea level rise

coming to terms with a tidal cityscape

In the wake of the widespread flooding that rocked Miami following Hurricane Irma, many began to seriously consider the potentially deadly combination of sea level rise and storm surge in low-lying south Florida, including the U.S. Army Corps of Engineers.

As part of a greater proposal for coastal adaption in Miami over the next forty years, the Corps suggested constructing six miles of twenty-foot-tall seawalls around parts of Brickell and downtown Miami. The proposed wall would have snaked through coastal neighborhoods and extended out into Biscayne Bay. Public backlash over this proposal prompted a series of revised design suggestions, with more recent designs featuring a series of mangrove-lined breakwater islands sited in the Bay itself. Realistically, either of these approaches would cost billions and have heavy social and environmental impacts.

The public conversation around sea level rise adaptation in Miami demonstrates the tension in coastal management between the engineered and the natural. This tension is integrally linked to both hybrid shoreline design and to urban development in the coastal zone more generally. Can south Florida have both a coastal paradise and protected urban coast?

Hybrid shoreline designs expecting to fully maximize all engineering and socio-ecological outcomes, and not provision for compromise in either direction, can expect to be inherently expensive. This is not to say that hybrid approaches are incapable of achieving win-win outcomes at competitive prices, nor meant to imply that their potential costs do not also include worthy benefits. In the short-term, socio-ecological benefits can come with incremental and collective changes to management, and any hybrid shoreline strategy represents a far more adaptive stance than "business as usual."

1 **detached breakwater levee**
could also be seawalls or spoil islands

2 **riprap revetment**
used here to stabilize seaward face of levee

3 **flood control gate & culvert**
supports control/management of tidal flows

4 **impounded tidal waterway**
low-energy area flushed by daily tides

5 **mangrove living shoreline**
provides stabilization and other benefits

urban micro-lagoons

But in the long-term, this tendency towards increasingly extreme designs seems as inevitable as a six-foot rise or more in sea levels. A likely result of either twenty-foot-tall seawalls or extensive living breakwaters for Miami, whether intentional or not, would be some amount of tidal impoundment, with tidewaters accumulating in urban areas. Both proposal would protect Miami from the more violent effects of storm surge but widespread flooding would likely persist, and may even increase, perhaps occuring in areas where it had not occurred before the structures were built.

Part of this issue is due to south Florida's unique geological situation. The porous limestone karst underlying the urban coastal zone, coupled with rising sea levels, will tend to push groundwater upwards, towards the surface, as an elevated ocean applies hydrostatic pressure. Ultimately, the only way for the urban environment to remain dry in the long-term is for the urban landscape itself to become both flood and salt tolerant. In essence, it will likely be impossible for urban south Florida to completely avoid tidal flooding in the long run, regardless of whether a hard or hybrid approach to coastal management is implemented.

Once long-term designs begin to embrace this reality of a wetter urban future, the tendency for some extensively armored features to create tidally impounded areas to their landward takes on new implications. The practice of intentionally impounding tidal areas is already widely used throughout more rural, coastal areas in Florida, and is done to help reduce mosquitos and protect coastal wetlands. Such design outcomes are also likey to be important to the emerging management of flooded and semi-flooded urban landscapes.

Urban "micro-lagoons" could be designed to blend strategic armoring features with coastal wetland restorations. The armoring aspects would protect impounded areas from storm surges and erosion while also allowing managers to more seamlessly control tidal water levels and flows at the landscape level. Incorporating extensively planted tidal wetlands would help to mitigate the many water quality issues likely to accompany flooded urban landscapes while also providing other ecosystem serivces.

Irrespective of their design specifics, long-term plans should consider the implications of any extensive armoring proposals, to not only the well-being of today's urban coast, but to that of the future's.

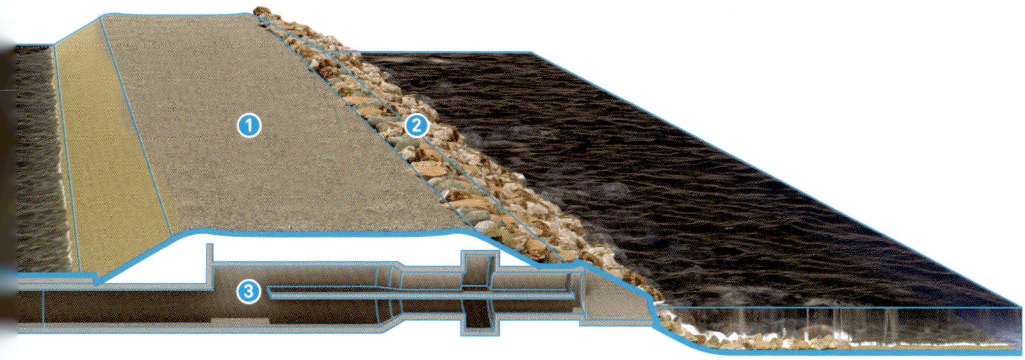

earthern berm, vegetated buffer, & path
integrates shoreline with inland urban area

tidal control gates

flow control at scale

Related to the shift in design considerations currently being experienced by local coastal managers, managers at more regional scales are similarly having to reconsider flow control strategies. Due to the gravity-driven nature of the regional canal network, the SFWMD and local partners are considering a series of large-scale projects that will seek to better integrate a complex network of floodwalls, canals, pumps, and tidal control gates to help manage the increases in flooding expected with rising seas. Tidal control gates are mechanical structures used to obstruct, slow, and/or alter tidal exchanges within enclosed or semi-enclosed waterways. The most relavent example in south Florida today is the "salinity control structures," but there are many other designs as well, each having unique uses, design scales, and considerations. Generally, tidal gate designs are considered either "passive" or "active."

passive flood gates

With "passive" gate designs, the action of the gate is controlled by the level and velocity of the waterway itself, and these types are considered "self regulating." The most common example of passive tidal control used in south Florida today is tidal check valves. Another, less common design safely integrates tidally impounded areas with more exposed waterways via culverts. The design shown at right is an example of this and is useful for managing flows in and out of tidal wetlands. In this design, the gentle change in water levels accompanying normal, daily tides causes the gate to float, allowing flows to freely transit the culvert in either direction under normal conditions. But during flood conditions, when the water level/velocity exceeds a certain elevation, pressure of water above shuts the gate, reducing the erosive energies within the protected area. Another design (below) employs the reverse of that strategy, floating a surge barrier sited in a seawall to protect inland areas under elevated conditions.

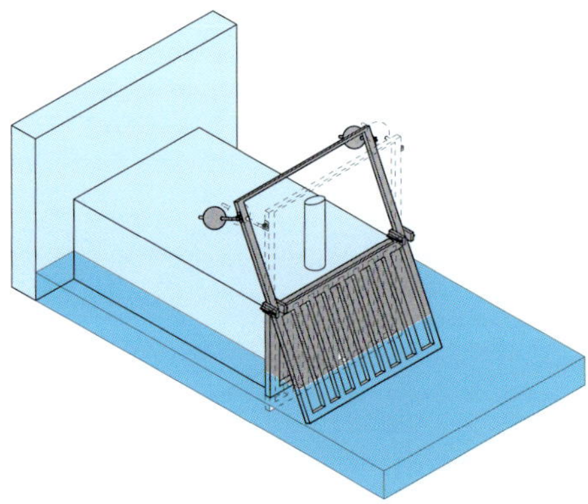

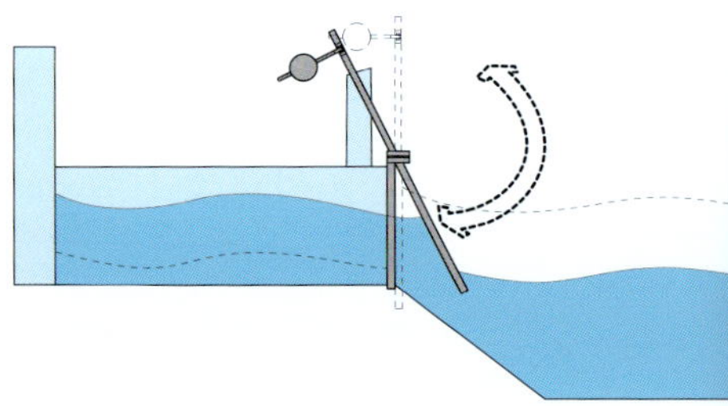

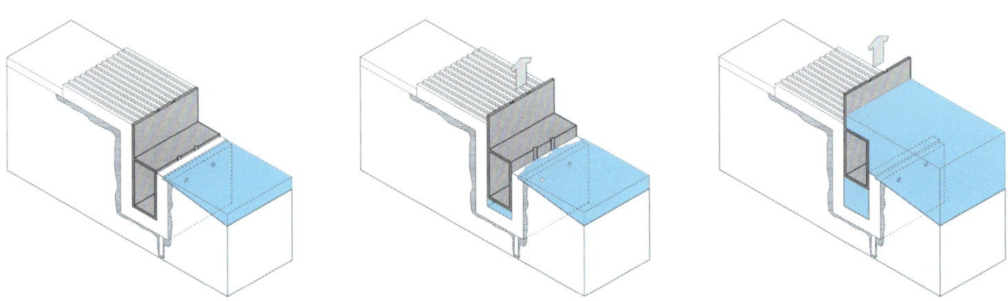

active flood gates

With "active" gate designs, a mechanical barrier is opened and closed on command, requiring electricity and a mechanical system to operate. These are normally sited within canals, rivers, channels, inlets, or similar waterways, and while some are meant for smaller scales (like that shown at top right), most are used at very large scales. The design shown at center right is similar to that of the regional control structures operated by the SFWMD. The main difference being the design shown here controls roughly equal water levels to either side, while the control structures have distinct "head" and "tail" elevations, with the landward "headwater" being considerably higher than the seaward "tailwater" under normal conditions. Some very large-scale designs, like that shown at bottom, only close in advance of storm events and are used to block surges from entering inlets.

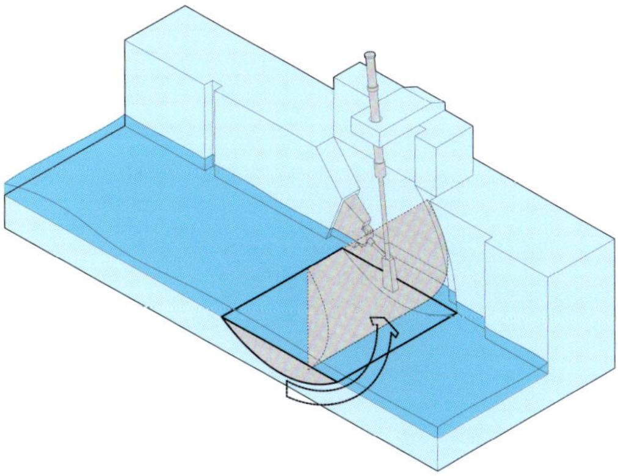

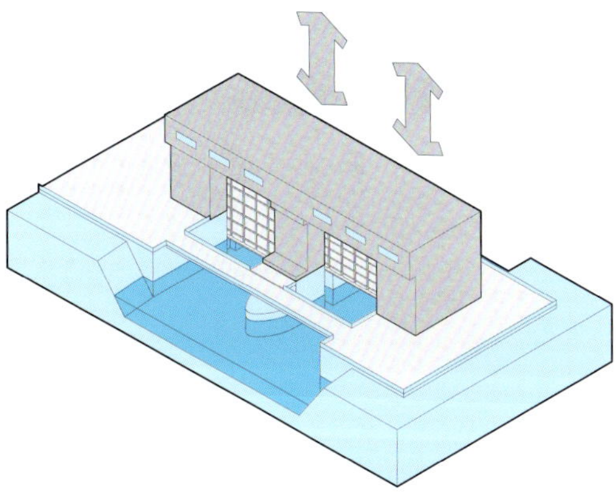

management & networking

Similar to advances in stormwater network management, some advances have been made in automation and system optimization for tidal networks managing sea level rise. For example, estimates of compound flooding under various scenarios for Norfolk, Virginia, found that gates could dramatically reduce flooding related to sea level rise and that predictive modeling and systems management of individual network nodes could improve outcomes even more. Similar assessment from China determined that tide gates could successfully improve coastal drainage networks experiencing compound flooding at a regional level, but that each gate is best opened/closed to control peak flows with respect to key water level criteria, determined for each gate. That study also indicated that regionally organizing network design by tidal, nontidal, and "transition" zones may farther improve management. Ultimately, any network that relies heavily on tidal gates will fail if the sea level surpasses gate design elevations.

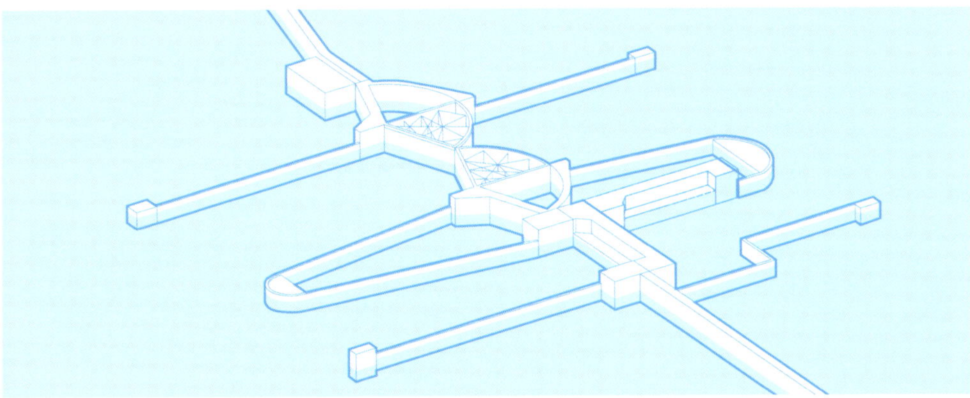

estuarine corridor design

The diverse environmental impacts of urban-climate cascades will be especially pronounced in the estuarine areas of south Florida as the "coastal squeeze" of rising sea levels drives the few remaining nearshore habitats against heavily armored shorelines. Although difficult to quantify in economic terms, the societal value of healthy nearshore ecosystems, both in south Florida specifically and at large, is quite high. For there to be any hope of saving these valuable environments for Florida's future, all aspects of coastal city design will need to change to prioritize the marine environment and minimize harm. One promising option may be to marry the emerging design of resilient "green-grey" stormwater facilities with coastal wetland migration corridors. Florida's coastal habitats, and urban green spaces, generally, provide a great variety of benefits to residents. Future urban planning might look to maximizing the accessibility of these important green spaces for urban residents while simultaneously improving landscape flood control by developing "restoration corridors," where some built features are removed or redesigned to receive migrating estuaries. Although this will be a challenging excercise in land use coordination, efforts should begin as soon as possible, as the success of such endeavors under future conditions will be more difficult and may depend heavily on any progress made today.

How do urban coasts even begin the work of merging the rigid structure of the built environment with the organic structure of the natural? A great many systemic and essential processes will need to change, but this need not happen overnight and does not mean that people should be forcably removed from the landscape to "save nature."

Conceptual work that mathematically predicts land use changes "cellularly," or inspired by geometric fractals, hold some promise to facilitating organic transitions at larger scales. But at the "ground-level", perhaps the most accessible option is to elevate key built aspects of the public realm while also reducing their intensity.

corridor "top" – tidal gardening

Due to the inherently complex and uncertain nature of predicting where estuarine corridors may arise, planning and design in upstream locations of adaptation action areas should focus on holistic approaches. Encouraging best management practices, nonstructural design improvements, and encouraging salt/tidal tolerant bioretention in inland esturaine areas will help regardless.

corridor "middle" – easement mosaics

Sea level rise inundation maps can help to identify inland areas that may be suitable for "conservation easement" programs or similar in the future, where property owners are encouraged to host targeted restoration efforts and/or explore "saltier" lifestyles by local governments. Emergent flooding issues and disaster response are other avenues of change as patches of repetitive losses may define corridors "naturally." Beneficial wetlands have been documented to accidentally occur in some urban contexts as a result of unintended changes to water management networks, and this is likely happen more in south Florida with sea level rise and should be planned for. Allowing "transition zones" to occur organically will be critical to building estuarine corridors but also complex, requiring the integration of hydrologic, ecologic, and community planning in creative and practical ways.

corridor "bottom" – natural estuaries

Shorelines and estuaries with existing mangrove forest, seagrass meadows, and oyster or coral reef must take primacy as these are the "seeds" of habitat that need to migrate inland and are generally rare in the coastal urban zone today. Estuarine parks and intact natural areas provide essential biotic infrastructure for nature-based solutions, and these areas must be conserved. Incentivizing the wider adoption of living and hybrid shorelines is also critical, but secondary, as existing native seed banks support the overall resilience of these features. New shoreline projects should always seek to enhance nearby habitats, not supplant them.

coastal corridor design

Nearly all of the sandy coastline separating urban south Florida from the Atlantic is considered "critically eroded" today. While sand "nourishments" have successfully mitigated local erosion rates in Florida for many decades, the practice is not without contention. Some experts claim it will continue to be an effective adaptation strategy against rising seas, while others point to the extreme costs associated with the apparent need to source ever increasing amounts of sand. "Sand borrowing" for nourishments from limited offshore reserves comes with many negative environmental costs, especially concerning sedimentation of reefs. Sand sourced from inland mines must be trucked to the beach overland at great expense, and these sources are not infinite. While an integrated system of sand nourishment and borrowing could theoretically result in a "closed loop" - with any eroded sand carried south by prevailing longshore currents relocated north again through future nourishments - in reality, this practice is not so simple. However, this kind of system may explain why observed rates of erosion in south Florida have not reflected observed rates in sea level rise. Reefs provide far more value than simply breakwaters, but continued nourishments are likely required to maintain the existing coast. Managers must consider the socio-ecological trade-off related to these choices carefully. Armoring of the coast is not a good solution either. While taller floodwalls may be effective at protecting areas from surge, such features could also worsen rates of beach erosion. Many of the Coastal Construction Control Line (CCCL) program's mandates are expressly concerned with mitigating this potential, limiting the amount of armoring that can occur on the coast, including that from building foundations. Ultimately, management of the coastline will require the holistic design coordination of a regional corridor, one that integrates management offshore, onshore, and inland, across stakeholders, design scales, and political boundaries.

6 the CCCL, buildings, & coastal realignment

The main regulating component of the CCCL is the Coastal Construction Control Line itself, a semi-political geographic boundary running roughly parrallel to the coast. The Line's exact distance from the ocean varies from location to location, determined by a variety of site-specific and political criteria and enforced by the FDEP. Generally, the CCCL seeks to reduce the impacts of construction activities and built features on coastal erosion and vulnerable coastal organisms, such as sea turtles. A newer but related state effort managed by the FDEP, the Sea Level Impact Projection Study Tool, or "SLIP Study," mandates that new construction in the coastal zone consider low-impact alternatives. While mitigating some of the most harmful types of development, both of these regulations still allow new construction in highly vulnerable areas. Climate change is expected to increase hurricane intensities by as much as 50 percent over the next century, and by the year 2100, a single category 5 hurricane could erode up to 47 percent of the beach area. Future managers should look to considering stronger setback regulations.

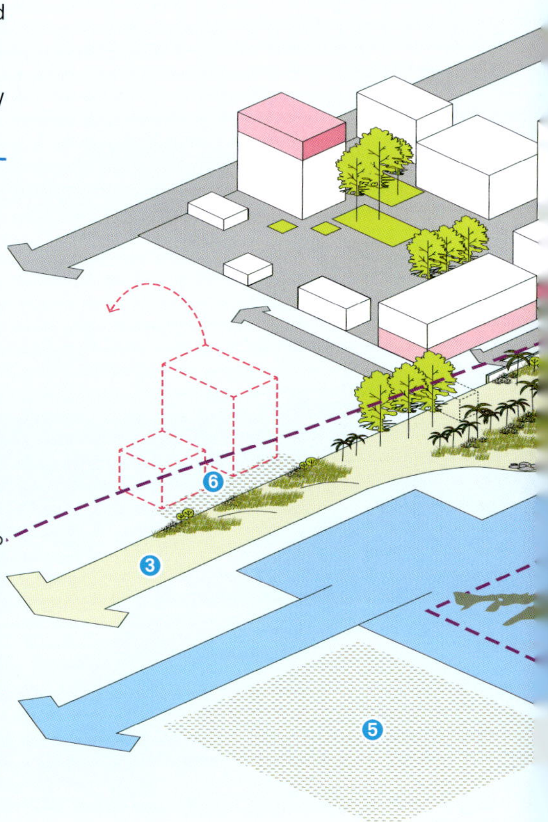

1 sand nourishment & vegetated beach dunes
Sand inputs are encouraged to integrate closely with dune restorations, as covering beach sands with densely planted, native vegetation can enhance outcomes of nourishment.

2 the regional "sand budget"
Waves and currents shape and reshape sandy coastlines, with lower energy waves tending to build up beaches and higher energy waves tending to relocate sand offshore and/or move it south – this ideally results in a balanced "sand budget," with eroded sand on any given beach being replaced by new sand seasonally.

3 man-made erosion
The main cause attributed to the presently eroded condition of south Florida's coast is urbanization, not sea level rise, as the dredging/armoring of inlets combined with the covering of dunes by impervious surfaces has collectively hindered the region's sand budget – beaches immediately south of jetties and inlets are especially bad off and often become "starved" of sand, even despite nourishments.

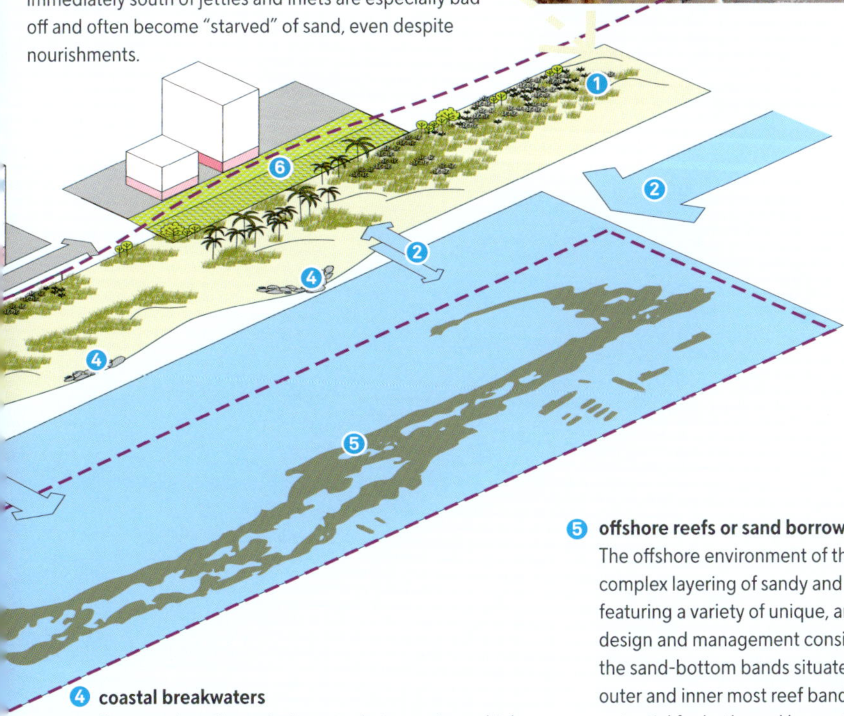

5 offshore reefs or sand borrowing
The offshore environment of the southeast coast is a complex layering of sandy and hard-bottom "bands," featuring a variety of unique, and often conflicting, design and management considerations. Generally, the sand-bottom bands situated between the outer and inner most reef bands have the greatest potential for both sand borrowing and artificial reef placement, but these are generally mutually exclusive by design. Where the enhancement of reef benefits are desired, protecting reefs from the impacts of over-fishing, urban runoff pollution, and sand borrowing/dredging is paramount.

4 coastal breakwaters
For some heavily eroded coasts that experience higher wave energies on average, strategic breakwaters can be used to mitigate localized erosion and maintain sand residence without impacting regional sediment transport. However, these features could also make future sand nourishments more challenging.

coastal stabilization

sediment transport & littoral currents

Sand and other loose particles on a beach are referred to as "sediment," and the movement of sediment by waves and currents is referred to as "sediment transport." Regional and seasonal trends in wave/current direction along coastlines creates unique patterns in sediment transport that can be leveraged to the benefit of coastal management. In some cases, waves will move sediment offshore through a "cross-shore drift." In others, sediment transport tends to move parallel with shore through a "longshore drift." For most beaches within a localized context, a complex combination of these patterns results and influences sediment transport. Individual design considerations for coastal adaptations can vary drastically from beach to beach based on the the interactive effect of localized currents and site conditions.

cross-shore drift

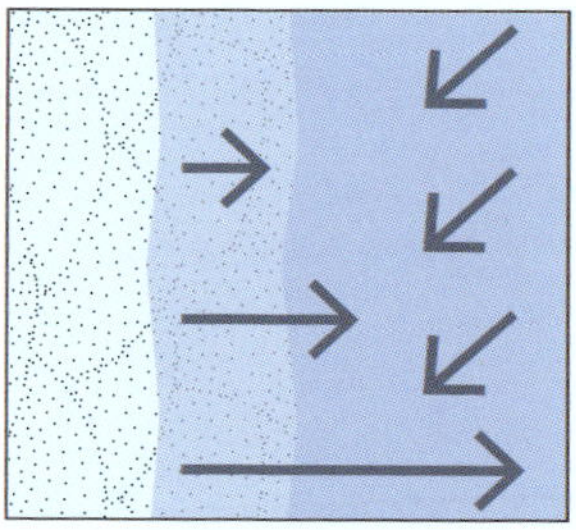

longshore drift

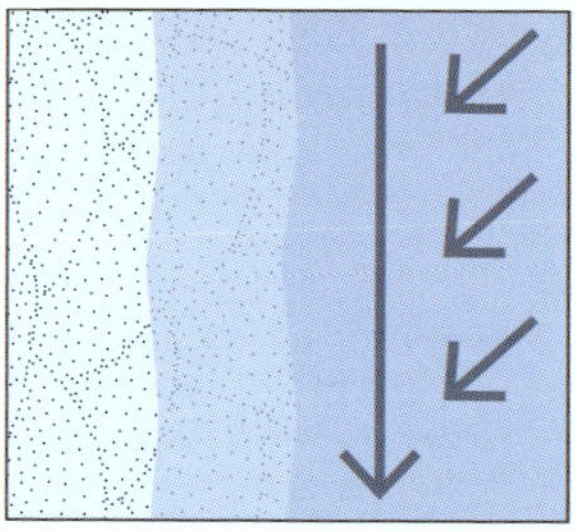

beach nourishment & sea level rise

While sand nourishments provide direct protection and stabilization to inland areas by way of buffering, intentionally losing sand to offshore erosion is also often a main consideration for design outcomes. When beach sand is eroded offshore, not only does it add to regional sand reserves, much of it eventually being deposited and benefiting beaches elsewhere, but the eroded sand can also create nearshore berms that function similar to breakwater features, causing larger waves to break well before shore, thereby mitigating erosion on the remaining beach sand. When simply considering rising seas and not increasing storms nor the associated costs/environmental impacts of sand sourcing, increasing nourishments could, theoretically, maintain many of south Florida's beaches into the future, even under the worst climate change scenarios.

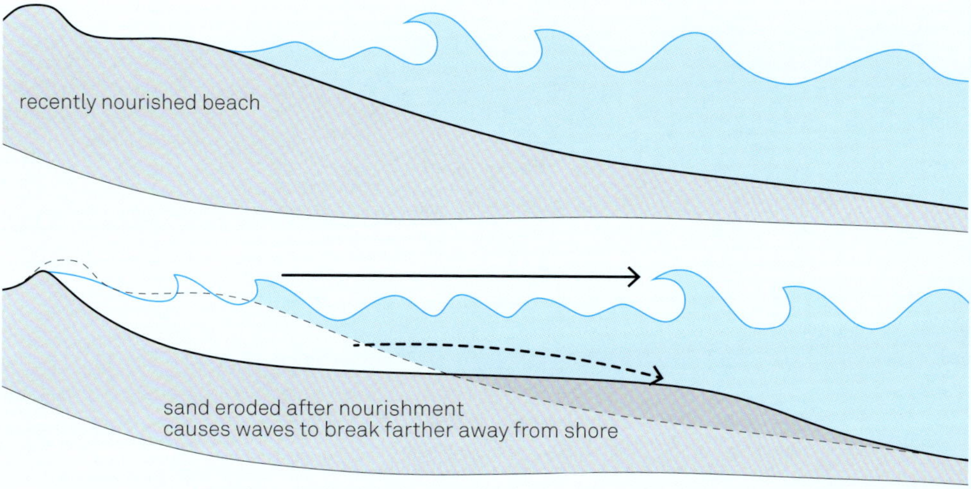

hybrid coastlines

While design options are not as flexible as those along protected tidal shorelines due to a variety of environmental, structural, and political constraints, hybrid designs that incorporate armored features are possible in some coastal areas. These tend to pair breakwater armor with soft stabilization strategies, but other armored designs may be considered in the future as sand reserves dwindle and erosion threats multiply.

detached breakwaters

Likely the most common hybrid shoreline facility in use along Florida coasts today are a combination of minor, detatched breakwaters, sandy beaches, and vegetated dune areas.

The breakwaters used in these designs are normally small groupings of relatively space-limited and low-lying features composed of limestone rock piles. These are sited below the mean tide line, and so are not "attached" to shore, but are also rarely sited very far from it. Protection provided by the breakwaters helps to retain and even collect sand along landward beaches through the manipulation of waves and currents, often resulting in a "platform" of sand that can extend from the beach all the way out to the breakwater itself, in some cases.

While this ability to passively collect sand is useful, the sandy beaches themselves and their vegetated dunes provide the bulk of protection benefits in these designs, the breakwaters are primarily used to support the residence and longevity of beach sand by reducing the rate of its erosion. Coastal breakwaters have traditionally only been necessary along very exposed shorelines that do not have good access to offshore sand reserves normally provided by regional sediment transport. Examples might include islands or beaches in disadvantageous locations with respect to inlets, both of which applies to the beach pictured above on Peanut Island in Palm Beach County. However, with a future of sea level rise, more intense storms, and dwindling sand sources, breakwaters may become more broadly used for preserving wide, recreational beaches.

"Groins" are a related feature sometimes used in similar settings to breakwaters and made of similar materials. Groins differ in that they are attached to shorelines, oriented perpendicular to them, while breakwaters are parallel. This relatively minor distinction results in a marked difference in outcomes, as groins impound sand to one side, while breakwaters encourage sand deposition but still allow sand to transport by with currents. Groins are discouraged for their propensity to "starve" beaches of sand, both nearby and regionally.

Breakwaters can be complex to design. The considerations detailed here are broad, apply equally to both estuaries and coasts, and are strictly meant to help orient designs by possibilities and not directly inform them.

reefs & sills

Breakwater features designed to have low overall heights and that are sited below mean tide to encourage waves to break offshore are called either "reefs" or "sills." "Sill" tends to be used more to refer to uses in low energy settings. If for low-energy (sills), siting should be very close to shore, ideally within ten feet waterward of MHW. Sills are useful for stabilizing living shorelines. If for high-energy areas (reefs), siting will vary by context and desired outcomes, but the material used should be relatively massive while also being ecologically compatible. The total height of either sill or reef should be more than 16 percent of the water depth to impact wave energies.

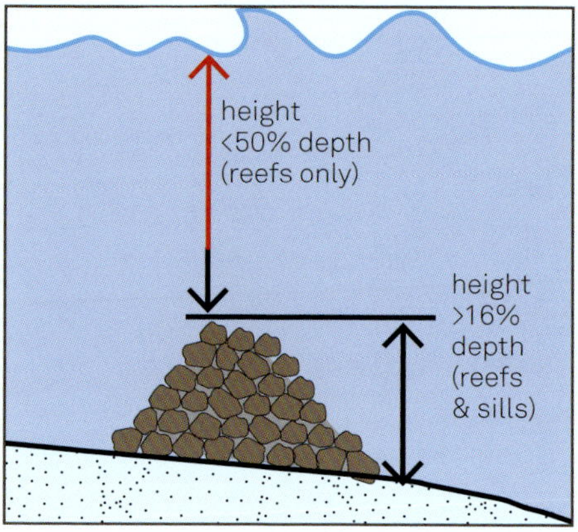

breakwaters & headlands

Detached breakwaters designed to be above water during most conditions reduce wave energy but also are designed to mimic natural seaward rocks or land that inspire beach formation to their protected sides. These are usually sited farther from shore than sills, but closer to shore than reefs, and compared to either, tend to block more incoming wave energy beacause they are above water. "Headlands" specifically refers to breakwaters that encourage beach platform formation in protected areas.

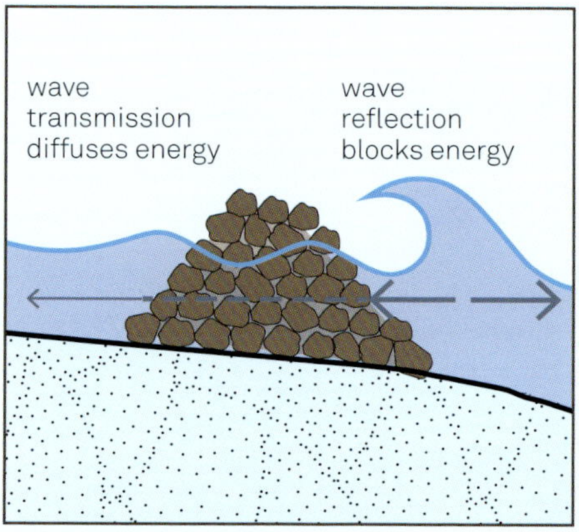

breakwater design & beach influence

A primary consideration of any breakwater is its influence on landward beaches. Sills are used to help stabilize localized littoral areas, while reefs are used to reduce wave energy more generally and at larger scales. Headlands and breakwaters above water produce different types of beach platforms depending on their design and positioning. When the resulting platform extends from shore but does not reach the breakwater itself, it is called a "salient," and these are used to build beach while still facilitating sediment transport. When a platform reaches all the way out to a breakwater it is called a "tombolo," and these are used to support wide beaches locally. Whether a tombolo or salient forms is mostly determined by a given breakwater's proximity to shore.

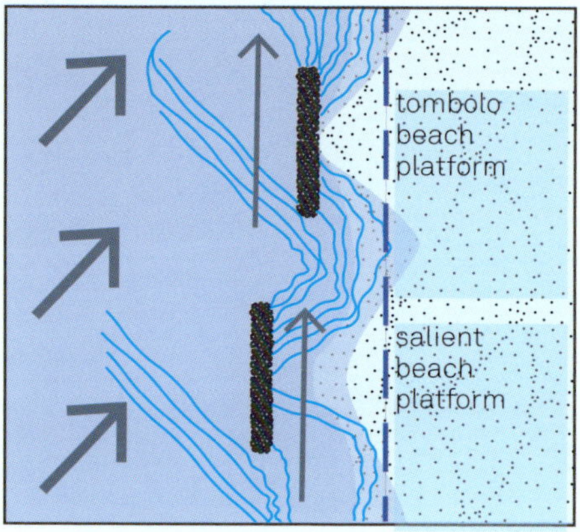

breakwater materials

Materials used to create breakwaters can vary as greatly as their design intent. Sills are generally smaller overall, with "oyster bags" (mesh bags filled with oyster shale) and "ReefBallsTM" (pre-cast, naturalistic shapes made of proprietary calcareous concretes) being among materials commonly used in estuarine settings. In some lower-energy estuaries, large pieces of driftwood may be used as breakwaters, and a few shorelines in Florida retain old dock pilings or the dead stumps of invasive Australian pines following their removal to provide protection for landward native plants. Limestone rocks piled into various riprap formations are the most commonly used material for breakwaters/headlands in south Florida as these are best for resisting energies associated with high boat activity and storm surges. Concrete rubble or similar materials may be used in a similar manner if sufficiently cleaned, presenting unique reuse potential. Any breakwater material will be directly interfacing with aquatic ecosystems and should be designed accordingly, but this is especially important for reef designs. The material used for a breakwater, sill, or reef can also influence the way wave energies interact with it and how localized erosion occurs. The figure series at right demonstrates different results for some sill materials common to various contexts.

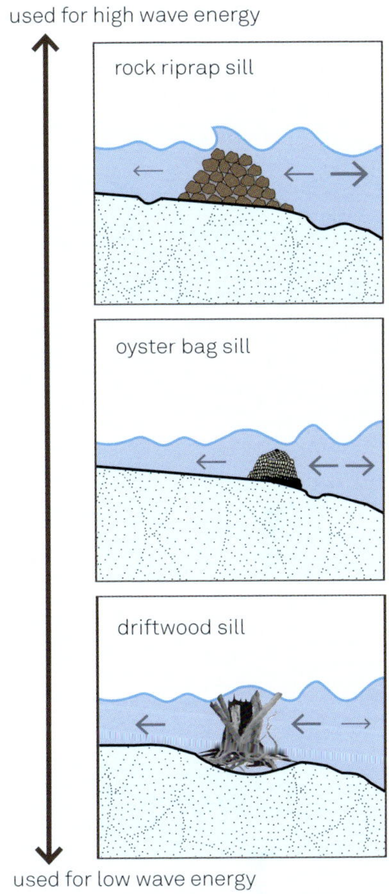

size & spacing

Projects should be less than 500 feet in total length to reduce shoreline impacts and permitting constraints. Generally, longer individual units spaced farther apart produce more pronounced beach platforms and bays, while smaller units spaced closer together produce a more consistent beach area. A minimum of a one-foot gap every seventy-five feet is required.

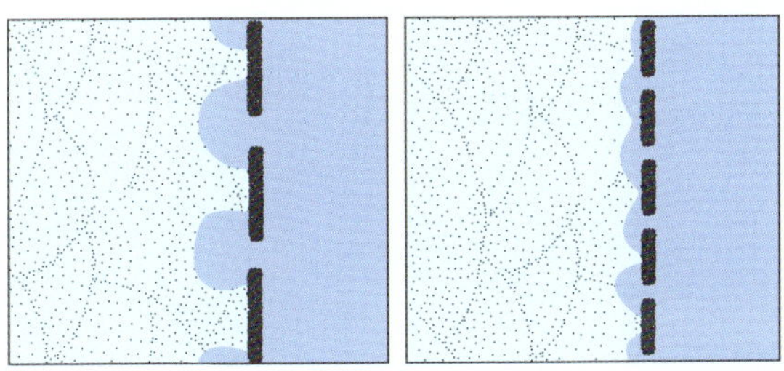

shapes & groupings

A variety of different breakwater shapes and configurations are possible, each with unique design outcomes related to beach formation, wave reduction, and current influence.

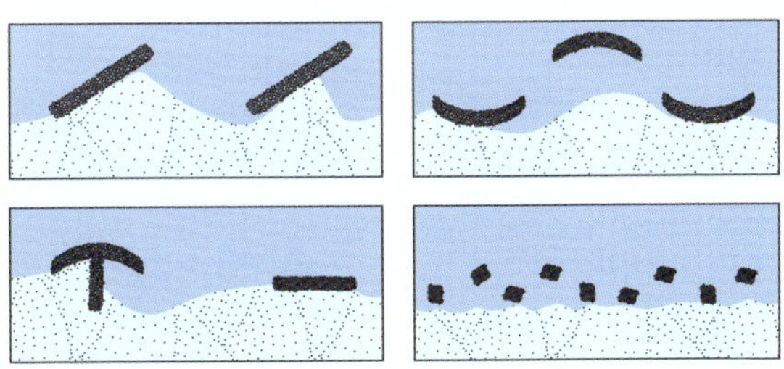

artificial reefs

In response to mounting environmental concerns over nearshore habitat and fisheries degradation, Florida has developed one of the nation's most progressive artificial reef programs of recent decades. Despite extensive regulations on their design and implementation, artificial reefs are common along Florida's hundreds of miles of coastline today, ranging from scuttled watercraft to purpose-built "reef towers," and providing a variety of co-benefits in addition to breakwaters, such as fisheries habitat and recreational diving tourism. As sea levels rise and climate change continues to ravage reef-building coral populations, the importance of artificial reefs may evolve and combine with concurrent efforts in coral restoration. Designs for "hybrid reefs," that directly couple breakwater benefits with coral restorations and climate change adaptations, should recieve closer scrutiny as these may become increasingly critical to the survival of this important ecosystem.

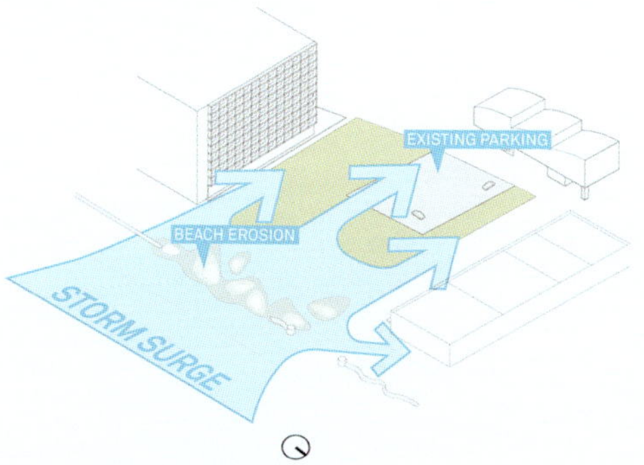

EXISTING PARK

PROPOSED PARK

Example showcasing adaptation of coastal dunes at DC Alexander Park by Brooks + Scarpa. The proposed coastal dunes amplify ecosystem services and provide a robust and vegetated hybrid dune system to help protect the park and surrounding development from future storm surge.

hybrid reef design & future possibilities

Recent investigations into hybrid artificial reef designs, directly merging considerations of wave attenuation with those of coral reef restoration, illuminate a variety of promising future directions. For example, submerged, trapezoidal breakwaters that encourage both offshore wave development and Acropora coral growth (pictured at above right) have the potential to reduce incoming wave heights by as much as 45 percent and wave energy by as much as 77 percent. The benefits of such structures to coral restoration includes increased flexibility for outplanting locations of corals, providing clear areas with beneficial current and sun exposures, while also creating calm areas to their lee where coral nurseries might be sited, improving outplanting success rates. Although far more expensive than traditional designs, hybrids reefs this have such varied and valuable co-benefits that unique financing options may be possible that are not with any other design. However, new permitting exemptions will likely be needed for depths.

hybrid coastal dunes

While most hybrid designs appropriate for exposed coasts utilize some kind of breakwater feature as the armored element, a few emerging designs have also considered the potential feasibility of armored enhancements on shore. In an apparent effort to marry the protective benefits of levees with the recreational benefits of natural beaches, one innovative concept proposes a "hybrid structural dune system" that utilizes a core levee feature sited underneath and/or behind of coastal sand dunes. While most onshore armoring, especially seawalls and floodwalls, are likely to worsen erosion along their exposed sides, causing sand to be eroded at much higher rates during storm conditions than it would be otherwise, the sloped faces of a levee may help to mitigate some of this potential. As recent hurricanes have painfully demonstrated, storm surge can easily enter coastal urban centers, causing direct devastation with violent currents while also causing a myriad of indirect issues through water damage and the spreading of sand inland. Following both Hurricanes Sandy and Irma, for example, Fort Lauderdale Beach saw tons of beach sand redistributed across coastal roadways and urban areas. While much of this sand was initially placed on the beaches at great expense through nourishments, once it contacts impervious urban surfaces, the sand must be collected and removed to landfills at equally great expense as oils and toxins associated with the urban environment cannot be placed back onto the beach due to its ecological implications. A hybrid coastal dune with a levee core would have likely prevented both surge and sand from entering the urban realm, and while it would have caused more erosion of beach sand to offshore than was otherwise experienced, that erosion would have recharged regional sand reserves, rather than represent a net loss from the sand budget to landfills. Such a design could also integrate well with "sand engines" that mechanically relocate sand from inland areas to the coast, helping to reduce some costs associated with inland-sourced sand nourishments. Several outstanding questions remain for such an approach, not least of which are concerns over the actual performance of these theoretical hybrid features under storm conditions. Other crucial design concerns for urban south Florida, specifically, include finding the space necessary to site such large-scale features and along a meaningful amount of coastline. Navigating the likely political backlash from coastal residents regarding beach views and property values would likely be the most challenging consideration. Still, despite these high barriers to feasibility, the reality of sea level rise and increasing storm intensity may warrant closer scrutiny of hybrid designs like these to protect vulnerable urban coasts.

levee with frontal dune
-less sand nourishment required
-takes up less space to landward
-erosion along seaward edge could cause levee to become exposed

dune - covered levee
-better protection provided
-feature height readily adjusted
-seaward erosion replenished
-requires more sand initially
-require ample space landward

dune - covered levee with internal floodwall and rock rubble facing
-internal wall strengthens core
-rock facings catch sand better
-otherwise same as above

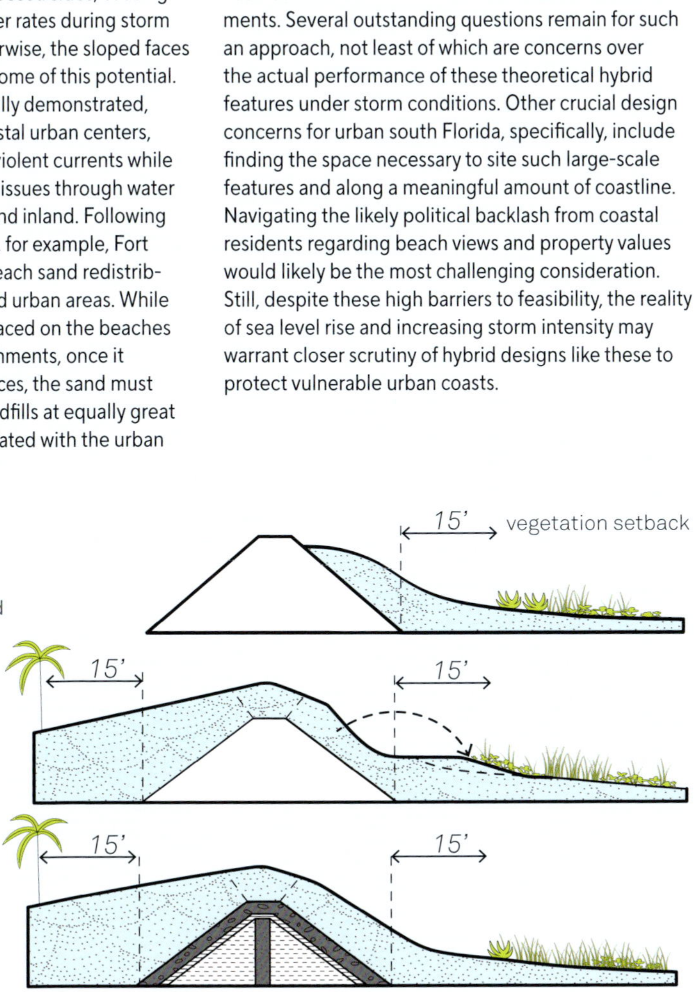

archi- **tecture**

seed
hammock veil
pollinator
CO_2
H_2CO_3
refuge/ orchidari
CH_4
rubber dunes
carbonic acid scrubber

Architecture should be designed to flood, create no impact **on surrounding flooding, and adapt to changing conditions and technologies.**

architecture and landscape design and planning principles

flood-adaptive architecture

Salty Urbanism contributes to the creation of flood-adaptive architecture and buildings by considering the following approaches:

1. Elevation and Design: Salty Urbanism promotes the use of elevated designs to mitigate and adapt to flood risks. Buildings can be constructed on stilts or raised platforms to elevate them above flood-prone areas. The design of structures can also incorporate flood-resistant materials and construction techniques that can withstand water exposure and minimize damage. Other strategies include amphibious and floating structures.

2. Floodwater Management: Salty Urbanism emphasizes effective floodwater management strategies. This can include implementing green infrastructure solutions such as permeable pavements, rain gardens, and bioswales to absorb and manage excess water. Additionally, incorporating features like flood barriers, flood walls, and drainage systems can help redirect and control floodwater.

3. Resilient Materials and Systems: Salty Urbanism promotes the use of resilient materials and systems that can withstand flooding. This can involve utilizing waterproofing techniques (wet and dry floodproofing), corrosion-resistant materials, and innovative building technologies that are capable of resisting water damage and facilitating quick recovery after flooding events.

4. Adaptive Design and Flexibility: Salty Urbanism emphasizes adaptive design principles that allow buildings to respond and adapt to changing flood types and conditions. This can involve flexible layouts, modular construction, and movable components that can be adjusted based on flood forecasts and rising sea and ground water levels. The idea is to create buildings that can dynamically respond to flood events without suffering extensive damage—design for flooding and exceedence.

5. Community Engagement and Awareness: Salty Urbanism recognizes the importance of community engagement and awareness in flood adaptation. The process encourages collaboration between architects, landscape architects, urban planners, engineers, and local residents to ensure that flood-adaptive strategies are well understood and implemented effectively. Public education and awareness campaigns can also play a role in promoting flood preparedness and resilience. By engaging communities at the scale of a neighborhood and smaller, allows the wicked and multifaceted problems to be better absorbed and addressed.

By incorporating these principled line of thinking can help create flood-adaptive architecture and buildings that are better equipped to withstand and recover from flood events, thereby increasing the resilience of coastal cities in the face of climate change and rising sea levels.

extreme heat and saltier conditions

In addition to flood adaptation, architecture also needs to take into consideration extreme heat and salty conditions, which are common challenges in coastal areas. Here are some ways in which architecture can address these issues:

1. Heat-Resilient Design: Salty Urbanism promotes heat-resilient design principles that help mitigate the effects of extreme heat. This includes incorporating shading elements such as awnings, green roofs, and vegetation to reduce solar heat gain. Buildings can be designed with natural ventilation strategies and the use of heat-reflective materials to minimize heat absorption. Large overhangs and brise soleil systems can farther shade and protect interior architecture and spaces.

2. Coastal Landscape Planning: Salty Urbanism recognizes the importance of coastal landscape planning to mitigate the impact of extreme heat. This can involve the strategic planting of trees and vegetation to provide shade, create cooling microclimates, and reduce the urban heat island effect on buildings and the public realm. Incorporating green spaces and parks in coastal areas also provides residents with natural cooling areas in addition to flood storage areas.

3. Salt-Resistant Materials and Infrastructure: Construction materials and methods must consider the

corrosive effects of salty conditions on buildings and infrastructure. Architecture should employ the use of materials that are resistant to saltwater corrosion, such as marine-grade stainless steel and fiber-reinforced composites. Proper maintenance and protective coatings for structures in coastal areas can also help prevent damage caused by saltwater exposure. Building codes that only allow for the use of steel reinforced concrete construction with no provisions for innovation using alternative concrete mixes or reinforcement are extremely limited. The effects of heat, saltwater, and salt-ladened air can have devastating effects on buildings as see with the Surfside building collapse on June 24, 2021. This will become a more common problem until alternative structural materials are allowed by code and regulation.

4. Climate-Responsive Urban Planning: Salty Urbanism emphasizes climate-responsive urban design that takes into account the specific challenges of extreme heat and salty conditions. This includes the strategic placement of buildings and infrastructure to optimize shading, airflow, and access to cooling breezes. Urban design and planning can also incorporate the use of water bodies or water features to provide natural cooling effects.

By integrating these strategies, Salty Urbanism thinking aims to create coastal cities that are better equipped to withstand extreme heat and salty conditions, ensuring the well-being and comfort of residents while adapting to the challenges posed by a changing climate.

hurricanes and extreme storm events

Since August 24, 1992, when Hurricane Andrew devastated south Florida the Florida Building Code has created building that have a high survivability rate to high velocity wind and debris impacts. Architecture must take into consideration the impact of hurricanes and other storm events in coastal areas. It must address these challenges through various approaches. First, resilient building design is emphasized, focusing on construction techniques, reinforced materials, and storm-resistant features such as impact-resistant windows and elevated foundations. Additionally, evacuation planning, emergency response systems, and community engagement are important in ensuring the safety of residents during storm events. Salty Urbanism also promotes the implementation of nature-based solutions with architectural and urban design strategies, such as the restoration and protection of coastal ecosystems like mangroves and wetlands, which act as natural buffers against storm surges.

However, post storms and flood events will continue to have challenges. Do buildings which have fire protection and suppression equipment also include floatable devices to ensure evacuation is possible in the event of long-term and unexpected flooding as was seen on April 12, 2023 when over twenty-five inches of rainfall fell in Fort Lauderdale in less than twenty-four hours?

Through the above strategies and principles and proceeding pages, Salty Urbanism aims to enhance the resilience of coastal architecture and safeguard both the well-being of residents and the integrity of infrastructure and buildings. The following pages include flood-adaptive techniques that also address a hotter, saltier, and more extreme weather future.

flood-adaptive architecture menu

flood type

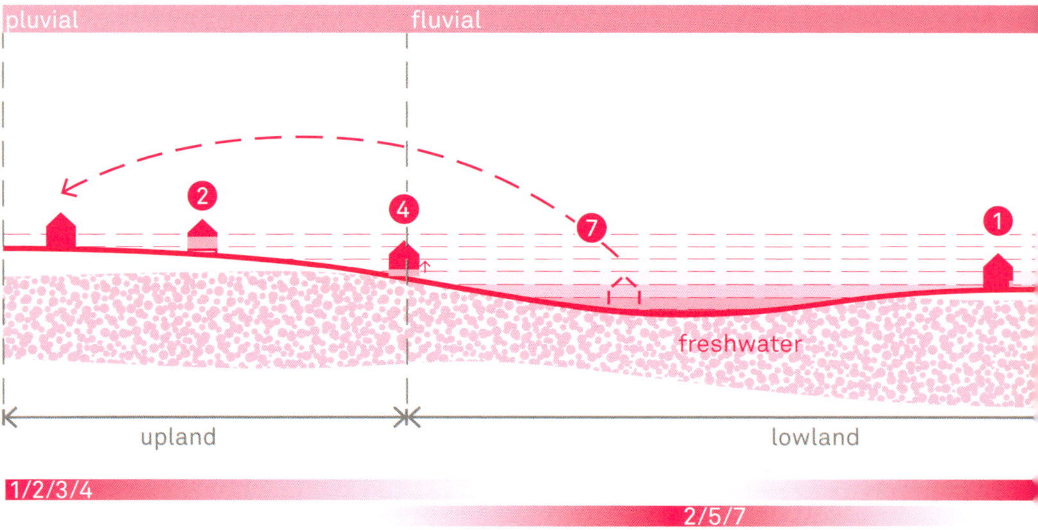

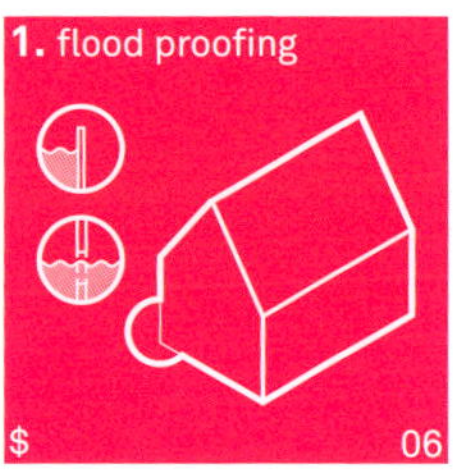

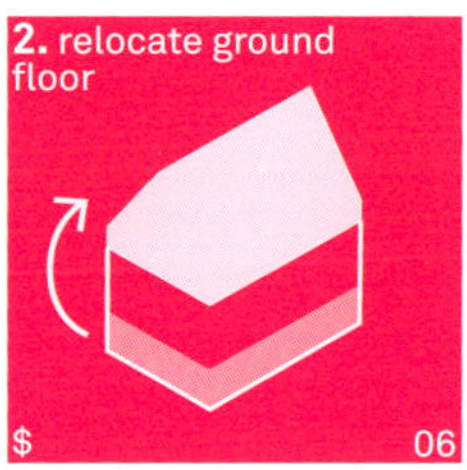

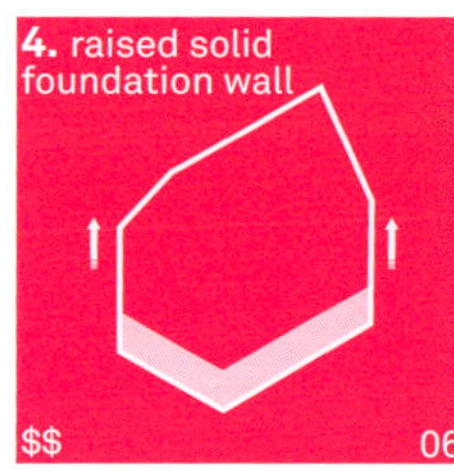

1. Dry flood-proofing: utilizes water-resistant materials and panel systems at openings to prevent water intrusion.

2. Wet flood-proofing: utilizes flood vents or breakaway walls to allow flooding to pass through.

3. Or increase the floor to ceiling dimension at ground level and raise floor.

Structure is built to accomdate retreat over time by abandoning lower-floor levels.

Building is raised above bfe on stilts. Keep in mind that nfip criteria does not account for future land development, coastal erosion and subsidence, or sea level rise. These would have to be factored in to ensure lifespan considerations. Consideration of what happens under the building should be addressed.

Structure is bulit on the raised platform. The raised platform can increase in elevation over time as adaptation demands.

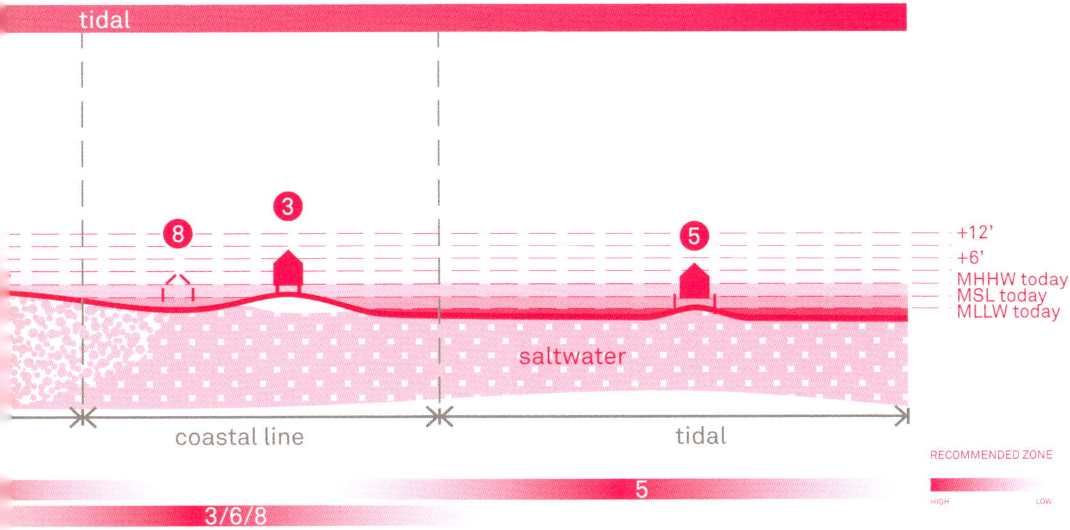

5. floating structure

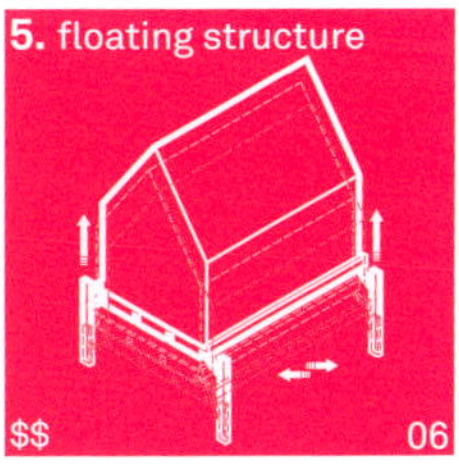

Structure is built to float on water and tethered to a mooring or anchoring device while allowing the building to move freely in multiple directions

6. amphibious structure

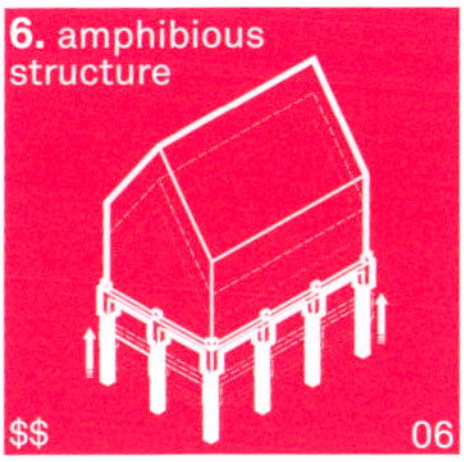

Structure is built to float on elevated flood water. The piles anchor the structure in place while the buoyant base floats up and down. The building rests atop the ground during non-flood events.

7. retreat

Relocation of buildings to higher elevations where flooding is less likely to occur. This could be a few hundred feet or miles.

8. abandon

Abandoned structures can be reclaimed or re-purposed, for example, the building could become an artificial reef or breakwater once materials that can pollute waterways are removed.

flood proofing

description

Involves implementing measures to protect buildings from flooding. This can include elevating structures, using flood-resistant materials, applying waterproofing techniques, installing flood barriers or vents, ensuring proper drainage, and incorporating backup power systems. These strategies aim to minimize damage and enhance the resilience of buildings in flood-prone areas.

summary

cost	$$$
building type	commercial and mixed-use
locations	coastal and low-lying areas

opportunities & challenges

Opportunities of flood proofing include mitigating property damage, enhancing resilience, ensuring safety, and potentially lowering insurance costs. Challenges include high costs, technical complexity, aesthetic considerations, and regulatory compliance.

design considerations

Considerations include incorporation of flood-resistant openings, effective drainage systems, barrier systems, protection of electrical and mechanical systems, and ensuring accessibility and evacuation measures.

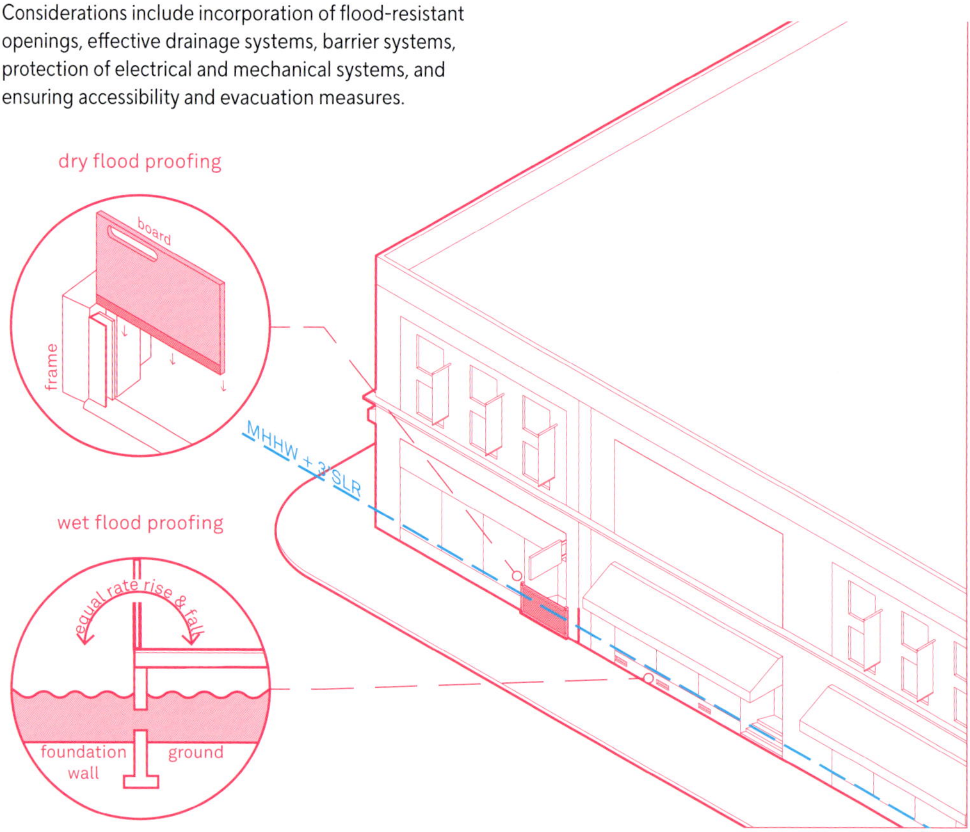

relocate ground floor

description

Flood adaptation, specifically in the context of abandoning lower floors, refers to a strategy where buildings or structures in flood-prone areas are designed or retrofitted to allow for the intentional abandonment of lower levels. This approach recognizes the vulnerability of ground-level spaces. Ground floors can also be designed with higher ceilings to allow floor to be raised instead of entire floor being abandoned.

opportunities & challenges

By intentionally sacrificing lower floors, buildings can enhance their resilience to floods, reduce repair costs, and expedite post-flood recovery. The feasibility and effectiveness of this strategy depend on various factors.

design considerations

This approach uses flood-resistant materials and construction techniques to allow water intrusion, thus designating lower floors for non-habitable or less critical functions. Retrofitting measures, such as flood barriers and sealed-off zones, are implemented to prevent water entry during flood events. Never place building systems at ground level.

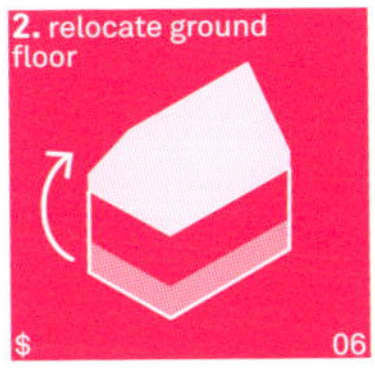

summary

cost	\$-\$\$\$
building type	any type
locations	coastal and low-lying areas

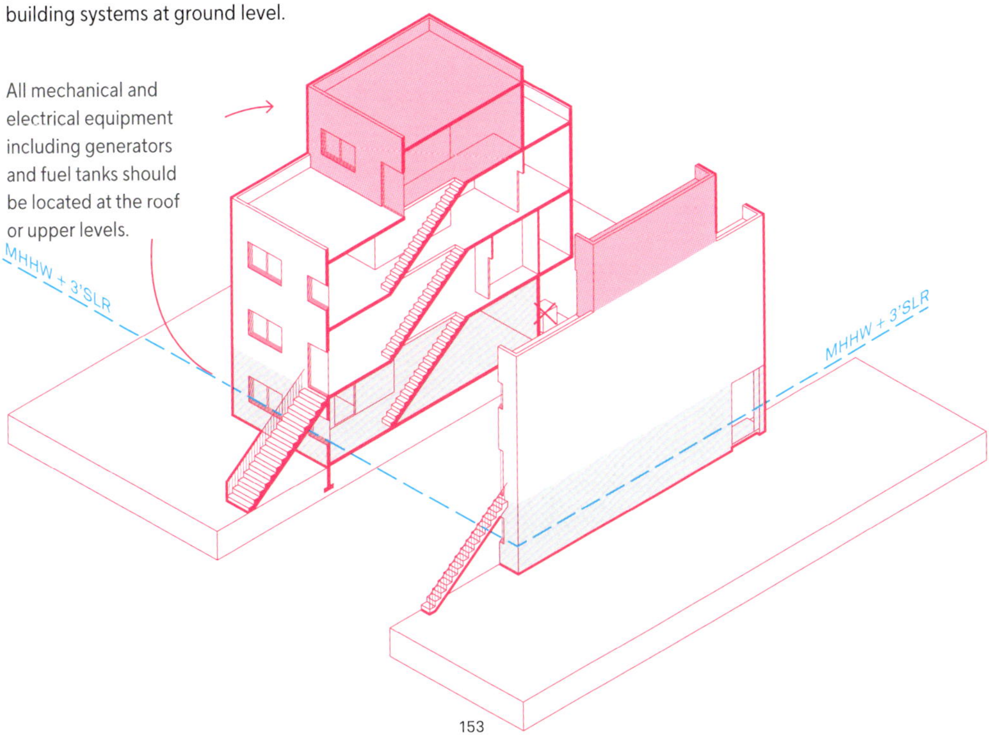

raised stilts

description

Stilted architecture is a design approach where buildings are constructed on columns or stilts, lifting the habitable spaces above the ground level. This architectural style is commonly employed in flood-prone areas as a flood adaptation strategy.

opportunities & challenges

By elevating the building above the potential flood level it helps protect the structure from floodwater damage allowing floodwaters to pass underneath the building, reducing the risk of water entering the living or working spaces and minimizing damage to the structure and its contents.

design considerations

Provides a practical solution for areas where recurrent flooding is a concern. In addition to flood adaptation, it offers other advantages like ventilation and natural cooling, improved views, and increased privacy, especially in densely populated areas. Designers should take into account the lifespan of the structure to ensure it raised high enough for current and future conditions. The underbelly activiation is critical as well.

summary

cost	$$
building type	single family, multi-family
locations	coastal and low-lying areas

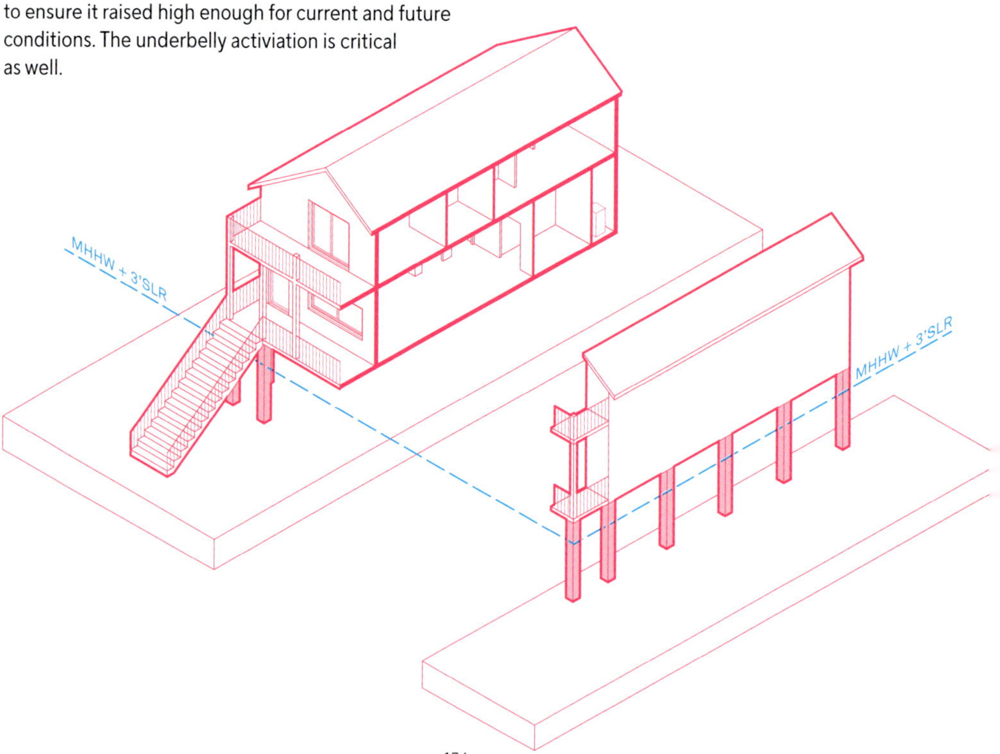

raised solid foundation

description

Stemwalls or a solid foundation is another approach to flood adaptation. Stemwalls are short walls constructed around the perimeter of a building, typically made of reinforced concrete, which elevate the structure above the ground. This method provides a raised platform for the building while maintaining a solid foundation.

opportunities & challenges

Consider the specific site conditions and the potential impact of floodwaters on the surrounding area. Adequate drainage systems should be implemented to ensure that water does not accumulate around the stemwalls or beneath the raised structure.

design considerations

Several advantages are it allows for a more secure and stable structure, providing a level of protection against both shallow and deep floods. It also enables easier access to the building during flood events, as well as facilitates post-flood cleanup and recovery efforts. Additional benefits include improved ventilation, enhanced views, and increased durability against other environmental factors like moisture and pests.

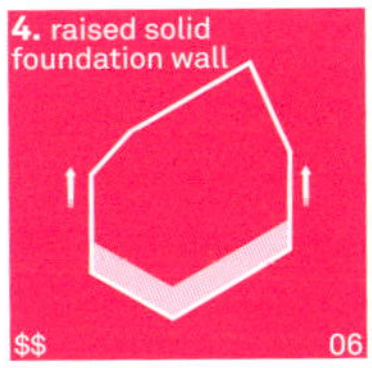

summary

cost	$$
building type	single family mostly
locations	coastal and low-lying areas

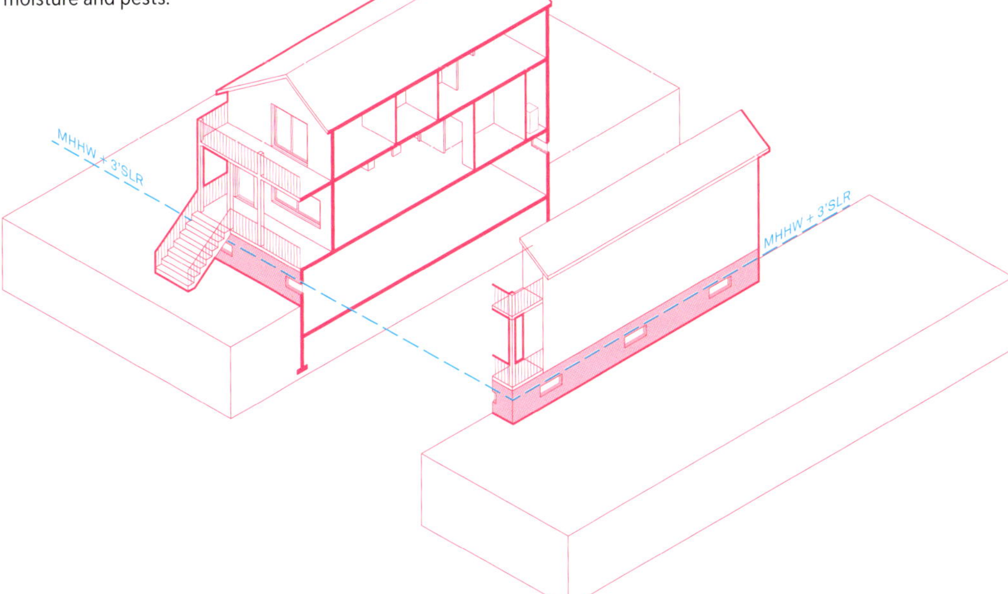

floating structure

description

Offer an innovative approach to flood adaptation. Instead of being firmly anchored to the ground, these structures are designed to float on water or be buoyant during flood events. This design concept allows buildings to rise and fall with changing water levels, minimizing the risk of damage and providing a resilient solution to flood-prone areas.

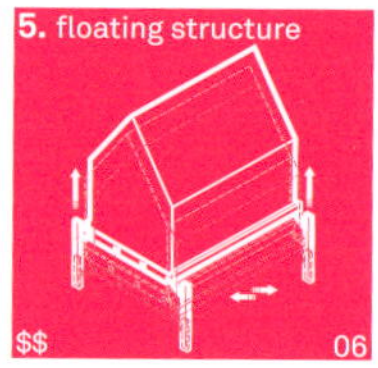

summary

cost	$$
building type	single family, townhouses
locations	coastal or open water areas

opportunities & challenges

Floating structures typically consist of buoyant materials and are engineered to withstand the forces exerted by water. They can be constructed using materials like reinforced concrete, steel, or specialized buoyant materials such as foam or hollow pontoons. The buoyancy is carefully calculated to ensure stability while accommodating variations in water levels.

design considerations

Considerations include infrastructure integration, stability, and accessibility.

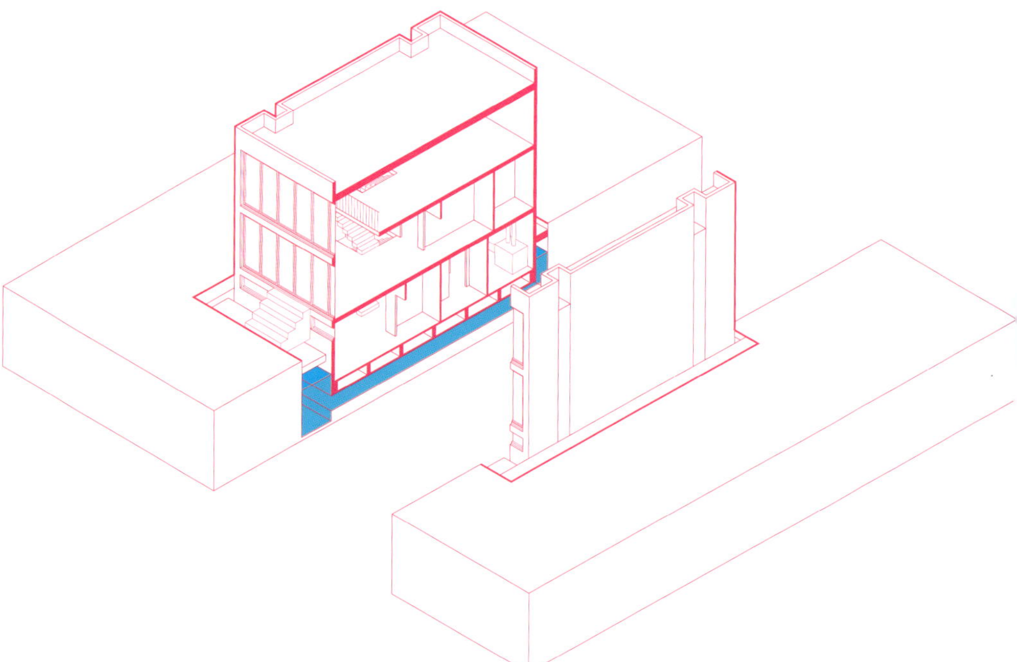

amphibious structure

description

Structures are designed to be partially or fully buoyant, capable of rising with floodwaters while remaining securely anchored to the ground during normal conditions. This adaptability allows them to withstand and mitigate the impact of flooding. Typically feature a combination of buoyant elements and traditional building techniques.

summary

cost	\$\$\$
building type	single family, townhouses
locations	open water or wetland areas

opportunities & challenges

During flood events, they float on the rising water level, reducing the risk of flood damage. When water recedes, they settle back onto their foundations. Structure, mooring, and utility connections can be challenging.

design considerations

They offer cost-effective and environmentally compatible solutions, but require careful structural design, anchoring, and utility integration.

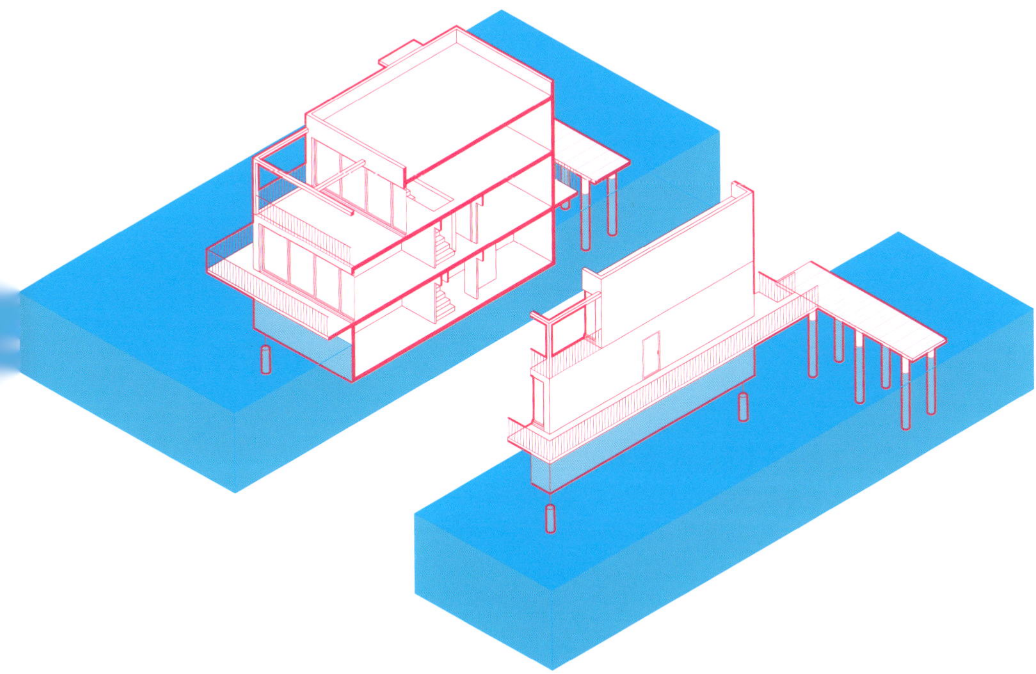

retreat (relocate)

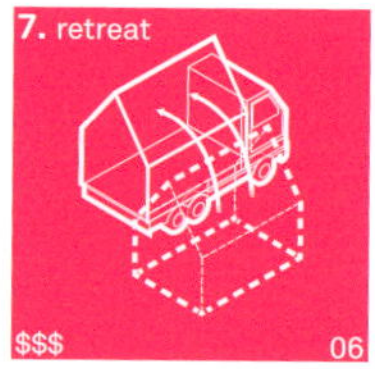

description

Relocating or moving structures is another strategy for flood adaptation. Instead of modifying the existing building, this approach involves physically moving the structure to a safer location outside the flood-prone area.

opportunities & challenges

Relocating or moving structures ensures safety, long-term resilience, and preservation of historical/cultural buildings, but challenges include cost, site availability, disruption, and ensuring building integrity.

design considerations

Relocating structures requires careful planning, coordination with relevant authorities, and engagement with professional consultants, logistics, and building code compliance. Considerations such as site selection, cost analysis, and community engagement should be evaluated to determine the feasibility and viability of relocating structures as a flood adaptation strategy.

summary

cost	$$$
building type	single family, small structure
locations	move to higher ground

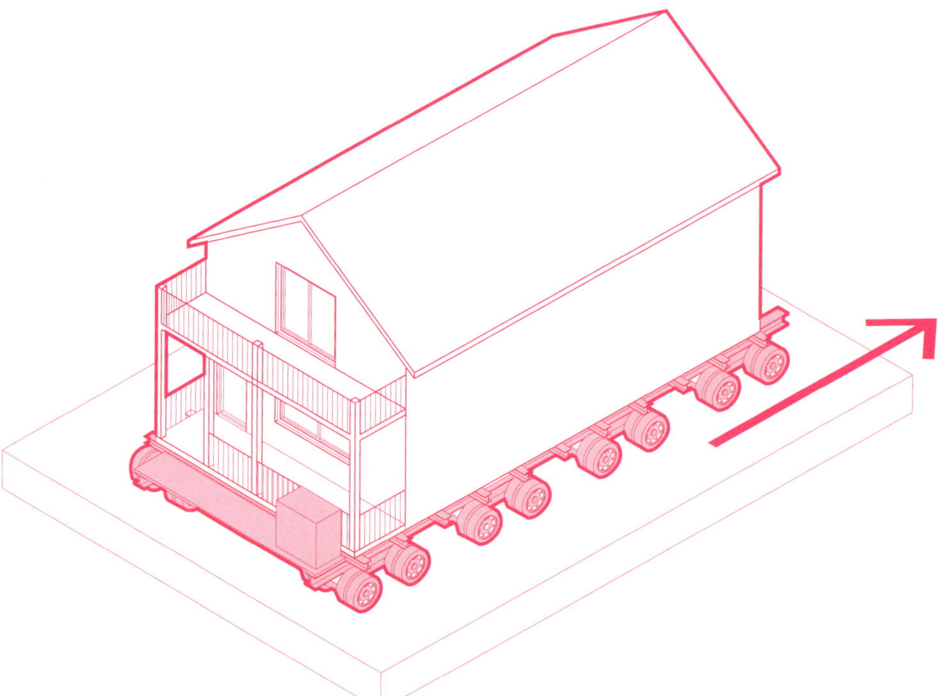

abandon

description

Abandoning buildings involves permanently vacating and ceasing the use of buildings located in flood-prone areas. Instead of implementing extensive flood-proofing measures or relocation, this strategy acknowledges the high flood risk and makes a deliberate decision to abandon the affected structures.

opportunities & challenges

Abandoning buildings ensures safety, reduces costs, and supports environmental preservation, however, toxic materials or carcinogenic materials should be removed, abated or encapsulated. Challenges of abandoning buildings include community displacement, potential property value decline, land use planning, and cultural/historical loss.

design considerations

The decision to abandon requires careful consideration, including the severity and frequency of flooding, cost-benefit analysis, community engagement, and long-term land-use planning. Alternative strategies such as relocation or adaptive reuse should be explored.

summary

cost	$$
building type	single family, townhouses
locations	coastal areas

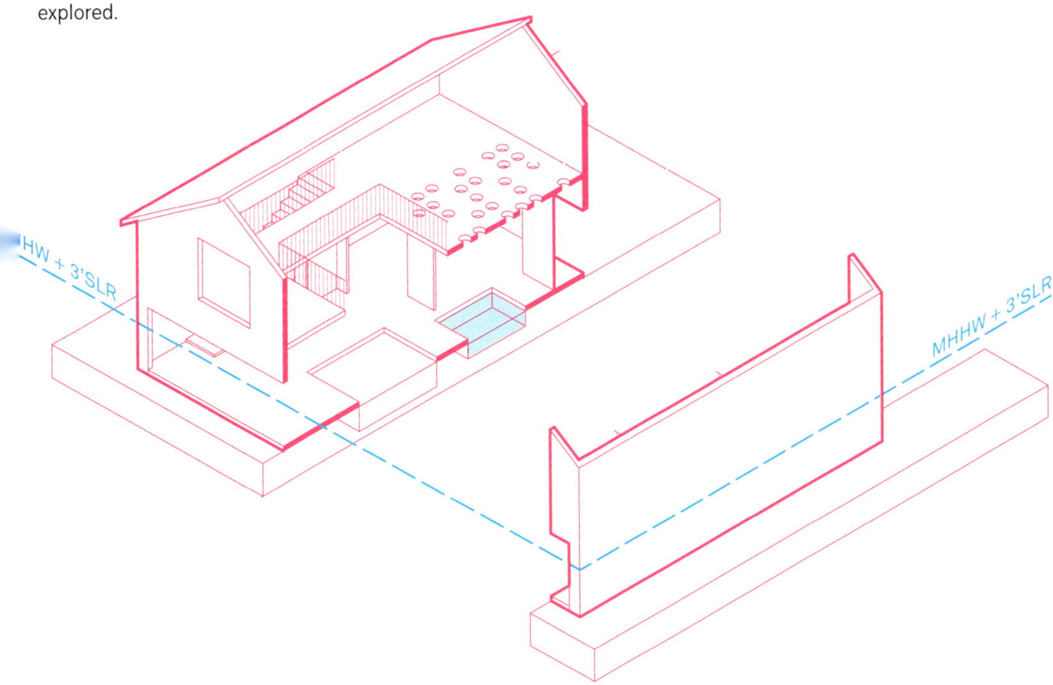

metabolist architecture

The metabolist architecture movement that emerged in Japan in the 1960s was characterized by its vision of urban planning and architecture as flexible, organic, and adaptable structures that could grow and change over time. It emphasized the use of modular units and megastructures that could be expanded or replaced as needed, reflecting a dynamic and evolving approach to urban development. The movement was influenced by ideas of metabolism, which referred to the biological concept of organisms constantly growing, changing, and renewing themselves. Metabolist architecture sought to apply this concept to urban environments, envisioning cities as living entities capable of regeneration and adaptation.

When applied to flood adaptive architecture, the principles of metabolist architecture can provide valuable insights and approaches. By leveraging this concept in Salty Urbanism could formulate a strategy where the existing and future built environment is designed to be disassembled, or reformatted so that the architecture does not need to be abandoned, discarded, demolished or destroyed. The concept of adaptability and flexibility inherent in metabolist architecture aligns with the need for buildings to withstand and adapt to flood events. Here's how metabolist architecture can be applied to flood adaptive architecture:

1. Modular and Flexible Design: Metabolist architecture's emphasis on modular units and flexible design can be employed to create buildings that can easily adjust to changing flood conditions. Modular components can be designed to be quickly assembled or disassembled, allowing for the easy reconfiguration of spaces in response to flooding.

2. Megastructure Concept: The idea of megastructures, which are large-scale structures composed of smaller units, can be employed to create flood adaptive buildings. These megastructures can be designed with the capability to adapt and modify their lower levels during flood events, while maintaining the functionality and safety of upper levels. Farthermore, structures can be designed to bridge across areas freeing up the ground for park or other ecological functioning.

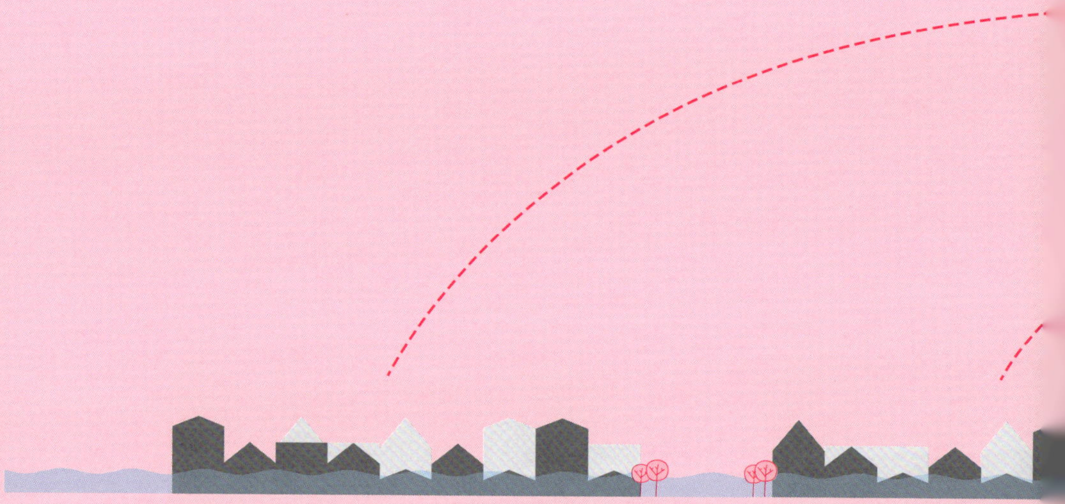

Current Community

3. Vertical Development: Metabolist architecture's focus on vertical development and high-rise structures can be advantageous in flood-prone areas. By elevating habitable spaces above flood levels, buildings can reduce the risk of damage and enable occupants to safely shelter during flood events. Densifying development through vertical means also frees up more land to serve as sponge parks or hydric zones to better filter, absorb and evapotranspriate flood water.

4. Adaptive Infrastructure: Metabolist architecture encourages the integration of infrastructure systems within buildings. In flood-adaptive architecture, this can involve incorporating flood mitigation measures, such as flood barriers, water drainage systems, and flexible utility connections, to adapt to changing flood conditions. It can also lay out a scaffolding for utilities and farming.

By incorporating the principles of metabolist architecture into flood-adaptive design, buildings can be better equipped to withstand and respond to flood events. This approach emphasizes flexibility, adaptability, and modular construction, allowing structures to evolve and adjust as needed while ensuring the safety and functionality of the built environment.

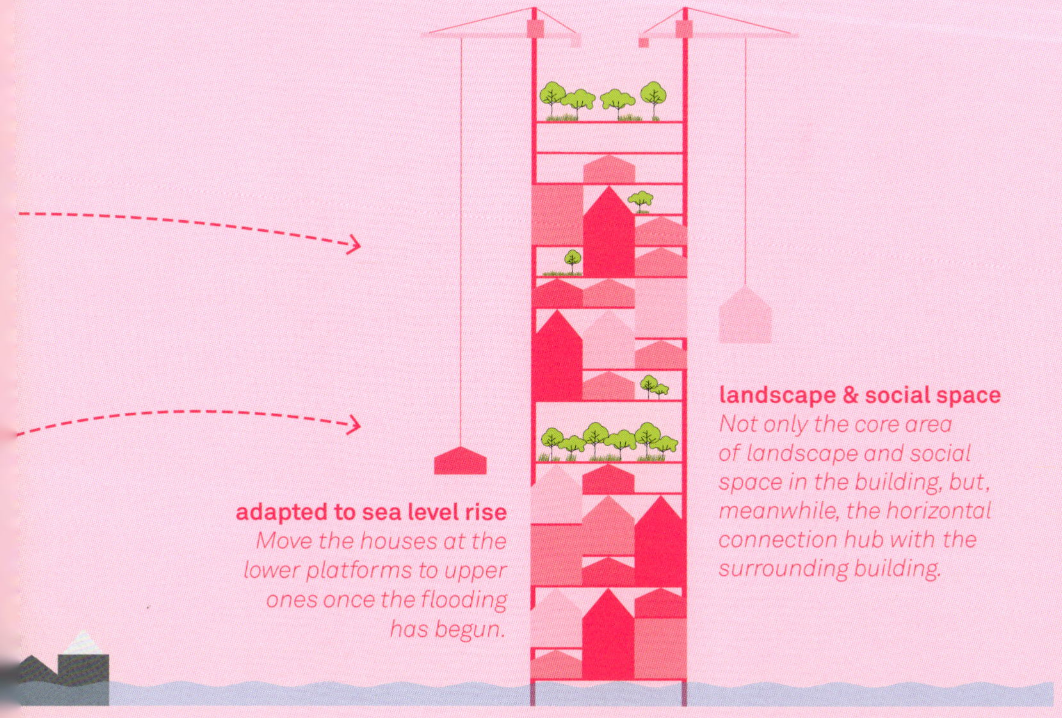

Vertical Community in the Future

THE BLUE ZONE

Vista Breeze, an affordable housing project under construction in Miami Beach, exemplifies architectural flood adaptation through its innovative "blue zone" strategy—where the base of the building is designed with enhanced waterproofing and corrosion-resistant materials that exceed FEMA standards, creating a durable barrier against saltwater intrusion in coastal conditions where current and future flooding are concerns.

freshwater ecologies
anaerobic
digester
mosquito control
mangrove mud flat
BioMat

vertical farming
enaergy production
amphibious dwellings
floating boardwalk
oyster nursery
mangrove nursery

BOAT CHARGING
alternative transportation
boyant walkway

rainwater collectors

materials

Materials in flood prone areas will require careful consideration. Choosing water-resistant materials (materials that will be fully submerged or in the tidal/littoral zone, or may become part of those zones due to future sea rise), managing moisture effectively, and selecting corrosion-resistant options in a heavy salt-laden environment are essential. Farthermore, hotter temperatures and extreme heat will mean faster chemical reactions and thus faster degradation. Durability, ease of cleaning and maintenance, and sustainable choices are other important factors. By balancing these considerations, architects and builders can select materials that withstand flooding, promote resilience, and minimize environmental impact.

environmental impact and corrosion

Materials and their environmental impact and corrosion are important considerations. Regarding environmental impact, the choice of materials used in flood adaptation should aim to minimize ecological consequences. Sustainable and environmentally friendly materials, such as recycled or low-impact materials, can help reduce the overall carbon footprint and resource consumption associated with construction. Corrosion is a particular concern in flood-prone areas due to the prolonged exposure to moisture and, in some cases, saltwater. Corrosion-resistant materials, such as stainless steel or treated metals, can be utilized to ensure the longevity and structural integrity of flood-adaptive architecture. Proper coating, sealing, or galvanizing methods can also enhance the resistance of materials to corrosion.

Balancing environmental impact and corrosion resistance is crucial in selecting appropriate materials for flood adaptation. Considering life cycle assessments, embodied energy, recyclability, and durability can help make informed choices that promote sustainability and mitigate the negative environmental impacts associated with flood-resistant materials.

environmental impact and corrosion

Structural considerations involve designing buildings to withstand flood forces and impacts. This includes ensuring load-bearing capacity to support floodwaters and debris, designing robust and elevated foundations, implementing efficient water flow systems, using resilient materials, and incorporating structural reinforcements. FEMA and NFIP regulate building design in floodplains, but does not account for future sea level rise. It is also important to consider alternative and innovation materials. Materials like conventional steel reinforcement steel or concrete mixes have

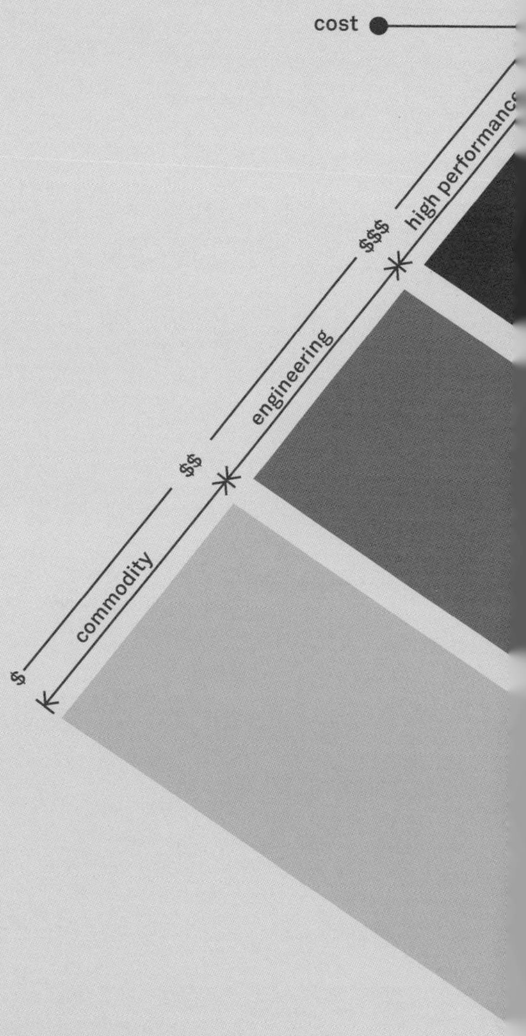

alternatives. Fiberglass or basalt have entered the market and provide non-corrosive alternatives to rebar, however, building codes and regulations have not kept up with the pace and are not currently accepted. Professional expertise is essential to meet building codes and standards, ensuring the safety and longevity of flood-adaptive structures.

global warming potential (GWP) [kg CO_2 eq/ m^3]

aluminum sheet *28242.0*
roof panel (steel) *26578.0*
galvanised steel *22923.1*
copper sheet *12433.6*
zinc *12209.4*

structural steel *8831.2*
epdm foil *5733.3*
vinyl flooring (pvc) *4095.5*
paint, matte *2851.0*
ceramic tiles *1725.3*
cement-bonded particle board *1694.0*
slate *1367.3*
aluminum framed window *1172.7*

brick, red, double-fired *898.2*
pir insulation *781.4*
wood-aluminum frame window *762.6*
fibre cement boards *699.0*
clinker-stoneware *618.0*
brick, red, single-fired *565.2*
fired clay brick *528.5*
wood frame window *474.1*
brick roof tiles 420.1
glass plane, triple-glazed *415.6*
roofing felt v60 *407.8*
plaster *375.1*
concrete roof tiles *366.1*

xps insulation *96.3*
unfired clay brick *93.6*
clay plaster *93.2*
gipsum fiber board (paper) *91.2*
linoleum *83.5*
eps insulation *80.4*
stone wool *70.4*
expanded perlite *60.1*
glass wool *21.6*
hemp fleece/pe *19.2*

rammed earth wall *9.3*
paper wool *6.2*
reused brick *4.9*

straw *-128.2*
wood fiber insulation *-173.1*
wood fier baord *-182.9*
modified wood *-519.0*
parquet floor, 14mm *-535.0*
glulam *-610.0*
plywood *-649.0*
cross-laminated-timber *-664.0*
mdf *-669.0*
construction timber *-680.0*
spruce *-777.5*
oak tree *-1063.0*

The construction material pyramid allows us to think about CO^2 and other embodied carbon in common materials used in the construction industry.

urban design

Salty Urbanism is an opportunity to create resilient coastal cities that adapt to the challenges

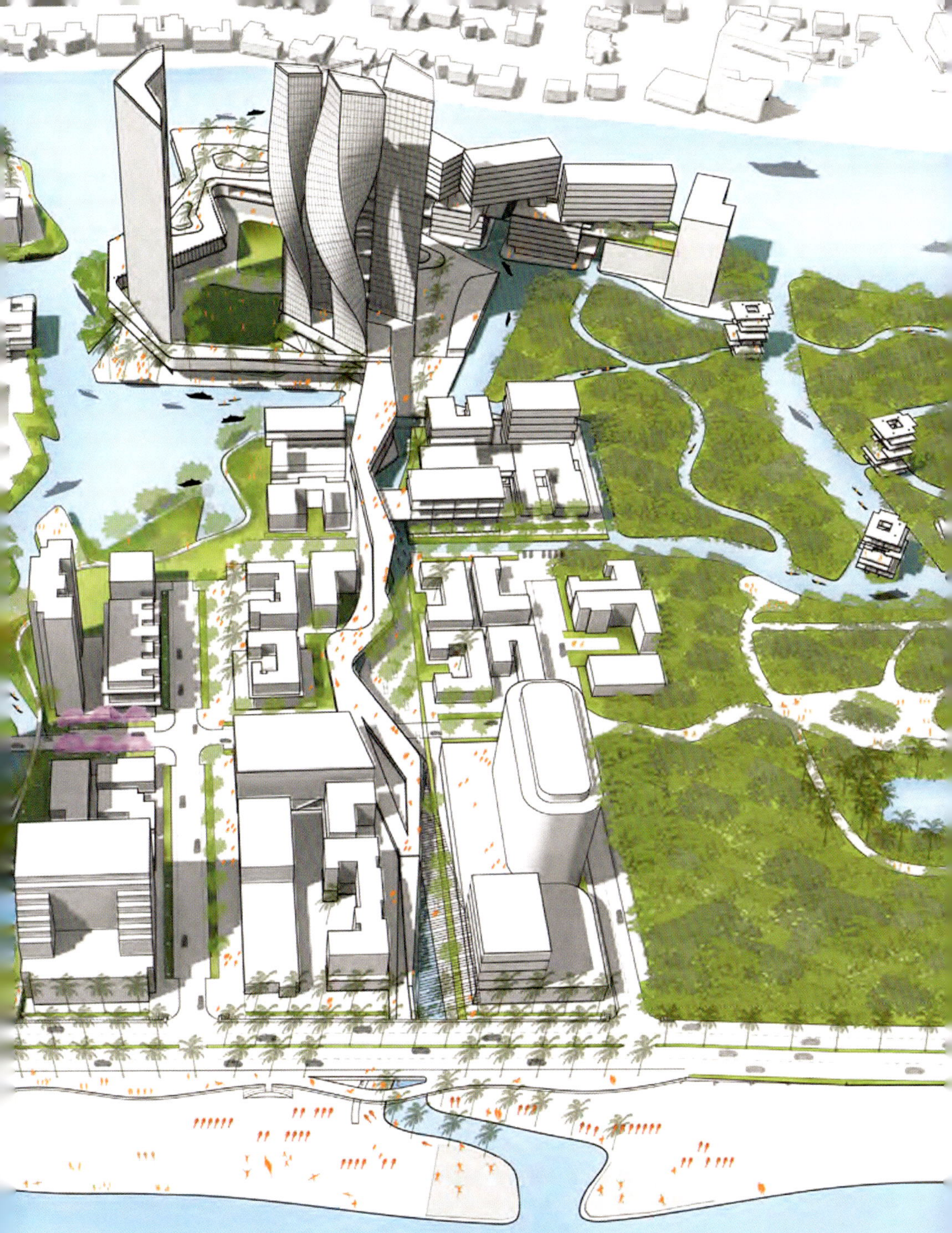

of rising seas and flooding while enhancing the quality of life for residents.

urban design

towards a Salty Urbanism

As an emerging urbanism framework for coastal adaptation, Salty Urbanism could be a form of new urban paradigm that aims to accomplish an integrated and multidisciplinary approach. In this regard, it strives to couple ecological processes within urban infrastructure, architecture, and public space networks to develop urban solutions at the scales of individual lots (what a property owner can do), public rights-of-way (what the municipality can do), and neighborhood (what coordinated public/private collaborations can do).

Placebuilding models, such as Salty Urbanism, engage socioenvironmental development and collectively yield a new ecology of the city necessary to address the greatest ongoing challenge to planning and design—ecological design within human-dominated ecosystems. By adopting ecological terms, architecture and urban design can achieve greater resilience and retool itself with the ability to adapt to changing conditions. Beyond composition, ecological thinking requires logics of assembly where timing, interactivity, sequencing, componentization, and recombination constitute another aesthetic and utilitarian intelligence. Urban design projects bring problems involving community-scaled systems. Only urbanism gives the architectural, landscape architectural, and planning professions a holistic framework through which these systems can be engaged, yet often urban design is the missing piece in discussions on resilience and sustainable planning.

Novel architecture with a new vision of adaptive urbanism lends itself to embracing historic and emerging technologies, especially in areas of low-lying floodplain conditions like south Florida or southern Louisiana. Flood-adaptive architecture can provide a robust catalog of building typologies from flood-proofing to amphibious techniques, the latter being fairly unrecognized in Southeast Florida (see Flood-Adaptive Architecture). The region has many examples of architecture and urbanism working in tandem, from Stiltsville in Biscayne Bay to new projects like the Perez Art Museum Miami, where the building is raised above parking area that acts as a sponge to capture rainwater and prevents flooding from storm surges.

coupling ecosystem and urban services

Coupling ecosystem services with urban development are at obvious odds with current planning and zoning regulations and the lifestyles of residents. We generally understand the need for utilities, police, fire, sanitation, but living shorelines and coastal dunes may impact our access or views. The situation summons creative approaches on how to retrofit traditional architecture, planning and urban design to address storm surge, sea level rise, and changing rainfall and runoff patterns on the heavily developed coastal zone. Defending against water from all directions is a particularly unique challenge in south Florida, but can be appropriated by other coastal communities.

the role of urban design

Urban design plays a crucial role in addressing flooding issues and implementing the principles of Salty Urbanism. Some key considerations in urban design related to flooding include:

Green and Blue Infrastructure: Integrating green and blue infrastructure elements, such as permeable surfaces, green roofs, rain gardens, and bioswales, can help manage stormwater runoff and reduce the risk of flooding. Tidal flooding and storm surge need equally important infrastructure elements and explained in Infrastructure. These features can absorb and store water, promoting natural drainage and preventing overwhelming the urban drainage system.

Waterfront Development: Designing waterfront areas in a flood-resilient manner is essential. Incorporating flood barriers or zones, raised promenades, or floodable public spaces can protect against floodwaters while maintaining access and connectivity to the waterfront.

Mixed-Use Development: Promoting mixed-use development can reduce the dependence on commuting and enhance walkability, reducing the carbon footprint and vulnerability to flood-related disruptions. By encouraging a diverse range of activities in a compact urban form, Salty Urbanism can foster self-sufficiency and decrease the need for extensive transportation and utility networks.

Land Use Planning: Strategically planning land use can help avoid building in high-risk flood zones and preserve natural floodplains. Zoning regulations can guide development away from flood-prone areas and incentivize resilient design practices. Practices related to Transfer of Development Rights or Land Adjustment can provide legal tools for communities to create greater adaptation and resilience.

Connectivity and Mobility: Designing well-connected and accessible urban environments promotes efficient evacuation routes during flood events, but good urbanism will also allow for sheltering in place since recent storms have proved it will be impossible to evacuate entire states like Florida in the future. Creating pedestrian-friendly spaces, prioritizing non-motorized transportation, and ensuring connectivity to public transportation can enhance mobility and emergency response capabilities.

Community Engagement: Engaging the community in the urban design process is crucial to ensure that flood adaptation measures reflect their needs and concerns. Encouraging community participation and integrating local knowledge can lead to more effective and culturally appropriate solutions.

By integrating these urban design considerations into Salty Urbanism principles, cities can enhance their resilience to flooding, create vibrant and sustainable urban environments, and improve the overall quality of life for their residents.

multi-scaled and multidisciplinary approach to change prevailing land development regulations and policies

In order to change the prevailing land-development models to favor integration of ecosystem functioning in urban development, Salty Urbanism proposes implementation of soft-engineering technologies within niche scales of the building, lot, public rights-of-way (streets, easements, parks, etc.), and neighborhood, to generate feedback between bottom-up design thinking and top-down policy and planning production.

Best management practices (BMPs) alone may address issues of urban stormwater quality and quantity, however, they will not lessen flood potential as environmental engineering and urban planning disciplines are practiced as separate fields. New tools and design methodologies that help connect segregated disciplines are needed to meet the complex challenges over the next 100 years.

The multi-scale approach (building, lot, public rights-of-way, and neighborhood) will provide a link between the large-scale policy-driven approach and bottom-up design thinking and scientific modeling to provide niche adaptation solutions.

salty urbanisms

A menu of ten urban adaptation strategies provide contextual, successive, and incremental approaches to land/coastline development. Each strategy responds to a particular land-use type to balance urban development, transportation and ecosystem services. Leveraging value-added infrastructure, these adaptation urbanisms balance resources to solve a communities desire for place-based adaptation utilities that create a robust public open space network.

The following menu provides specific land-use adaptation recommendations that will nest within the broader ecotypic response matrix outlined next. These include:

Surf and turf neighborhoods, where water and land ecotones are common. Green streets to blueways, that design for the intersection of urban runoff corridors and natural or man-made drainage ways. Strategic retreat neighborhoods that propose removing, abandoning or moving existing infrastructure out of low-lying areas. Ecological retrofit neighborhoods that botanize the asphalt and large impervious areas common in urban development. Inundation districts that are designed to flood. Transverse glades canal retrofits that follow the natural drainage ways and plan to make it an asset.

place-based adaptation

Place-based adaptation tailors adaptation strategies and measures to specific geographic locations and their unique characteristics in land use and ecology. It recognizes that different regions, cities, and communities have distinct vulnerabilities, risks, and assets in the face of climate change impacts, including flooding. Place-based adaptation involves understanding the local context, considering the specific socioeconomic and environmental conditions, and engaging with local stakeholders to develop and implement appropriate adaptation measures. This will be coordinated within the larger ecotypic condition as well be discussed next as a way to bridge land-use and ecological thinking.

In the context of flooding, place-based adaptation takes into account factors such as topography, hydrology, existing infrastructure, land use patterns, and community dynamics. It aims to develop context-specific strategies that address the specific challenges and opportunities presented by flooding in a particular location. This may include a combination of structural and non-structural measures, policy interventions, community engagement, and capacity-building initiatives.

Place-based adaptation recognizes that a one-size-fits-all approach is insufficient in dealing with the complex and site-specific impacts of flooding. It emphasizes the importance of local knowledge, participation, and collaboration among various stakeholders to develop adaptation solutions that are relevant, effective, and sustainable for the specific place.

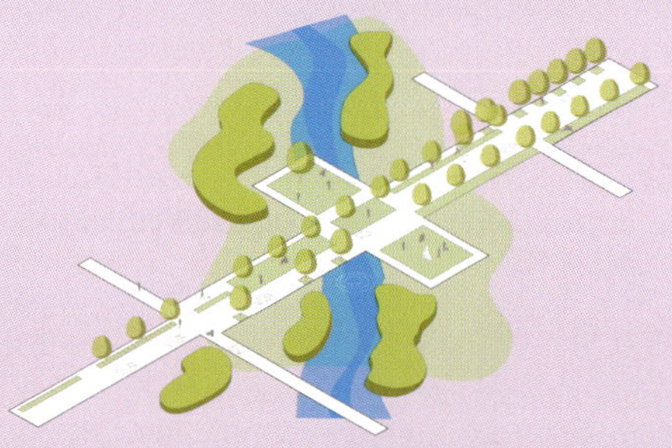

green streets to blueways

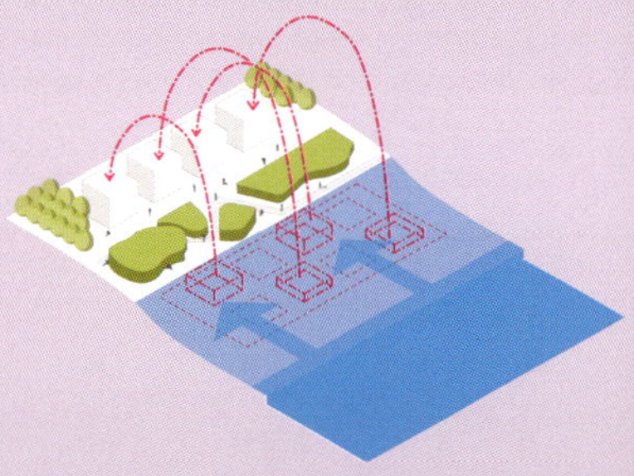

strategic retreat neighborhood

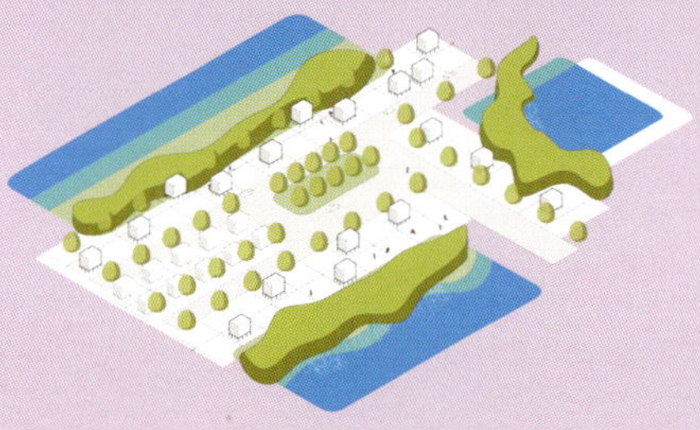

surf & turf neighborhood

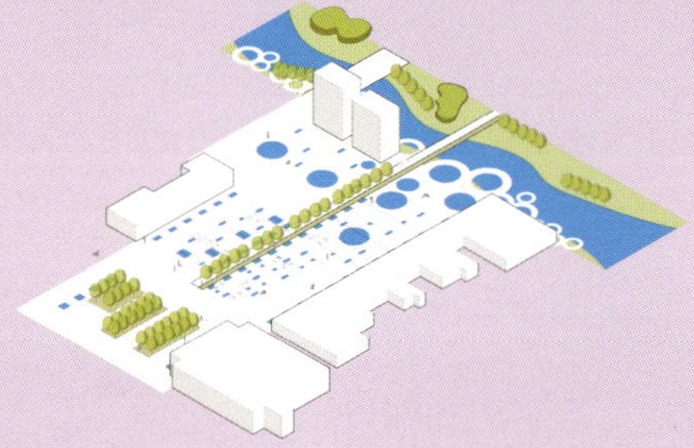

ecological retrofit neighborhood

By adopting place-based adaptation approaches, cities and communities can better identify and prioritize adaptation actions that account for the unique characteristics and needs of their environment and population. This tailored approach can lead to more resilient and successful outcomes in managing and adapting to the challenges posed by flooding and other climate-related hazards, especially in retrofit solutions.

ecotypic response matrix

An ecotypic response matrix is a tool used in ecological research and conservation to assess and categorize the responses of different plant species or ecotypes to environmental conditions or disturbances. It represents the relationship between environmental factors or stressors and the corresponding ecological responses or traits of different species. This thinking can be incorporated into an urban design response that factors in specific hydrological, ecological, and geological factors with place-based adaptation strategies. The following four ecotype responses represent the four main types of ecosystems found in south Florida:

inundation district

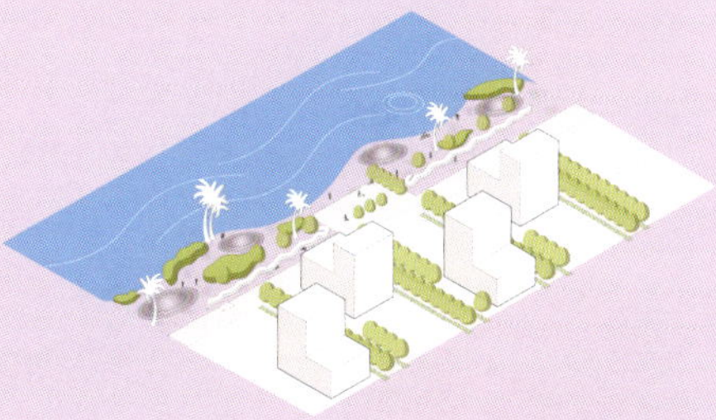

dunescape littoral defense

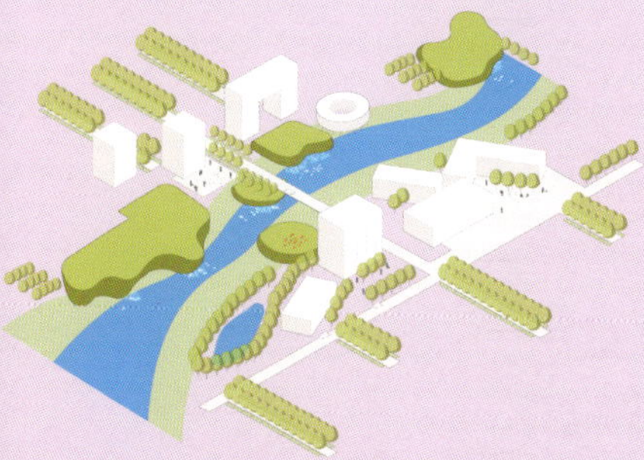

transverse glades canal retrofit

amphibious neighborhoods

living shoreline district

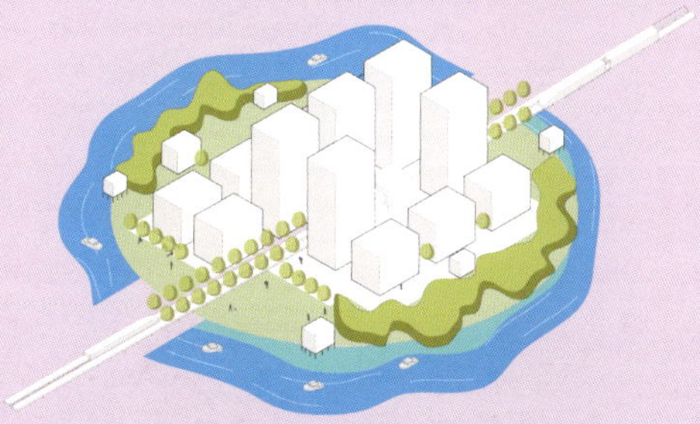

transit-oriented-development ridge

1) Glades, or the areas formerly connected and part of the Everglades; 2) Transverse Glades, areas between pineland and rockland ridges that served as drainage ways for water flowing southeast from Lake Okeechobee; 3) Coastal Ridge/Uplands that consists of the highest elevations regional that historically had

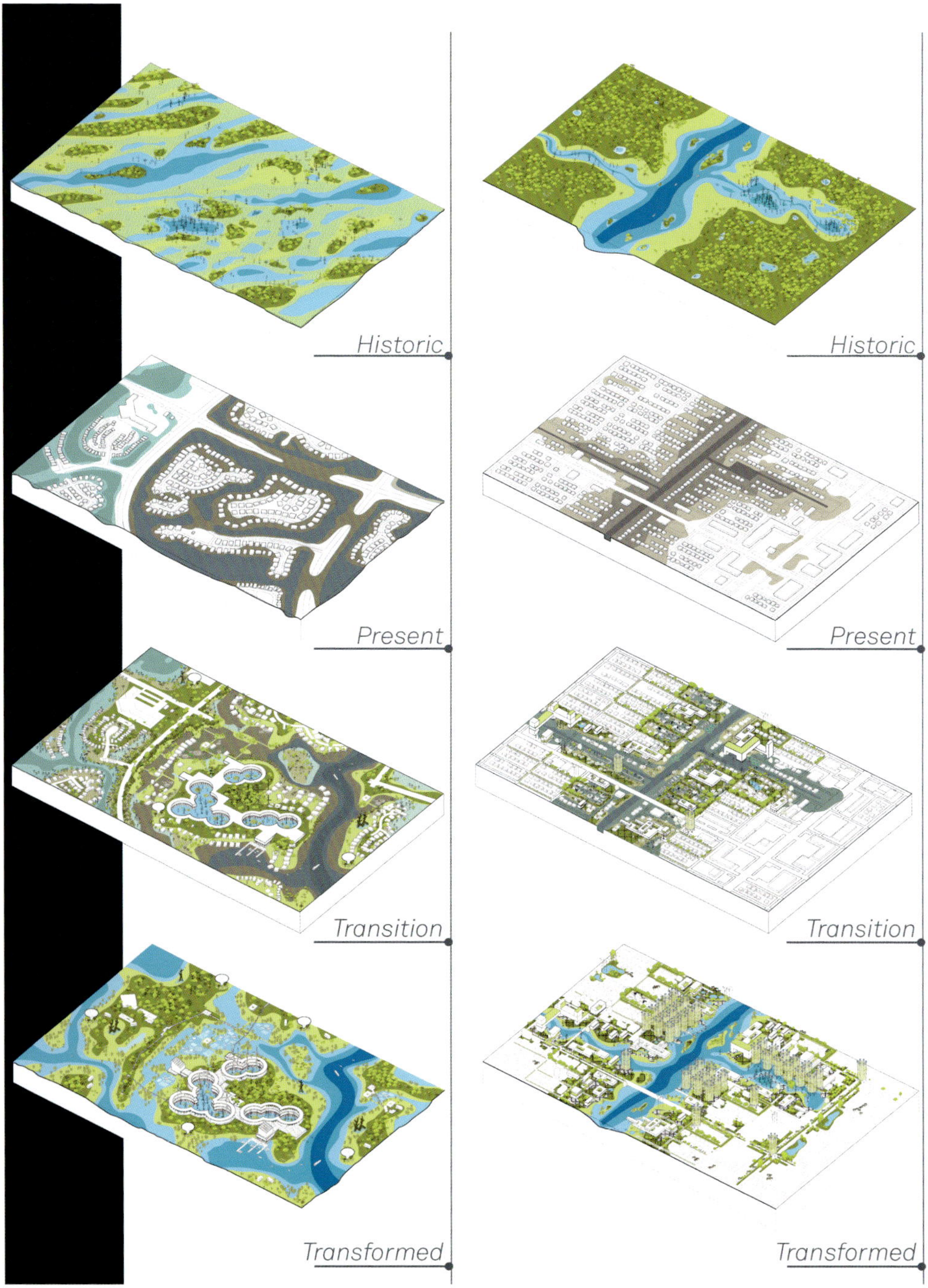

hardwood hammocks and pineland ecosystems; and 4) Barrier Island/Estuarine environments that offer a buffer to the mainland and contains a cross section in elevations that change considerably between the beach to intracoastal/bay areas. Overall all ecotypes will become more halophytic, or saltier.

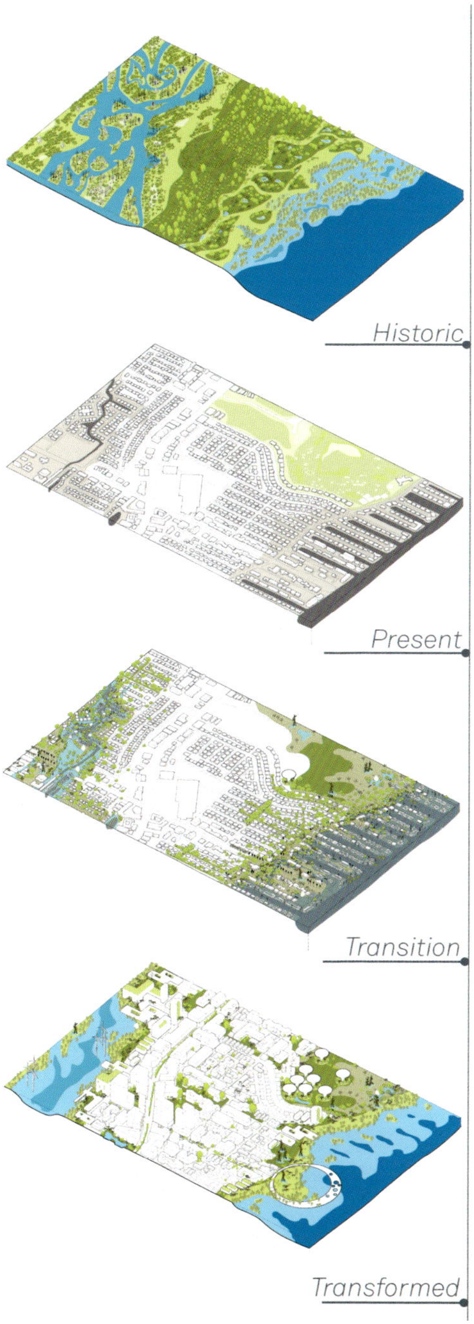

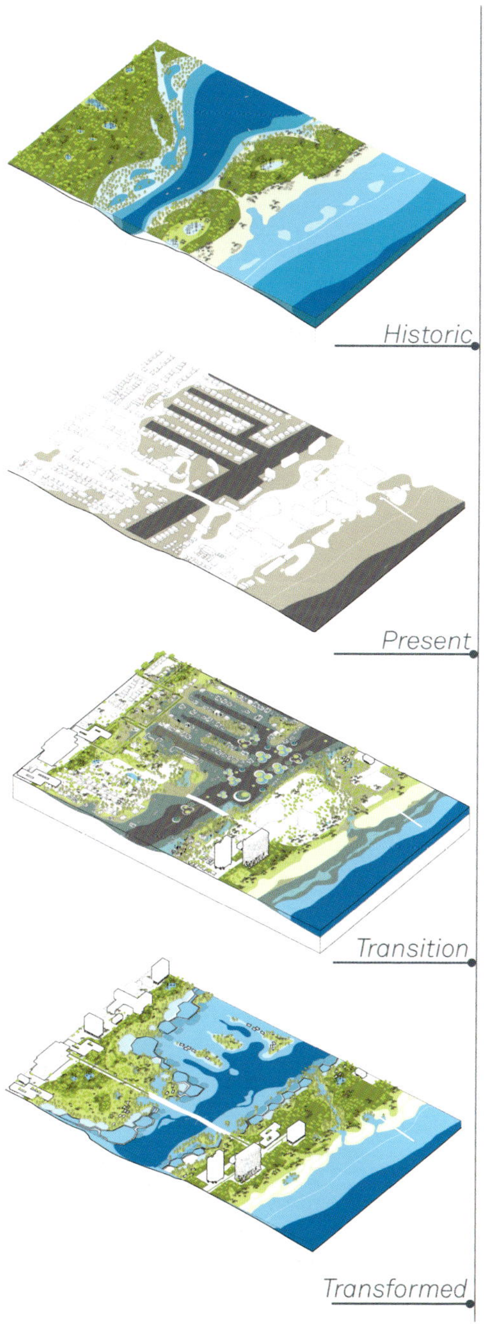

glades adaptation

glade problems

The Everglades and developed glades areas experience natural flooding due to its unique hydrological characteristics and the interaction between rainfall, surface water, and underground aquifers.

Flooding in the glades areas occurs due to its flat topography, heavy rainfall, natural water storage areas, and human alterations to the hydrological system. The Everglades' low-lying wetland terrain and slow water movement make it susceptible to prolonged inundation during intense rainfall events. Additionally, the ecosystem's natural storage areas become saturated, causing water to spread out and contribute to flooding. Human modifications, such as canals and levees, farther impact water flow and exacerbate flooding. While natural flooding is essential for the Everglades' ecological balance, managing and balancing the hydrological processes with human needs is crucial to mitigate adverse impacts on the ecosystem and surrounding areas.

glade solutions

Adapting glades areas to flooding involves implementing strategies that aim to manage and allow for the impacts of excessive water and preserve the ecological integrity of the wetland. Some key approaches for adapting the glades to flooding include:

Hydrological Restoration: Restoring the natural water flow patterns is essential. This can involve removing or modifying levees and canals to reestablish historic water flows and allow for more natural distribution and drainage of water during flood events.

Water Storage and Retention: As seas rise salt water and brackish conditions will emerge; implementing water storage and retention areas for freshwater can help retain native ecosystems, but more as islands.

Land Use Planning: Land use planning is crucial to adapt to flooding. Zoning regulations and development guidelines should be implemented to restrict construction and seek to develop a "Department of Unplanning" to decommission these urban areas into small hamlets of development.

By combining these approaches, the glades can be better prepared to handle flooding events.

Seed mangrove forests along western areas closest to the Everglades and along canal areas. Glade areas will become brackish and mangroves can help filter runoff and build land.

Certain roads should be raised to provide evacuation and routes for critical services, but transportation may need to adapt to water-based craft.

major flood type considerations:

rainwater | pollution | water table

Biomounds and bioswales can be installed to help with evapotranspiration rates. Vegetation will need to be installed that is salt tolerant or halophytic.

Single-family homes will need to be flood-adapted and structurally improved to prevent hydrostatic and hydraulic failure. Structures will need to be wet and dry flood proofed. Access to structures may be limited by extreme storm events.

Certain areas and neighborhoods may need to be decommissioned to allow for more room for water, especially to ensure freshwater recharge is maintained.

Rainwater harvesting and decentralized utilities will become critical to provide services to residents in these areas as infrastructure becomes too costly to serve entire areas.

transverse glades adaptation

transverse glades problems

The Transverse Glades are unique due to their distinct geological and hydrological characteristics. These include a series of limestone ridges and depressions, known as the Atlantic Coastal Ridge, which separate the Everglades from the Atlantic Ocean. The Transverse Glades play a vital role in south Florida's hydrological system, supporting diverse ecosystems, acting as wildlife corridors, and facing environmental challenges. Preserving and managing these areas are essential for maintaining the region's ecological balance and biodiversity. With both marl and peat, as well as some cypress strands these drainage ways are critical and low areas where dredged canals can be seen throughout the region. Though urban development has continued since the original dredging of canals in the turn of the twentieth century, the canals have never been widened or altered in any significant way.

transverse glade solutions

Adapting the Transverse Glades to flooding involves implementing strategies to manage and allow the impacts of excessive water in this specific region. Some key approaches include:

Understanding Geology, Hydrology, and Biodiversity: The Transverse Glades are characterized by a series of limestone ridges and depressions that run east-west across the southern part of the Florida Peninsula. These corridors should remove urban development and rewild the corridor. They act as natural barriers that control the flow of water from the north to the south, influencing the movement of surface and groundwater. The interaction between the shallow aquifer, wetlands, and canals in the transverse glades contributes to the unique water flow patterns and the delicate balance of freshwater and saltwater in the region. A diverse range of ecosystems and habitats, that include freshwater marshes, cypress swamps, hardwood hammocks, and pinelands. These habitats provide important refuge and nesting grounds for numerous plant and animal species, including rare and endangered species such as the Florida panther and the Cape Sable seaside sparrow, thus these areas serve as important wildlife corridors, allowing for the movement and migration of various species across the region, but more importantly, will regulate freshwater supply and flooding in the future and should be designed appropriately. A clear development edge that makes room for water must be implemented.

Seed mangrove forests along canals. Transverse glade areas will become brackish, and mangroves can help filter runoff and build land.

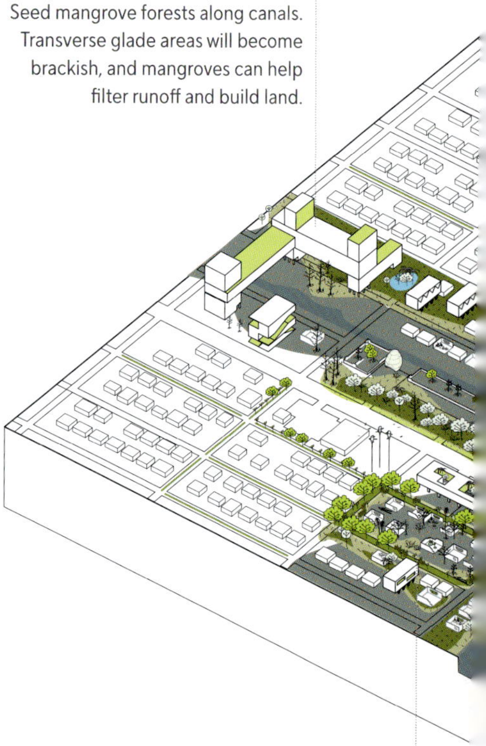

Certain roads will bridge over the transverse glades to provide evacuation and routes for critical services, but like glades areas, transportation may need to adapt to water-based craft.

major flood type considerations:

New development opens up the ground for ecological functioning and provides elevated spaces for recreation and outdoor activites. These rooftops can be linked to other developments to form a new elevated ground.

Expanded canal zones will require removal and decommissioning of built areas. These areas can allow for intensified development that is flood-adapted and offers access to water-based transporation.

Green and blue roofs help reduce ruoff and collect water for drinking or other building uses.

Rainwater harvesting and decentralized utilities will become critical to provide services to residents in these areas as infrastructure becomes too costly to serve entire areas.

Agriculture and plant nurseries will provide needed food and rewilding resources.

coastal ridge and uplands adaptation

uplands problems

The Atlantic Coastal Ridge possesses some unique characteristics. The interaction between the ridge's geological features and the surrounding hydrological system is of particular note and when viewed with all the other ecotypes that interface it. The Atlantic Coastal Ridge acts as a natural barrier, influencing the movement and flow of water across the region. The flat topography and underlying limestone formations of the ridge play a crucial role in water storage, retention, and flow patterns during flood events. The interplay between urban development, land use patterns, and the natural hydrological system poses unique challenges in managing and adapting to flood events.

uplands solutions

Adapting the Atlantic Coastal Ridge with flood resilient urban design features requires a combination of strategies. Effective drainage and stormwater management systems in these upland areas should be implemented to control water flow and prevent flooding downstream or in adjacent low-lying areas. Preserving and restoring natural water storage areas, such as wetlands and floodplains, is essential. These areas act as buffers, absorbing and retaining water during flood events, thereby reducing the risk of flooding along the Atlantic Coastal Ridge. Additionally, implementing land use planning and zoning regulations to restrict construction in flood-prone areas and intensifying development on higher ground that is less vulnerable. Monitoring systems and early warning systems provide crucial information for timely response and evacuation, while community education and preparedness play a vital role in building resilience.

Collaboration among various stakeholders is key to the successful adaptation of the Atlantic Coastal Ridge. Government agencies, local communities, and conservation organizations need to work together to implement and maintain these adaptation measures. By combining scientific knowledge, community engagement, and sustainable management practices, the Atlantic Coastal Ridge can be better equipped to handle and mitigate the effects of flooding, ensuring the long-term resilience of the region. One of the unique challenges will be to design and develop in a way that does not alienate, nor push out those populations that have occupied the land for generations—climate gentrification is an issue that will need to be solved at the neighborhood and community scale.

Transfer of development rights can be a powerful tool to incentivize development to the coastal ridge.

Allow for transportation to adapt to water-based craft and have new development provide access to public waterways.

major flood type considerations:

rainwater | **pollution** | **water table**

Transfer of development rights or TDR allow for intensification of development at the higher elevations. New development should still plan for flooding and design to integrate green and blue roofs, living walls, and green infrastructure.

Neighborhoods should implement green and blue streets and redevelop with flood-adpative architecture.

Certain areas and neighborhoods may need to be decommissioned to allow for more room for water, especially to ensure freshwater recharge is maintained.

Vulnerable properties along the intracoastal waterways should be decommissioned or redeveloped. Access should be converted to water-based transportation only.

coastal uplands-esturaine adaptation

coastal upland problems

Flooding of the coastal uplands and barrier islands presents several unique challenges. One significant aspect is the proximity to the ocean and the susceptibility to storm surge during hurricanes and other severe weather events. Barrier islands, in particular, serve as a protective barrier between the mainland and the open ocean, making them prone to coastal flooding and erosion. Storm surge, combined with high tides and heavy rainfall, can result in significant inundation.

The flat topography of the coastal uplands and barrier islands also plays a role in flooding dynamics. With minimal elevation changes, even relatively small increases in water levels can lead to widespread flooding. The permeability of the soils in these areas is another factor that affects flooding, as it can impact the rate of water infiltration and drainage.

Farthermore, the delicate balance between saltwater and freshwater in these coastal ecosystems makes them particularly vulnerable to flooding. Excessive flooding can cause saltwater intrusion into freshwater superficial aquifers, threatening drinking water supplies and impacting the delicate balance of coastal ecosystems.

coastal upland problems

Adapting to flooding in the coastal uplands and barrier islands of south Florida requires specific strategies that address the unique challenges posed by their coastal location, storm surge vulnerability, flat topography, and the delicate balance of saltwater and freshwater ecosystems. Coastal protection measures, such as dune restoration and beach nourishment, as well as the development of resilient infrastructure and land use planning, are vital for mitigating the impacts of flooding in these areas.

Adapting barrier islands to flooding involves a range of strategies. These include beach nourishment to restore eroded beaches, dune restoration to strengthen natural barriers, living shorelines to dissipate wave energy, elevated structures and flood-resistant infrastructure, strategic land use planning, monitoring systems and early warning systems, and public education. By combining these approaches, barrier islands can enhance their resilience to flooding, protecting coastal communities and infrastructure from the impacts of storm surge and wave action. Collaboration among stakeholders is vital to implementing these measures effectively and ensuring the long-term sustainability of barrier island ecosystems.

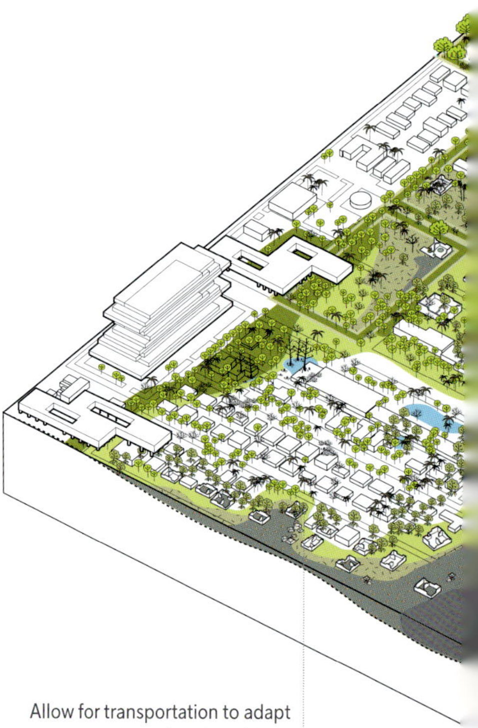

Allow for transportation to adapt to water-based craft and have new development provide access to public waterways.

major flood type considerations:

Low-lying areas should implement green and blue streets and redevelop with flood-adpative architecture. Repetitive loss properties in the finger islands should consider decommissioning or take extreme action to make them flood adaptive. Transportation should go to water-based.

Transfer of development rights or TDR allow for intensification of development at the higher elevations. New development should still plan for flooding and design to integrate green and blue roofs, living walls, and green infrastructure.

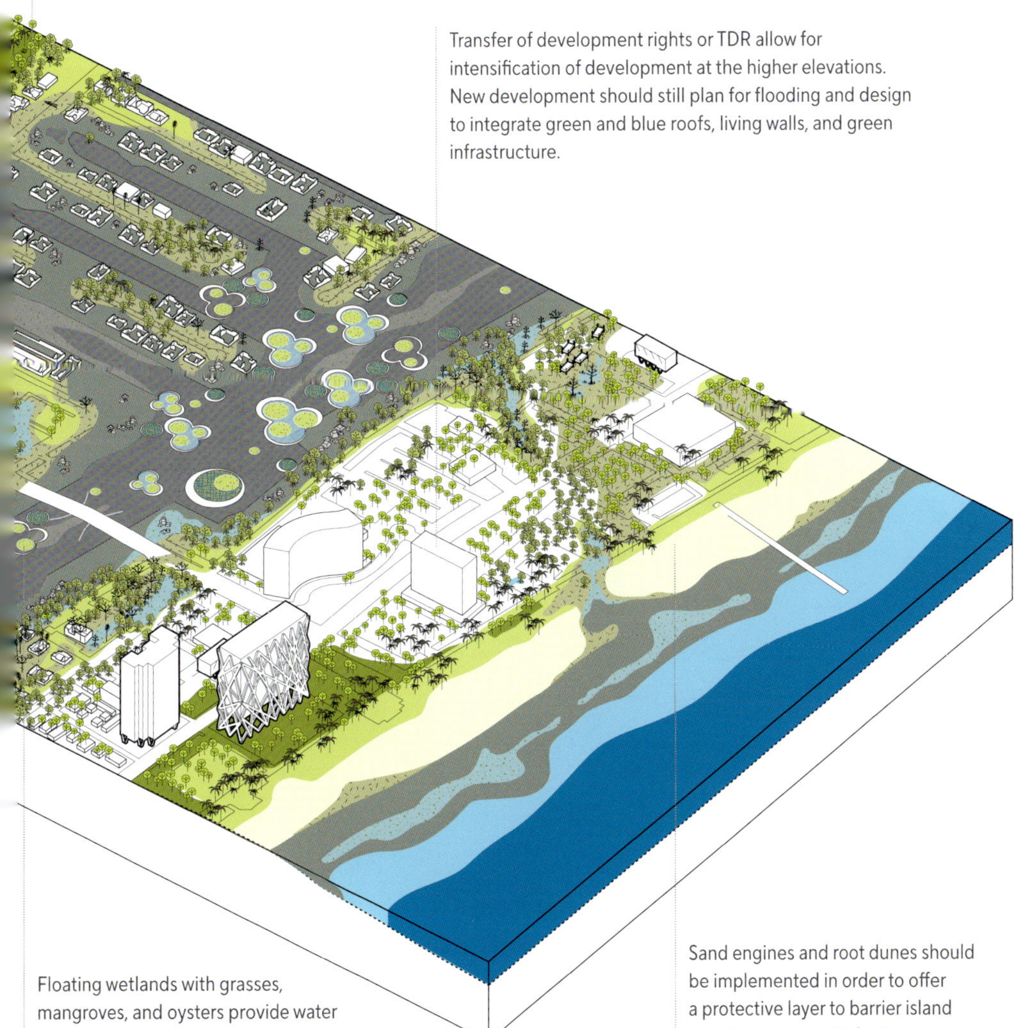

Floating wetlands with grasses, mangroves, and oysters provide water quality and habitat. These floating biodiversity mats will provide critical habitat that will not be able to keep up with rising seas.

Sand engines and root dunes should be implemented in order to offer a protective layer to barrier island developments and infrastructure. Sand and saltwater should be considered in any design.

A1A
A1A

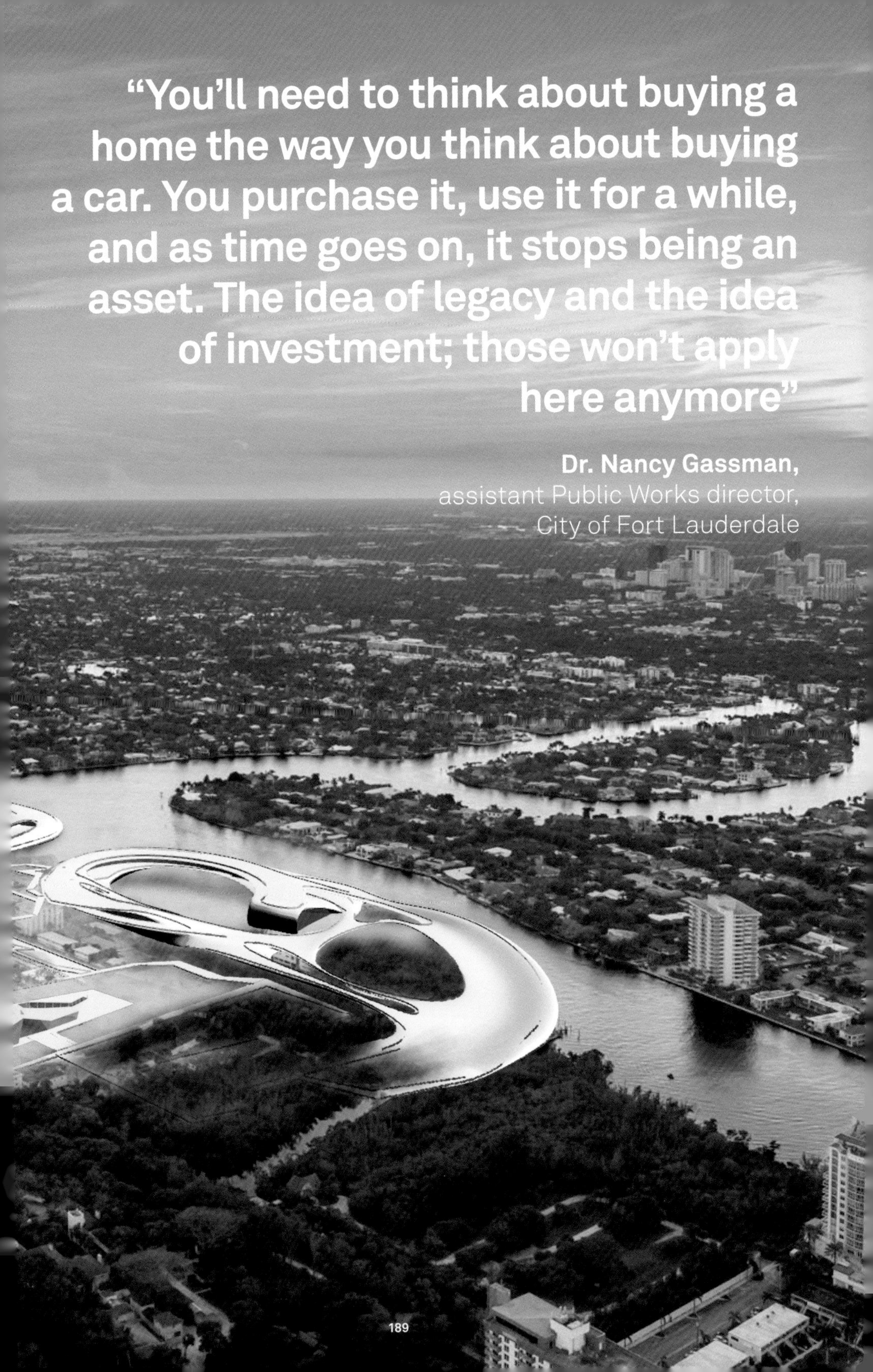

"You'll need to think about buying a home the way you think about buying a car. You purchase it, use it for a while, and as time goes on, it stops being an asset. The idea of legacy and the idea of investment; those won't apply here anymore"

Dr. Nancy Gassman,
assistant Public Works director,
City of Fort Lauderdale

case study: north beach village

North Beach Village, like all of south Florida, has distinct wet and dry seasons and a relatively flat topography. The topography slopes from the beach to the intracoastal by more than 12 feet. Seventy percent of the annual precipitation typically falls from June to September, just before the King Tides in late September and October (coincidentally this is also hurricane season). The soil capacity to store water is limited because the freshwater lens just below the surface in the wet season; it is this limited soil storage that leads to flooding, necessitating the extensive drainage facilities that discharge large volumes of water during the wet season. As a result, there is a nexus that drives the public demand for future development in North Beach Village, while protecting infrastructure and property from flood damage. Such impetus requires short and long-term planning and assessment of vulnerable areas. Long-term decision-making becomes critical because infrastructure and development is not temporal—it is expected to last fifty years or more. Hence, it is in the community's interests to develop a stormwater planning framework to adapt to rising seas and consider economic resilience through a long-term plan. Utilizing the tools and menus presented in the manual

Phase 1: 0-10 years

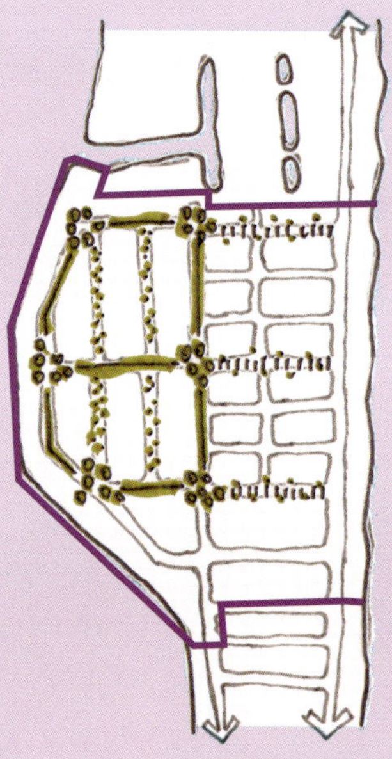

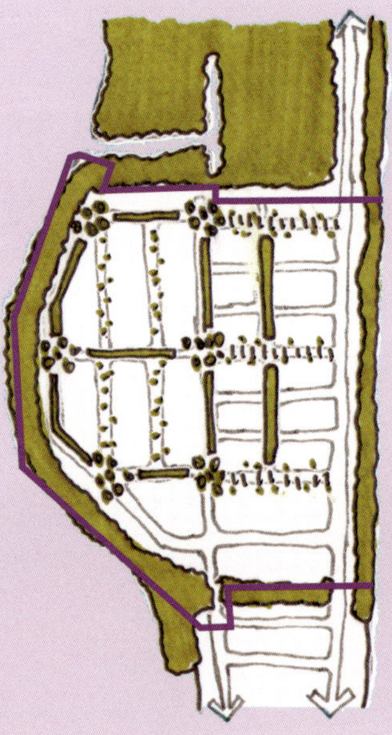

Botanizing the Asphalt of North Beach

Over the first ten years investments focus on streetscape improvements. These initial investments provide critical "botanizing" or softening infrastructure in an artful way to showcase techniques and provide pilot projects that aim to illustrate plausible ways forward toward a preferred adaptation solution.

Scenario 1: Soft Defense

Create a fortified ring of living shoreline at perimeter and ecological water management infrastructure within street right-of-ways. Areas will still be susceptible to tidal inundation, but green infrastructure will reduce residence time of standing water.

three scenario approaches were developed with neighborhood workshop; soft defense, strategic retreat, and land adjustment; and balance stakeholder buy in and political will. A first ten-year phase was also proposed that included public investments. The scenario visioning allows for plausible propositions that would be unimaginable otherwise. These scenarios forced in-depth conversations regarding how much flooding and investment will be tolerable or manageable with clear immediate and long-term solutions.

Phase 2: 10-60 years

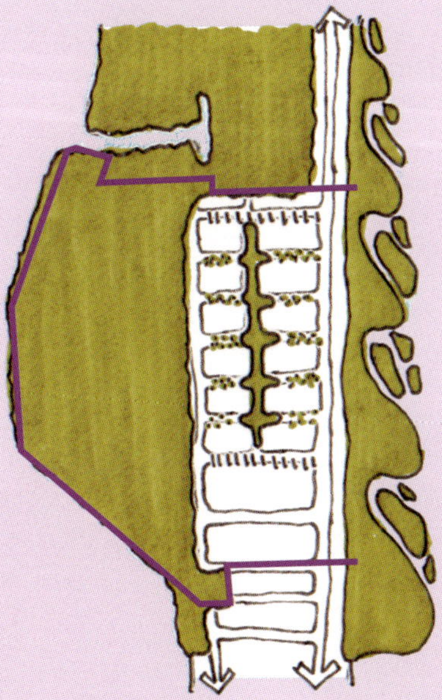

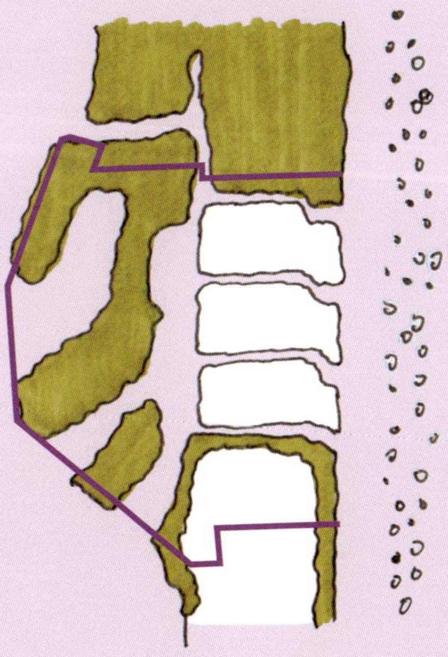

Scenario 2: Strategic Retreat

Rewild the lowland areas and densify the higher ground at coastal ridge. This provides critical and extensive green infrastructure that is able to absorb and manage sea level rise over the next one hundred years.

Scenario 3: Land Adjust

Reformat urban development to better integrate gray and green infrastructure solutions and create flood-adaptive architecture that reimagines living with, on, and over water. Hyrologic functioning provides corridors for flood waters and new amphibious and raised buildings minimize flood damage.

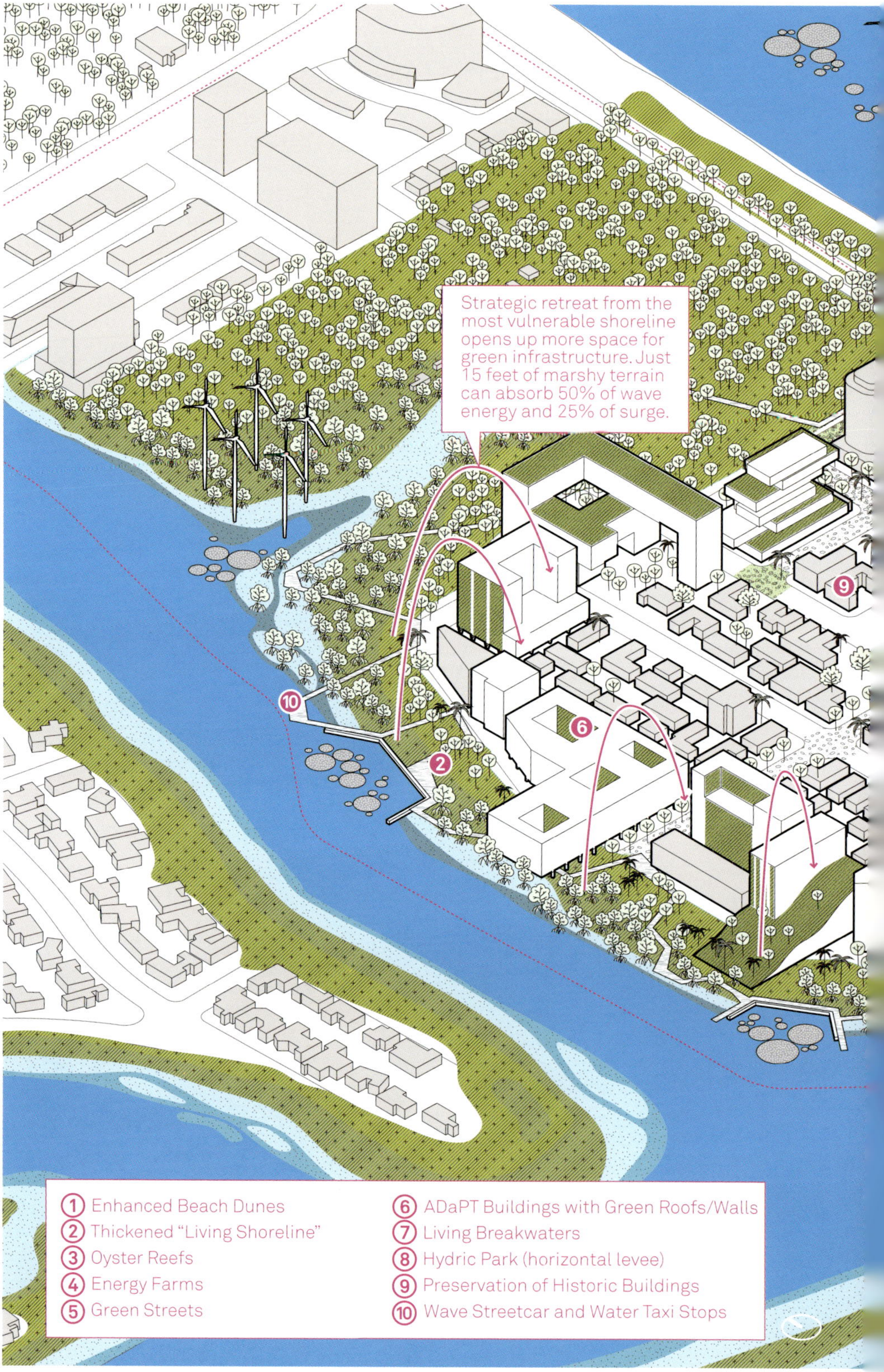

Strategic retreat from the most vulnerable shoreline opens up more space for green infrastructure. Just 15 feet of marshy terrain can absorb 50% of wave energy and 25% of surge.
(1) Enhanced Beach Dunes
(2) Thickened "Living Shoreline"
(3) Oyster Reefs
(4) Energy Farms
(5) Green Streets
(6) ADaPT Buildings with Green Roofs/Walls
(7) Living Breakwaters
(8) Hydric Park (horizontal levee)
(9) Preservation of Historic Buildings
(10) Wave Streetcar and Water Taxi Stops

1. *Soft Defense* (The Green Jacket)

The most conservative of all three scenarios where a fortified "green jacket" of living shoreline and breakwaters with green streets botanize the Village—parks, not pipes! Major infrastructural investments require development to simply pull back from the edge.

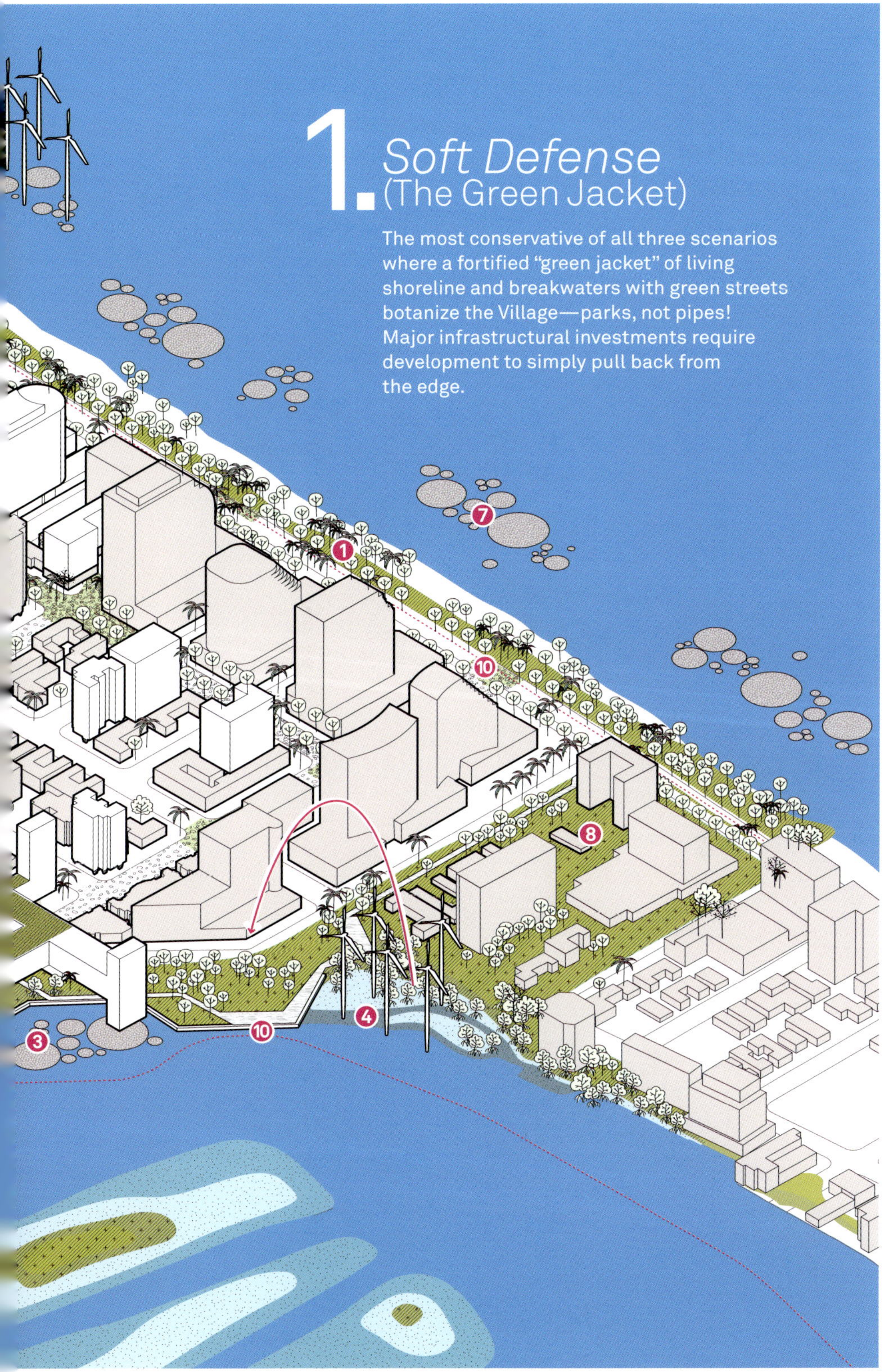

The recently completed DC Alexander Park in Fort Lauderdale serves as a model for coastal adaptation—where parks act as sponges, absorbing water and integrating ecosystems into urban infrastructure.

Streets can become
Eco-Boulevards.
New permeable median of bioswales and rain gardens can create oases within street corridors.

Transfer of Development Rights (TDRs) provide a legal framework to shift vulnerable development to the coastal ridge.
5
10
8
2
3
4
1 Enhanced Dunes and Sand Engine
2 Thickened "Living Shoreline"
3 Oyster Reefs
4 Energy Farms
5 Amphibious/Stiltsville Neighborhood
6 ADaPT Buildings with Green Roofs/Walls
7 Living Breakwaters
8 Enhanced Mangrove Forest
9 Stormwater Hydric Park
10 Wave Streetcar and Water Taxi Stops

2. *Strategic Retreat*

Retreating back from the lowest elevations and rewilding the beach and intercoastal shorelines ensures productive ecological services. The rewilding gives back critical biodiversity and refuge to the shoreline, essentially giving land back to nature.

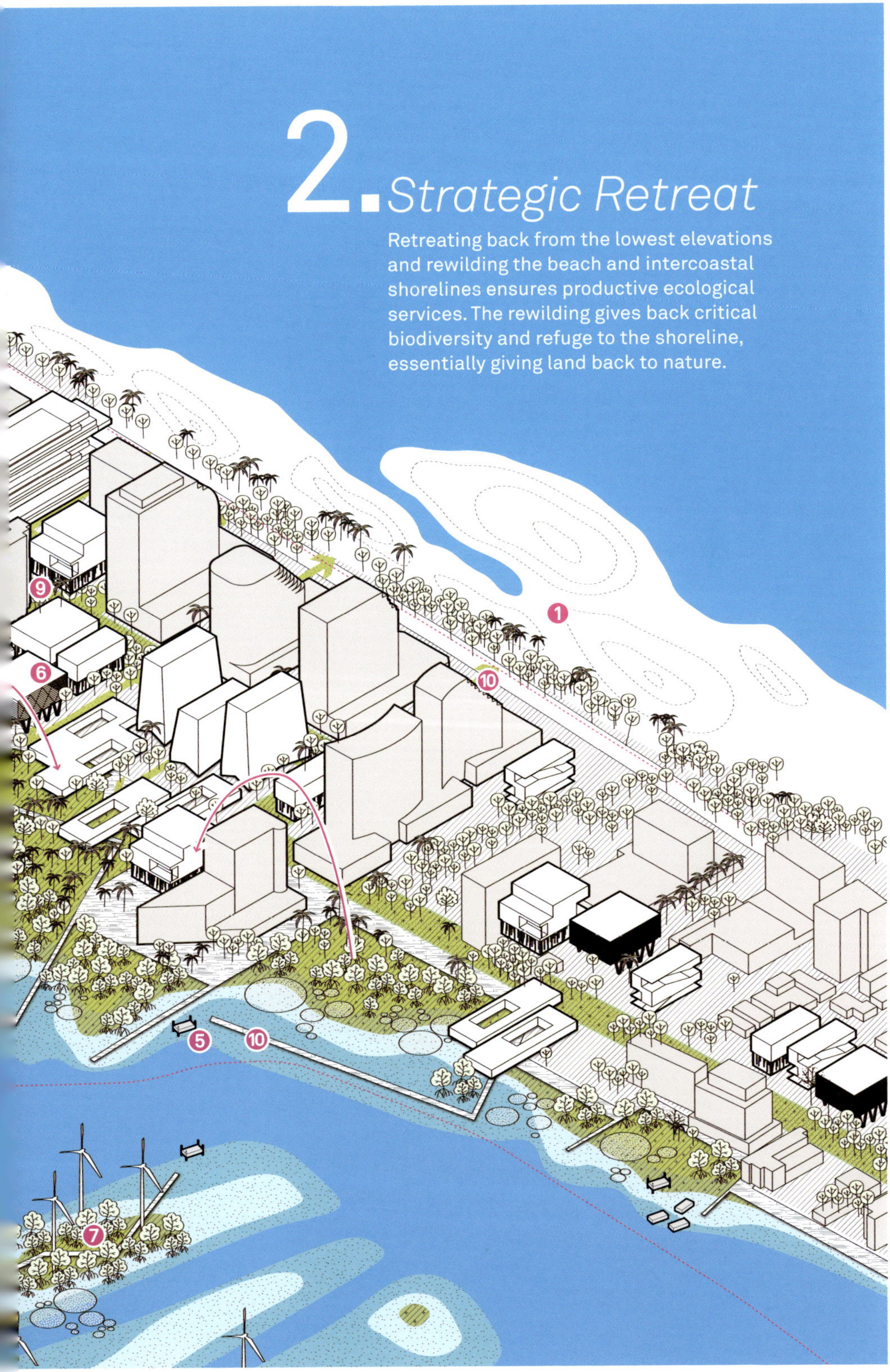

Celebrating the potential of a life "aquatic," opportunities for residents and tourists alike engage the water.

Rooftop Deck
Buyont Hull
aweed/Kelp
Submerged Bedroom With View
Amphibious Home

Designed by Brooks + Scarpa and built by Shiff Construction, DC Alexander Park exemplifies the Salty Urbanism framework by integrating ecosystem and urban services into resilient community infrastructure along Fort Lauderdale Beach.

Floating bioremediation islands integrate a system for farming food and energy, cleaning up pollution, managing waste from buildings and de-acidify saltwater.
5
10
6
3
2
4
1 Enhanced Dunes and Sand Engine
2 Saltwater Tidal Marsh and Nursery
3 Oyster Reefs
4 Energy Farms
5 Amphibious/Stiltsville Neighborhood
6 ADaPT Buildings with Green Roofs/Walls
7 Living Breakwaters and Coral Nursery
8 Waterway Blocks
9 Stormwater Hydric Park
10 Wave Streetcar and Water Taxi Stops

3. *Land Adjust* (Islands and Atolls)

The most radical scenario requires land assembly and adjustments. New development provides amphibious and submerged building typologies that create new lifestyle possibilities celebrating the water.

...a salty future will require Salty Urbanism.

“A salty future will require plants adapted to saltier conditions. The following palettes are appropriate to south Florida and other areas can take a similar approach with regionally appropriate plants that will be better adapted to local conditions.”

plant palettes

large trees

These are large landscape trees useful as hedgegrow screens, specimens, wide avenue plantings and/or for providing urban canopy and shade cover.

All grow taller than thirty feet at maturity and so must be set back at least thirty feet away from the nearest powerlines.

red maple Pr/D
Acer rubrum

45'- 50' FL
lime rock, sand, muck

willow bustic Pr/Ev
Sideroxylon salicifolium

30'- 50' FL
loam, lime rock

false mastic Pr/Ev
Sideroxylon foetidissimum

40'- 70' FL
lime rock, sand

royal poinciana Pr/D
Delonix regia

30'- 70'
loam, lime rock, sand, clay

Japanese fern tree Pr/Ev
Filicium decipiens

20'- 35'
loam, sand, clay

silk floss tree Pr/Ev
Chorisia speciosa

30'- 50'
loam, sand, clay

red mulberry Pr/D
Morus rubra

35'- 70' FL
loam, sand

avocado Pr/Ev
Persea americana

30'- 65'
loam, lime rock, sand

persimmon Pr/D
Diospyros virginana

35'-60' FL
loam, sand, clay

bridalveil tree Pr/Ev
Caesalpinia granadillo

25'-35'
loam, sand, clay

slash pine Pr/Ev
Pinus elliottii

80'- 100' FL
loam, lime rock, sand

bald cypress Pr/D
Taxodium distichum

50'- 100' FL
loam, muck, sand, clay

queen crape myrtle Pr/Ev
Lagerstroemia speciosa

35'- 60'
loam, sand, clay

banyans Pr/Ev
Ficus spp.

40'- 60'
loam, muck, sand, lime rock

live oak Pr/Ev
Quercus virginiana

40'-80' FL
loam, sand

low salt tolerance

preferred soil moisture

xeric — mesic — hydric

- caution advised siting near structures
- CAUTION - weedy exotic species
- caution - weedy native species
- #'- #' species mature height range
- FL indicates Florida native species

growth rate — slow / moderate / fast

preferred sun exposure — full sun / part shade / full shade

phenology
- Pr - long-lived perennial
- pr - short-lived perennial
- An - annual
- Ev - evergreen
- D - deciduous

West Indies mahogany Pr/D
Swietenia mahagoni

30'- 70' FL

loam, lime rock, sand, clay

paradise tree Pr/Ev
Simarouba glauca

30'- 50' FL

loam, sand, clay

red mangrove
Rhizophora mangle

20'- 50' FL

marine sediments, lime rock

wild tamarind Pr/Ev
Lysiloma latisiliquum

30'- 40' FL

loam, lime rock, sand

Jamaican dogwood Pr/D
Piscidia piscipula

15'- 50' FL

lime rock, sand

black mangrove Pr/Ev
Avicennia germinans

20'- 40' FL

marine sediments, sand

mango Pr/Ev
Mangifera indica

30'- 60'

sand, loam, clay

Florida soapberry Pr/Ev
Sapindus saponaria

30'- 40' FL

loam, sand, lime rock, clay

pitch apple Pr/Ev
Clusia rosea

25'- 50' FL

lime rock, sand

pond cypress Pr/D
Taxodium ascendens

50'- 85' FL

loam, muck, sand

yew podocarpus Pr/Ev
Podocarpus macrophyllus

20'- 60'

loam, sand, clay

eastern red cedar Pr/Ev
Juniperus virginiana

25'- 40' FL

loam, muck, sand

monkey apple Pr/Ev
Mimusops coriacea

20'- 40'

loam, sand, lime rock

green buttonwood Pr/Ev
Conocarpus erectus

30'- 50' FL

lime rock, sand

seagrape Pr/Ev
Coccoloba uvifera

25'- 50' FL

sand

high salt tolerance

growth forms — sprawling canopy / rounded canopy / vase-like canopy / irregular canopy / upright conifer / thicket forming

medium trees

These are moderately large landscape trees/tall shrubs that are useful as median and larger street-side plantings, as hedges and screens, or as shade/specimen trees in space-confined settings. Most of these have mature heights of thirty feet but some grow taller.

dahoon holly Pr/Ev
Ilex cassine

loam, muck, sand

redberry stopper Pr/Ev
Eugenia confusa

loam, lime rock, sand

wild cinnamon Pr/Ev
Canella winterana

loam, lime rock, sand

carombola Pr/Ev
Averrhoa carambola

loam, sand

atemoya Pr/Ev
Annona squamosa hybrids

loam, sand, clay

West Indies cherry Pr/Ev
Prunus myrtifolia

loam, lime rock

coastalplain willow Pr/D
Salix caroliniana

muck, sand

satinleaf Pr/D
Chrysophyllum oliviforme

muck, lime rock, sand

wild dilly Pr/Ev
Manilkara jaimiqui emarginata

sand, lime rock

sweetbay magnolia Pr/Ev
Magnolia virginiana

muck, sand

pink trumpet tree Pr/Ev
Tabebuia heterophylla

loam, lime rock, sand

yellow trumpet tree Pr/Ev
Tabebuia caraiba

loam, sand, clay

fiddlewood Pr/Ev
Citharexylum spinosum

lime rock, sand

crabwood Pr/Ev
Gymnanthes lucida

loam, lime rock, sand

wild lime Pr/Ev
Zanthoxylum fragara

lime rock, sand

low salt tolerance

preferred soil moisture

xeric — mesic — hydric

caution advised siting near structures

CAUTION - weedy exotic species

#'- #' species mature height range

FL indicates Florida native species

growth rate — slow | moderate | fast

preferred sun exposure — full sun | part shade | full shade

phenology
- Pr - long-lived perennial
- pr - short-lived perennial
- An - annual
- Ev - evergreen
- D - deciduous

Madagascar olive — Pr/Ev
Norohnia emarginata

loam, sand, clay

black ironwood — Pr/Ev
Krugiodendron ferreum

loam, lime rock, sand

white mangrove — Pr/Ev
Laguncularia racemosa

marine sediments, lime rock, sand

loquat — Pr/Ev
Eriobotrya japonica

loam, lime rock, sand

pomegranate — Pr/Ev
Punica granatum

loam, sand, clay

pond apple — Pr/Ev
Annona glabra

loam, muck, sand

lancewood — Pr/Ev
Damburneya coriacea

loam, lime rock, sand

Krug's holly — Pr/Ev
Ilex krugiana

loam, sand, lime rock

pigeon plum — Pr/Ev
Coccoloba diversifolia

sand

blolly — Pr/Ev
Guapira discolor

loam, lime rock, sand

verawood — Pr/Ev
Bulnesia arborea

loam, sand

silver buttonwood — Pr/Ev
Conocarpus erectus var. sericeus

lime rock, sand

white frangipani — Pr/D
Plumeria alba

loam, sand, clay

geiger tree — Pr/Ev
Cordia sebestena

loam, sand, lime rock, clay

gumbo limbo — Pr/Ev
Bursera simaruba

loam, sand, lime rock, clay

high salt tolerance

growth forms — spreading canopy | rounded canopy | vase-like canopy | irregular canopy | columnar canopy | thicket forming

small trees & tall shrubs

These are small trees and tree-like shrubs that rarely grow taller than twenty feet and are excellent for smaller street-side and urban uses.

Many of the shrubs in the bottom rows, like the stoppers (*Eugenia* spp.), can be pruned to be either hedges or small trees.

bitterbush Pr/Ev
Picramnia pentandra

10'-15' FL
sand

spicewood Pr/Ev
Myrcia neopallens

10'-20' FL
lime rock, sand

seven-year apple Pr/Ev
Casasia clusiifolia

8'-20' FL
lime rock, sand

strongbark Pr/Ev
Bourreria succulenta

10'-15' FL
lime rock, sand

red bottlebrush Pr/Ev
Callistemon citrinus

10'-15'
loam, sand, clay

dwarf poinciana Pr/Ev
Caesalpinia pulcherrima

8'-15'
loam, sand, clay

strawberry tree Pr/Ev
Arbutus unedo

6'-18'
loam, sand, clay

red frangipani Pr/D
Plumeria rubra

15'-20'
loam, sand, clay

myrsine Pr/Ev
Myrsine cubana

10'-20'
loam, sand

Simpson's stopper Pr/Ev
Myrcianthes fragrans

5'-20' FL
loam, lime rock, sand

white stopper Pr/Ev
Eugenia axillaris

6'-20' FL
loam, lime rock, sand

Florida privet Pr/Ev
Forestiera segregata

5'-15' FL
loam, lime rock, sand

tropical lilac Pr/Ev
Miconia bicolor

10'-25' FL
loam, lime rock

spanish stopper Pr/Ev
Eugenia foetida

12'-20' FL
loam, lime rock, sand

white indigoberry Pr/Ev
Randia aculeata

12'-15' FL
loam, lime rock, sand

low salt tolerance

preferred soil moisture

xeric — mesic — hydric

caution - weedy native species
#'-#' species mature height range
FL indicates Florida native species

growth rate — slow / moderate / fast

preferred sun exposure — full sun / part shade / full shade

phenology
- Pr - long-lived perennial
- pr - short-lived perennial
- An - annual
- Ev - evergreen
- D - deciduous

blackbead Pr/Ev
Pithecellobium unguis-cati

10'-15' FL
lime rock, sand

lignum-vitae Pr/Ev
Guaiacum sanctum

10'-20' FL
loam, lime rock

joewood Pr/Ev
Jacquinia keyensis

4'-10' FL
loam, lime rock, sand

Japanese privet Pr/Ev
Ligustrum japonicum

8'-12'
loam, sand, clay

cinnecord Pr/Ev
Vachellia choriophylla

6'-10' FL
lime rock, sand

sweet acacia Pr/Ev
Vachellia farnesiana

8'-20' FL
lime rock, sand

oleander Pr/Ev
Nerium oleander

6'-18'
sand, loam, clay

Florida boxwood Pr/Ev
Schaefferia frutescens

15'-25' FL
loam, lime rock, sand

bay cedar Pr/Ev
Suriana maritima

6'-20' FL
sand

wax myrtle Pr/Ev
Morella cerifera

10'-20' FL
loam, lime rock, sand

marlberry Pr/Ev
Ardisia escallonioides

8'-20' FL
sand, lime stone

varnishleaf Pr/Ev
Dodonaea viscosa

10'-20' FL
lime rock, sand

Jamaican Caper Pr/Ev
Quadrella jamaicensis

6'-12' FL
loam, lime rock, sand

green pittosporum Pr/Ev
Pittosporum tobira

8'-12'
loam, sand

saltbush Pr/D
Baccharis halimifolia

7'-15' FL
loam, sand

high salt tolerance

growth forms — spreading canopy / rounded canopy / vase-like canopy / columnar canopy / thicket forming / rounded shrub / irregular shrub

palms & palm-like shrubs

These are a variety of both native and exotic palms and palm-like shrubs that are commonly grown in south Florida landscapes.

The tallest-growing species are in the top rows while progressively shorter species are displayed in descending rows.

royal palm Pr/Ev
Roystonea regia

50'-100' FL
loam, sand

foxtail palm Pr/Ev
Wodyetia bifurcata

30'-60'
loam, sand

majesty palm Pr/Ev
Ravenea rivularis

60'-80'
loam, sand

traveler's palm Pr/Ev
Ravenala madagascariensis

15'-35'
loam, sand

carpentaria palm Pr/Ev
Carpentaria acuminata

35'-40'
loam, sand, clay

areca palm Pr/Ev
Dypsis lutescens

20'-30'
loam, sand, clay

Macarthur palm Pr/Ev
Ptychosperma macarthurii

15'-25'
loam, sand

christmas palm Pr/Ev
Adonidia merrillii

6'-25'
loam, sand

yellow butterfly palm Pr/Ev
Chrysalidocarpus lutescens

20'-30'
loam, sand, clay

pygmy date palm Pr/Ev
Phoenix roebelenii

6'-10'
loam, sand

king sago Pr/Ev
Cycas revoluta

8'-15'
loam, sand

bottle palms Pr/Ev
Hyophorbe spp.

8'-15'
loam, sand

dwarf palmetto Pr/Ev
Sabal minor

4'-9' FL
loam, sand

lady palm Pr/Ev
Rhapis excelsa

4'-9'
loam, sand

coontie Pr/Ev
Zamia integrifolia

2'-5' FL
sand

low salt tolerance

preferred soil moisture

xeric — mesic — hydric

CAUTION - weedy exotic species
caution - weedy native species
#'-#' species mature height range
FL indicates Florida native species

growth rate — slow, moderate, fast

preferred sun exposure — full sun, part shade, full shade

phenology
Pr - long-lived perennial
pr - short-lived perennial
An - annual
Ev - evergreen
D - deciduous

bismarck palm — Pr/Ev
Bismarckia nobilis

loam, sand

canary date palm — Pr/Ev
Phoenix canariensis

loam, sand

cabbage palm — Pr/Ev
Sabal palmetto

loam, sand

paurotis palm — Pr/Ev
Acoelorraphe wrightii

loam, muck, lime rock, sand

screw pine — Pr/Ev
Pandanus utilis

loam, sand, clay

coconut palm — Pr/Ev
Cocos nucifera

sand, lime rock

buccaneer palm — Pr/Ev
Pseudophoenix sargentii

lime rock, sand

pindo palm — Pr/Ev
Butia odorata

loam, sand

thatch palm — Pr/Ev
Thrinax radiata

loam, lime rock, sand

ponytail palm — Pr/Ev
Bearcarnea recurvata

loam, sand, clay

spanish bayonet — Pr/Ev
Yucca aloifolia

sand

silver thatch palm — Pr/Ev
Coccothrinax argentata

loam, sand, clay, lime rock

cardboard cycad — Pr/Ev
Zamia furfuracea

loam, sand, lime rock

saw palmetto — Pr/Ev
Serenoa repens

loam, sand

false sisal — Pr/Ev
Agave decipiens

sand

high salt tolerance

growth forms — long-frond palm, wide-frond palm, multi-trunk palm, shrubby palm / palm-like shrub, agave / agave-like

shrubs & vines

These are shrubs and shrub-like plants useful as borders and hedges. Most are fairly hedge-tolerant but a few, such as giant leatherfern, prickly pears, and shell ginger, are not. The bottom row shows vining species that can be used to create green façades..

firebush Pr/Ev
Hamelia patens

loam, sand

cocoplum Pr/Ev
Chrysobalanus icaco

sand, clay

Florida privet senna Pr/Ev
Senna ligustrina

sand

beautyberry Pr/Ev
Callicarpa americana

loam, lime rock, sand

wild sage lantana Pr/Ev
Lantana involucrata

sand

dwarf schefflera Pr/Ev
Schefflera arbicola

loam, sand, clay

buttonbush Pr/Ev
Cephalanthus occidentalis

loam, muck, sand

wild coffee Pr/Ev
Psychotria nervosa

loam, lime rock, sand

shell ginger Pr/Ev
Alpinia zerumbet

loam, sand, clay

splitleaf philodendron Pr/Ev
Philodendron selloum

loam, lime rock, sand

false indigobush Pr/D
Amorpha fruticosa

sand

snowberry Pr/Ev
Chiococca alba

loam, lime rock, sand

monstera Pr/Ev
Monstera deliciosa

loam, sand, clay

passionvines pr/Ev
Passiflora spp.

loam, sand, clay

wild allamanda Pr/Ev
Pentalinon luteum

loam, lime rock, sand

low salt tolerance

preferred soil moisture

xeric — mesic — hydric

- CAUTION - weedy exotic species
- caution - weedy native species
- #'- #' species mature height range
- FL indicates Florida native species

growth rate — slow | moderate | fast

preferred sun exposure — full sun | part shade | full shade

phenology
- Pr - long-lived perennial
- pr - short-lived perennial
- An - annual
- Ev - evergreen
- D - deciduous

blacktorch Pr/Ev
Erithalis fruticosa

lime rock, sand

necklacepod Pr/Ev
Sophora tomentosa var. tomentosa

sand

beach sea lavender Pr/Ev
Heliotropium gnaphalodes

sand

coastal pricklypear Pr/Ev
Opuntia stricta

sand

maidenberry Pr/Ev
Crossopetalum rhacoma

lime rock, sand

beach inkberry Pr/Ev
Scaevola plumieri

sand

copperleaf Pr/Ev
Acalypha wilkesiana

lime rock, sand

silver sea-oxeye Pr/Ev
Borrichia arborescens

sand

marshelder Pr/Ev
Iva frutescens

sand

crotons Pr/Ev
Codiaeum variegatum

loam, sand

giant leatherfern Pr/Ev
Acrostichum danaeifolium

loam, muck, sand, clay

christmasberry Pr/Ev
Lycium carolinianum

marine sediments, sand

bougainvellias Pr/Ev
Bougainvillea spp.

loam, sand, clay

skyblue clustervine Pr/Ev
Jacquemontia pentanthos

lime rock, sand

beach morning glory Pr/Ev
Ipomoea imperati

sand, lime rock

high salt tolerance

growth forms — rounded shrub | irregular shrub | upright shrub | sprawling shrub | cactus cactus-like | fern fern-like | vine vine-like

groundcovers

These are low-growing shrubs and herbaceous plants useful for groundcovering and small border-massing applications. Some species, such as those shown in the bottom-most row, grow in ways that make them suitable as alternatives to turfgrass..

Florida peperomia Pr/Ev
Peperomia obtusifolia

0.5'-1' FL
lime rock, sand

quailberry Pr/Ev
Crossopetalum ilicifolium

1'-2' FL
lime rock, sand

"horizontal" cocoplum Pr/Ev
Chrysobalanus icaco var. horizontal

1'-2' FL
loam, sand, lime rock

blue mistflower pr/Ev
Conoclinium coelestinum

1'-2' FL
loam, muck, sand

blue porterweeds pr/Ev
Stachytarpheta spp.

2'-8'
lime rock, sand

blanket flower pr/Ev
Gaillardia pulchella

1'-2'
loam, sand

swamp fern Pr/Ev
Telmatoblechnum serrulatum

2'-3' FL
loam, muck, sand, clay

southern shield fern Pr/Ev
Thelypteris kunthii

1'-3' FL
loam, lime rock, sand

wild plumbago Pr/Ev
Plumbago zeylanica

1'-2' FL
lime rock, sand

lizard's tail Pr/Ev
Saururus cernuus

0.5' FL
loam, muck, sand, clay

wild petunia Pr/Ev
Ruellia caroliniensis

1'-2.5' FL
sand

soap aloe Pr/Ev
Aloe maculata

1'-2'
loam, sand, clay

sunshine mimosa Pr/Ev
Mimosa strigillosa

creeping FL
lime rock, sand

baby sunrose Pr/Ev
Aptenia cordifolia

creeping
loam, sand

frogfruit Pr/Ev
Phyla nodiflora

creeping FL
loam, sand, clay

low salt tolerance

preferred soil moisture

xeric — mesic — hydric

CAUTION - weedy exotic species
caution - weedy native species
#'-#' species mature height range
FL indicates Florida native species

growth rate — slow | moderate | fast

preferred sun exposure — full sun | part shade | full shade

phenology
- Pr - long-lived perennial
- pr - short-lived perennial
- An - annual
- Ev - evergreen
- D - deciduous

wild gold lantana — Pr/Ev
Lantana depressa var. depressa

lime rock, sand

beach verbena — Pr/Ev
Glandularia maritima

lime rock, sand

railroad vine — pr/Ev
Ipomoea pes-caprae brasiliensis

sand

eastcoast dune sunflower — pr/Ev
Helianthus debilis var. debilis

loam, sand

sea-oxeye daisy — Pr/Ev
Borrichia frutescens

loam, lime rock, sand

coastal searocket — pr/Ev
Cakile lanceolata

loam, sand, clay

seaside goldenrod — pr/D
Solidago sempervirons

sand

sea purslane — Pr/Ev
Sesuvium portulacastrum

loam, sand, lime rock

beach bean — Pr/Ev
Canavalia rosea

sand

beach creeper — Pr/Ev
Ernodea littoralis

lime rock, sand

mangrove spiderlily — Pr/Ev
Hymenocallis latifolia

loam, sand

beach marshelder — Pr/Ev
Iva imbricata

sand

perennial peanut — Pr/Ev
Arachis glabrata

sand, loam, clay

gopher apple — Pr/Ev
Licania michauxii

sand

turtleweed — Pr/Ev
Batis maritima

sand

high salt tolerance

growth forms — sprawling shrub | bunching herb | showy flower herb | flowering bulb | ground-running | agave agave-like | fern fern-like

grasses

These are grasses and grass-like plants that grow well in south Florida. The top two rows are mostly bunching varieties useful as borders while the bottom two rows are turf-tolerant groundcovers. The right-most column and middle row have specialty uses.

purple lovegrass pr/D
Eragrostis spectabilis

sand

fakahatchee grass Pr/Ev
Tripsacum dactyloides

loam, sand

dwarf fakahatchee grass Pr/Ev
Tripsacum floridanum

lime rock, sand

lopsided indiangrass Pr/D
Sorghastrum secundum

sand

lemongrass pr/Ev
Cymbopogon citratus

loam, muck, sand

lilyturfs Pr/Ev
Liriope spp.

sand, lime rock, muck

horsetail Pr/Ev
Equisetum hyemale var. affine

loam, sand

soft rush Pr/Ev
Juncus effusus

loam, muck, sand, clay

bushy bluestems Pr/D
Andropogon spp.

loam, muck, sand

maidencane Pr/Ev
Panicum hemitomon

muck, sand

blue maidencane Pr/Ev
Amphicarpum muhlenbergianum

sand, muck

pinewoods fingergrass Pr/Ev
Eustachys petraea

loam, sand

bahiagrass Pr/Ev
Paspalam notatum

loam, sand

St. Augustine grass Pr/Ev
Stenotaphrum secundatum

loam, sand, clay

zoysiagrass Pr/Ev
Zoysia spp.

loam, sand

low salt tolerance

preferred soil moisture

xeric — mesic — hydric

CAUTION - weedy exotic species

caution - weedy native species

#'-#' species mature height range

FL indicates Florida native species

growth rate — slow, moderate, fast

preferred sun exposure — full sun, part shade, full shade

phenology
- Pr - long-lived perennial
- pr - short-lived perennial
- An - annual
- Ev - evergreen
- D - deciduous

sand cordgrass — Pr/Ev
Spartina bakeri

sand

muhly grass — Pr/Ev
Muhlenbergia capillaris

lime rock, sand, clay

sea oats — Pr/D
Uniola paniculata

sand

bulbine — Pr/Ev
Bulbine frutescens

loam, sand

Elliot's lovegrass — Pr/D
Eragrostis elliottii

loam, sand

bitter panicgrass — Pr/Ev
Panicum amarum

loam, sand

basketgrass — Pr/Ev
Oplismenus setarius

loam, sand

beachstar — Pr/D
Cyperus pedunculatus

sand

smooth cordgrass — Pr/Ev
Spartina alterniflora

loam, sand

whitetop sedge — Pr/Ev
Rhynchospora colorata

loam, muck, sand

saltmeadow cordgrass — Pr/Ev
Spartina patens

sand

seashore dropseed — Pr/Ev
Sporobolus virginicus

marine sediments, sand

bermudagrass — Pr/Ev
Cynodon dactylon

loam, sand

seashore paspalum — Pr/Ev
Paspalum vaginatum

sand

saltgrass — Pr/Ev
Distichlis spicata

lime rock, sand, clay

high salt tolerance

growth forms — bunching grass, rhizomatous grass, grass-like herb

saltwater-brackish aquatics

These obligate wetland plants are native to Florida and useful for vegetating wetlands expected to either occasionally or frequently exhibit salty conditions.

Species in the left-most columns prefer salinities <10ppt while species to the right can tolerate up to 35ppt.

string lily Pr/Ev
Crinum americanum

loam, muck, sand

bald cypress Pr/D
Taxodium distichum

loam, muck, sand, clay

pond cypress Pr/D
Taxodium ascendens

loam, muck, sand

dwarf papyrus Pr/Ev
Cyperus haspan

loam, muck, sand

coastal spikerush Pr/Ev
Eleocharis cellulosa

loam, muck, sand

sawgrass Pr/Ev
Cladium jamaicense

lime rock, sand, clay

jointed flatsedge Pr/Ev
Cyperus articulatus

loam, sand

saltmarsh mallow Pr/Ev
Kosteletzkya pentacarposcarpos

sand

seashore paspalum Pr/Ev
Paspalum vaginatum

sand

water hyssop Pr/Ev
Bacopa monnieri

sand, muck

grassy arrowhead Pr/Ev
Sagittaria graminea

muck, sand

marsh sea lavender Pr/Ev
Limonium carolinianum

muck, silt, sand

soft rush Pr/Ev
Juncus effusus

loam, muck, sand, clay

tapegrass Pr/Ev
Vallisneria americana

muck, sand, silt

widegeongrass Pr/Ev
Ruppia maritima

marine sediments, sand, muck

low salt tolerance

preferred water depth

onshore emergent offshore

caution - weedy native species

#'-#' species mature height range

FL indicates Florida native species

growth rate: slow | moderate | fast

preferred sun exposure: full sun | part shade | full shade

phenology:
Pr - long-lived perennial
pr - short-lived perennial
An - annual
Ev - evergreen
D - deciduous

saltgrass — Pr/Ev
Distichlis spicata

lime rock, sand, clay

turtleweed — Pr/Ev
Batis maritima

sand

red mangrove — Pr/Ev
Rhizophora mangle

marine sediments, lime rock

black needlerush — Pr/Ev
Juncus roemerianus

marine sediments, sand

pond apple — Pr/Ev
Annona glabra

loam, muck, sand

black mangrove — Pr/Ev
Avicennia germinans

marine sediments, sand

gulf cordgrass — Pr/Ev
Spartina spartinae

loam, sand

glassworts — Pr/D
Salicornia spp.

muck, loam

white mangrove — Pr/Ev
Laguncularia racemosa

marine sediments, lime rock, sand

sea-oxeye daisy — Pr/Ev
Borrichia frutescens

loam, lime rock, sand

giant leatherfern — Pr/Ev
Acrostichum danaeifolium

loam, muck, sand, clay

smooth cordgrass — Pr/Ev
Spartina alterniflora

loam, sand

shoal grass — Pr/Ev
Halodule wrightii

marine sediments, sand

manatee grass — Pr/Ev
Syringodium filiforme

marine sediments

turtle grass — Pr/Ev
Thalassia testudinum

marine sediments

high salt tolerance

canopy forms: thicket forming, upright conifer, sprawling canopy, irregular canopy, rounded canopy

understory forms: rounded shrub, upright shrub, bunching herbs, fern fern-like

groundcovers: bunching grass, rhizome grass, creeping herb

true-aquatics: emergent vegetation, submerged vegetation

brackish-freshwater aquatics

This seleciton of obligate wetland species is best suited for wetlands and ponds not likely to experience inundation by saltwater, however, species on the right-hand page will tolerate occasional salinities. All are useful species for wet bioretention features.

coastalplain willow Pr/D
Salix caroliniana

muck, sand

wapato Pr/Ev
Sagittaria latifolia

muck, sand

buttonbush Pr/D
Cephalanthus occidentalis

loam, muck, sand

prairie iris Pr/D
Iris savannarum

loam, sand

swamp rosemallow Pr/Ev
Hibiscus grandiflorus

loam, sand

scarlet hibiscus Pr/Ev
Hibiscus coccineus

loam, sand

golden canna Pr/Ev
Canna flaccida

loam, muck, sand, clay

pickerelweed Pr/Ev
Pontederia cordata

muck, sand

arrow arum Pr/Ev
Peltandra virginica

muck, loam

lizard's tail Pr/Ev
Saururus cernuus

loam, muck, sand, clay

maidencane Pr/Ev
Panicum hemitomon

muck, sand

American lotus Pr/Ev
Nelumbo lutea

loam, clay, silt, muck

American frogbit Pr/Ev
Limnobium spongia

banana lily Pr/Ev
Nymphoides aquatica

muck, silt, sand

Florida water-lilies Pr/Ev
Nymphaea spp.

muck, silt, sand

low salt tolerance

preferred water depth

onshore emergent offshore

⚠ caution - weedy native species

#'-#' species mature height range

FL indicates Florida native species

growth rate: slow | moderate | fast

preferred sun exposure: full sun | part shade | full shade

phenology
Pr - long-lived perennial
pr - short-lived perennial
An - annual
Ev - evergreen
D - deciduous

alligator flag — Pr/D
Thalia geniculata

loam, muck, sand

duck potato — Pr/Ev
Sagittaria lancifolia

muck, sand

bald cypress — Pr/D
Taxodium distichum

loam, muck, sand, clay

dwarf papyrus — Pr/Ev
Cyperus haspan

loam, muck, sand

string lily — Pr/Ev
Crinum americanum

loam, sand

pond apple — Pr/Ev
Annona glabra

loam, muck, sand

jointed flatsedge — Pr/Ev
Cyperus articulatus

loam, sand

coastal spikerush — Pr/Ev
Eleocharis cellulosa

loam, muck, sand

sawgrass — Pr/Ev
Cladium jamaicense

lime rock, muck, sand, clay

creeping primrose willow — Pr/Ev
Ludwigia repens

muck, sand

lemon hyssop — Pr/Ev
Bacopa caroliniana

sand, muck

water hyssop — Pr/Ev
Bacopa monnieri

sand, muck

spatterdock — Pr/Ev
Nuphar advena

muck, loam, silt, sand, clay

guppy grass — Pr/Ev
Najas guadalupensis

muck, sand

tapegrass — Pr/Ev
Vallisneria americana

muck, sand, silt

high salt tolerance

canopy forms: thicket forming, upright conifer, sprawling canopy, irregular canopy, rounded canopy

understory forms: rounded shrub, upright shrub, bunching herbs, low-lying shrub

groundcovers: bunching grass, rhizome grass, creeping herb

true-aquatics: emergent vegetation, submerged vegetation

glo–ssary

glossary

100-year storm
A weather event, typically a heavy rainfall or storm, that historical referred to having a 1% chance of occurring in any given year. Reflects statistical probability used for planning and flood risk assessments.

Aerobic
Having or providing oxygen.

Aggregate
A broad category of particulate material used in construction, including sand, gravel, crushed stone, slag, recycled concrete, and geosynthetic aggregates, and is often available in various particle sizes for differing purposes.

Anaerobic
Lacking oxygen.

Anoxic
Soils or habitats that contains little or no dissolved oxygen. These conditions arise in some wetlands and water bodies due to a lack of water circulation, but also occur within saturated soils.

Aquatic Buffers
Areas with vegetation suitable for nutrient uptake and soil stabilization that are set aside between developed areas and a water body or wetland for stormwater treatment purposes.

Aquifer
A subterranean geologic formation, group of formations, or part of a formation that contains sufficient groundwater within permeable material to supply useful quantities of water to wells, springs, surface water, drinking water, irrigation, industry, or other uses.

Armor Layer
Refers to the protective layer on coastal protection features, such as a breakwaters, revetments, or seawall. Is composed of armor units.

Artificial Reef
Objects of natural or human origin deployed purposefully on the seafloor to influence physical, biological, and/or socioeconomic processes related to living marine or estuarine resources.

Attenuation
1) The lessening of wave height by coastal protection features OR 2) the reduction in flow and/or discharge rate of water moving through or out of a stormwater management feature.

Backdunes
A generic term for an established and/or stabilized set of dunes in a coastal setting that are separated from the shoreline by another set of less established dunes (see "foredune").

Barrier Island
A coastal landform consisting of an narrow strip of unconsolidated sediment (primarily sand) lying parallel to the mainland coast and being separated from the mainland by a lagoon, salt marsh, or bay. Historically dominated with dunes, vegetation, and swamp-like terrain.

Base Flood Elevation
The elevation of the base flood, including wave height, relative to a geodetic elevation datum (e.g, NAVD88) specified by a Flood Insurance Rate Map (FIRM). Often based on a "100-year flood" or the "1-percent-annual chance flood," which is a flood having a one percent (1 percent) chance of occurring at a specified location in any given year.

Bathymetry
The measurement of water depth at various places in a wetland, lake, lagoon, ocean, or other water body.

Beach Nourishment/Re-nourishment
The process of replenishing a beach with material (usually sand) obtained from another location.

Benthic
Pertaining to the sub-aquatic bottom.

Berm
An impermeable earthen mound designed to resist the flow of floodwaters through it and used to shield adjacent properties or public right-of-ways.

Best Management Practices (BMPs)
State-of-the-art methods or techniques used to manage the quantity and improve the quality of wet weather flow.

Biochar
A carbon-rich material produced by pyrolysis (combustion at high temperatures and low oxygen levels) of organic feedstocks, particularly municipal, agricultural, and domestic vegetation wastes. Similar to charcoal but has less volatile compounds, presents an extremely high surface area, and can be used to enhance soil aggregation, water holding capacity, plant growth/tolerances, and can provide similar benefits to engineered media as activated charcoal or compost.

Biomass
The amount of living and organic matter, in the form of organisms and their waste products, present in a particular habitat or area.

Bioretention
Landscape stormwater features that use leverage plants or living ecosystems to accomplish all or some of their designed goals. Includes such stormwater features as rain gardens, bioswales, green roofs, and bioretention planters.

Blue Carbon
Refers to the proportion of biological carbon that is found in the oceans and coastal areas of the world.

Brackish
Refers to a mixture or mixing of marine and freshwater. Generally used to refer to the water contained within lagoons, estuaries, marine river deltas, and other water bodies where freshwater outflows from inland sources are continually mixing with saltwater delivered by ocean winds and tides.

Building Alteration
Any change or modification of construction, space arrangement, size, occupancy, or use of a building or structure, including the addition or removal of hard features in landscaping and cosmetic changes to historic buildings.

Building Façade
That portion of any exterior elevation of a building extending vertically from the grade to the top of a parapet wall or eaves and horizontally across the entire width of the building elevation. Essentially refers to the exterior most portion of building walls, those that are not the structural and/or load bearing walls.

Bulkhead
Vertical structures or partitions parallel to shore, normally sited directly at the shoreline, designed to hold or prevent soil from sliding seaward and reduce land erosion. Providing protection to shorelines from light-to-moderate wave action is considered a secondary function of bulkheads, which are generally less massive and not as resistant to high wave energy-settings as other design types (see "Seawalls").

Canopy (vegetation)
1) The upper portion of a tree consisting of limbs, branches, and leaves. "Canopy trees" are large trees that have a canopy sufficient to form a shade cover over the ground, creating a shaded and cool environment, as in a forest. 2) The highest stratum of a natural plant community or forest composed of tall, woody plants and palms.

Carbon Sequestration
The process by which atmospheric carbon dioxide (CO^2) is removed from the atmosphere and stored in the ocean, landscapes, geological formations, buildings, or in any other setting where it is not likely to return to its atmospheric state in the near term.

Catch Basin
Box-like underground structures constructed of concrete and sited at key junctures within a stormwater sewer system, generally located beneath a street or other impervious surface.

Catchment
An area of land draining to a single reference point (see "Drainage Basin"); similar to a drainage basin, but on a smaller scale.

Climate Change
Refers to regional or global changes in mean climate state or in patterns of climate variability ranging over decades to millions of years, often identified using statistical methods and sometimes referred to as changes in long-term weather conditions. Climate is influenced by many processes, including changes in plate tectonics, variations in Earth's orbit, axial tilt and precession, atmospheric greenhouse gas (GHG) concentrations, solar variability, volcanism, internal variability resulting from interactions between the atmosphere, oceans and ice (glaciers, small ice caps, ice sheets, and sea ice), and anthropogenic activities such as greenhouse gas emissions and land use changes to carbon cycling.

Coastal Flood Wall
A wall parallel to an exposed coastline, sited some distance inland from the crest of a beach or the edge of a seawall, and used to prevent more extreme floodwaters from flowing onto the land areas behind it.

Coastal High Hazard Area/Zone
Area within the special flood hazard area extending from offshore to the inland limit of a primary dune along an open coast and any other area that is subject to high-velocity wave action from storms or seismic sources, and shown on a Flood Insurance Rate Map (FIRM) or other flood hazard map as velocity Zone V, VO, VE or V1-30.

Complete Street
A street where the entire right-of-way is planned, designed, and operated for all modes of transportation and all users, regardless of age or ability, as defined by the National Complete Streets Coalition (NCSC). Pedestrians, bicyclists, transit riders, and motorists of all ages and abilities must be able to safely move along and across a Complete Street.

Conceptual Site Plan
A plan (to scale) delineating any physical structures, including dimensions.

Confining Unit
A geologic strata or layer of clay, hardpan, organic mucks, or other material that restrict the movement of water below that strata or layer. Often used to refer to boundaries above or below an aquifer.

Control Elevation
The lowest elevation at which water can be released through a water control device or landscape features.

Conveyance
The movement of water from one location to another.

Corridors
Spatially discrete components of an ecosystem that are longer than they are wide and which provide a continuous transect of habitat through an area of different habitats and/or non-habitat and which often connect two geographically isolated, larger units of similar habitat (see also "Patches").

Cultural Ecosystem Services
The nonmaterial benefits people obtain from ecosystems through spiritual enrichment, cognitive development, reflection, and aesthetic experience, including, for example, knowledge systems, social relations, and aesthetic values.

Curb Cuts/Curb Cut-outs
Breaks along the length of a curb system or street edge that allow water to flow into an adjacent landscape and/or stormwater feature.

Datum
Any permanent line, plane or surface used as a reference of measure for vertical distances and elevation. For the present work, there are two main categories of datum planes to consider: the "geodetic" and those that reference some measurement of sea-level. The important geodetic datum commonly used is the North American Vertical Datum of 1988 (see "NAVD88"). Of the many datum planes available, the ones most relevant to resilient adaptation design are likely Mean Higher-High Water and Mean High Water, which reference planes that determined by taking an average of the high tides.

Dead Load
The weight of materials incorporated into the building, including but not limited to walls, floors, roofs, ceilings, stairways, built-in partitions, finishes, cladding, and other similarly incorporated architectural and structural items, and the weight of fixed service equipment, such as cranes, plumbing stacks and risers, electrical feeders, heating, ventilating, and air-conditioning systems and automatic sprinkler systems. Particularly important to design considerations for green roofs and rainwater harvesting systems that store water on the roof (see also "Blue Roofs").

Deep Injection Well
The transmission of materials through a well that discharges to the Boulder Zone. The Boulder Zone lies approximately three thousand (3,000) feet below the land surface of Broward County and contains water of greater than ten thousand (10,000) parts per million (ppm) total dissolved solids (TDS).

Design Flood
The flood associated with the greater of the following two areas: 1) An area with a floodplain subject to a 1 percent or greater chance of flooding in any year; OR 2) an area designated as a flood hazard area on a community's flood hazard map, or otherwise legally designated.

Design Flood Elevation
The vertical elevation of the "design flood," including wave height, relative to the datum specified on a community's legally designated flood hazard map (e.g, NAVD88). In areas designated as Zone AO, the design flood elevation shall be the elevation of the highest existing grade of the building's perimeter plus the depth number (in feet) specified on the flood hazard map. In areas designated as Zone AO where a depth number is not specified on the map, the depth number shall be taken as being equal to two feet (610 mm).

Design Storm
1) A hypothetical extreme storm whose waves coastal protection structures will often be designed to withstand, OR 2) a hypothetical extreme storm whose volume and rate of rainfall stormwater management features will often be designed to accommodate. In either case, the severity of the storm (see "Return Period") is chosen in view of some legally agreed upon level of acceptable risk (see "Flood Insurance Study").

Detention
The temporary delay of stormwater runoff through the storage of a specified volume of stormwater. Chiefly meant to attenuate floodwaters while providing some amount of water quality treatment (i.e, sedimentation). Contrasts with "Retention" in that designs prioritize discharge to downstream features and/or waterways over on-site storage.

Directly Connected Impervious Area
A continuously connected surface area covered by buildings, roadways, or other impervious surfaces. Without pervious landscape interruptions.

Discharge
The purposeful or unintentional flow of floodwater from one property, water body, pipe, and/or landscape feature into another

Drainage Basin
The common location where the total upland area drains to (see "Catchment") by way of streams, tributaries, and/or other surface features (see also "Watershed").

Drainage Layer
A functional layer in a stormwater management feature that absorbs excess runoff by draining it from a surface through a hollow space or permeable material. Some notable features that require a drainage layer include tree boxes, permeable pavements, green roofs, and bioretention planters. With certain other features where a drainage layer is not required, such as swales, the inclusion of elements with similar design can greatly enhance the feature's efficacy (see "Underdrains"). With appropriate design and material selection, a drainage layer can also serve as a water storage unit that acts as a small-scale retention or detention feature (see also "Reservoir Layer"). For landscape features that incorporate plants into drainage designs, a drainage layer can help to increase the space available to the root zone. Additionally, a drainage layer can act as a protective layer for underlying structures (e.g, roof membranes beneath green roofs).

Dredging
The removal of submerged bottom material and sediments beneath surface waters by any means.

Dry Floodproofing
A combination of design modifications that results in a building or structure, including the attendant utilities and equipment and sanitary facilities, being water tight with walls substantially impermeable to the passage of water and with structural components having the capacity to resist loads associated with flood events.

Dry Retention
A landscape basin having a bottom elevation of at least one foot above the control elevation of the area, intended to store all of a specified amount of runoff from a given catchment area on-site (see "Retention").

Easement
Any strip of land or body of water created by a property owner for public or private travel, access, utilities, drainage, sanitation, or other specified uses having limitations, the fee title to which shall remain in the name of the property owner subject to the right of use designated in the document granting the easement, generally granted to the owner by the relevant municipal and/or state agency. Easements differ from right-of-ways in that they are not necessarily defined in service of preserving the essential function of an infrastructure or infrastructural element (see "Right-of-Way").

Ecological Niche
An abstract concept that represents the total physical space and/or behavioral potential realized by a species, or individuals of a species, in a given ecosystem. The dimensions or limits defined for this space often include, but are not limited to, habitat use, food preference, and interactions with other organisms. An animal or plant is said to be "occupying an ecological niche" when it is carrying out certain patterns of activity necessary to it's day-to-day survival, growth, and reproduction within a specific habitat area.

Ecological Succession
Refers to the sequential replacement of species, communities, or ecosystems over time or following notable disturbances to a given area (e.g, a fire). When applied to a given site/habitat, "succession" can also refer to specific changes in communities and ecosystems (e.g, structural, functional, etc.).

Ecosystem
A dynamic complex of plants, animals, microorganisms, and the non-living environment interacting as a functional unit.

Ecosystem-Based Management (EBM)
An integrated approach to landscape and/or ecological management that considers the entire ecosystem, including humans. The goal of ecosystem-based management is to maintain an ecosystem in a healthy, productive, and resilient condition so that it can provide the services humans want and need (see "Ecosystem Services") while also supporting essential natural processes (see "Ecosystem Function"). Ecosystem-based management differs from more traditional approaches in that it considers the cumulative impacts of different sectors and does not focus solely on a single species, sector, activity, or concern.

Ecotype (genetic)
A population of a species that survives as a distinct group from others of the same species due to environmental selection and isolation pressures inherent to the given geography they inhabit. For example, a plant species with a large geographic distribution can vary considerably in such characteristics as height, growth habits, maturation, leaf appearance, and reproduction across their range. These characteristics are rarely distributed randomly but are typically clustered into ecological regions (ecoregions). Plants within these ecological regions and representing genetic adaptation unique to the biotic and abiotic conditions of that region are known as "ecotypes."

El Niño
A climatic cycle wherein warm, equatorial water in the eastern Pacific flows southward along the coast of Peru and Ecuador during February and March of certain years, influencing the climate elsewhere around the globe. During many El Niño years, storms, rainfall, and other meteorological phenomena in the Western Hemisphere are measurably different than during non-El Niño years.

Endemic Species
A native species that is confined to a specific geographic area and only found within that limited extent and nowhere else in the world.

Erosion
The wearing of land and/or terrestrial sediments by the action of natural forces. On a beach or exposed shoreline, the carrying away of sediments is mainly perpetrated by wave action, tidal currents, littoral currents, and winds.

Estuary
A semi-enclosed, naturally coastal water body that has a free connection with the open sea and within which saltwater is measurably diluted with freshwater and is affected by tides.

Eutrophication
An increase in the rate of supply of organic matter and/or nutrients (such as nitrogen) to an aquatic ecosystem. Eutrophication often leads to an array of cascading changes in ecosystem structure and function such as decreased dissolved oxygen levels (see "Anoxic") and increased algal growth rates (see "Harmful Algal Blooms").

Evaporation
The physical process whereby water (liquid) is converted to vapor (gas) through the transfer of heat energy.

Evapotranspiration
The combined loss of water to the atmosphere from land and water surfaces by both physical evaporation and the biological transpiration of plants. This includes evaporation from water surfaces and moist soils, interception of rainfall by canopy where it evaporates from the surfaces of leaves and branches, water absorbed and retained within the living plant tissues themselves, as well as water transpired (given off) or evaporated from the living tissues of plants. Measured in terms of depth of water per unit area during a specified period (e.g, mm/day).

Exfiltration
The percolation and downward movement of collected water through a soil, substrate, or media located either at the bottom of or beneath a natural landscape or designed feature. Differs from "infiltration" principally in that stormwater is collected from one site and then conveyed to another location by way of a central conduit, where it is then released into a reservoir layer and/or bottom elevation of a landscape feature, rather than being infiltrated into the ground/drainage layer directly at the surface of the catchment area.

Exfiltration Trench
A subsurface retention system designed to collect and convey surface waters underground. Consists of a central conduit, normally perforated pipe, surrounded by a "Reservoir Layer" of natural or artificial aggregate that retains stormwater below ground while also encouraging it to percolate into the native soil as soon as possible (see "Exfiltration"). A common example is a French Drain.

Exotic Species
Species introduced into an ecosystem where they do not occur naturally.

Extensive Green Roof
A roof mainly created for supporting biodiversity or providing other environmental benefits, and which is not intended to be used frequently by humans.

Facultative Plants
Plant species that have adapted to thrive equally in both wetland and upland conditions.

FDEP
(Acronym) Florida Department of Environmental Protection. The state agency that oversees and manages EPA regulations at the state level for Florida, as well as providing many other environmental and permitting services.

FEMA
(Acronym) Federal Emergency Management Agency. The federal agency that, in addition to carrying out other functions, administers the National Flood Insurance Program.

Fetch
The area in which rough seas are generated by wind having a fairly constant direction and speed. "Fetch" also refers to "fetch length," which describes the uninterrupted, horizontal distance that wind can travel over water. Generally, the more expansive a water body the greater potential it has to produce rough conditions because wind will have more uninterrupted distance — or fetch — over which to contact the water surface and generate wave action.

Fill
A miscellaneous mixture of substrate material, namely various soils, rock, sediments, and debris, which are intended for use as a sub-structural foundation to buildings, roads, and/or certain infrastructural features.

Filter Layer
1) For stormwater management: a functional layer within an infiltration or retention stormwater feature that prevents finer soil and substrate from entering into a drainage layer (see "Drainage Layer"). OR 2) For coastal stabilization: an intermediate layer placed beneath certain coastal protection features that prevents fine materials of an underlying layer or substrate from being washed away through the voids of a comparatively course upper layer.

Flood Gate
A gravity outlet fitted with vertically-hinged doors, opening if the inner water level (the "head water") is higher than the outer water level (the "tail water"), so that drainage takes place during low water.

Flood Hazard Area
The area within a floodplain subject to a 1 percent or greater chance of flooding in any year, or the area designated as a flood hazard area on a community's flood hazard map, or otherwise legally designated. Whichever of these definitions covers a greater geographic area within a given context takes precedent.

Flood Insurance Rate Map (FIRM)
The official map of the community on which FEMA has delineated both special flood hazard areas and the risk premium zones applicable to the community.

Flood Insurance Study (FIS)
The official report provided by FEMA that contains the FIRM (see "Flood Insurance Rate Map"), the Flood Boundary and Floodway Map (if applicable), the water surface elevations of the base flood, and supporting technical data.

Floodplain
The flat land area adjacent to a water body, such as a river, canal, estuary, or ocean, and subject to occasional or periodic inundation by floodwaters from said water body. Floodplains are delineated according to their estimated frequency of flooding.

Florida-Friendly Landscaping TM
A Florida state-wide standard for landscape design and management. Refers to a set of criteria that assure quality landscapes that conserve water, protect the environment, are appropriate for local conditions, and are drought, wind, or salt tolerant.

Flow Control Device
A mechanical element of a conveyance system or discharge structure which allows the gradual release of water under controlled conditions. Includes bleed-down systems, or "bleeders."

Flushing Time
The turnover time of water in an estuary, that is, the time required to replace the freshwater or saltwater contained in an estuary with freshwater inflow from upstream or saltwater from the ocean.

Fluvial
Of or pertaining to rivers; produced by the action of a river or stream.

Forebays
A pretreatment option suitable for street-side stormwater features that readily integrates with curbs, driveways, and similar features.

Foredune
A foredune is a shore-parallel dune ridge that forms on the back beach of an ocean, estuary, or bay by wind deposits. Part of the beach zone, it is generally dominated by sand and very hardy beach dune plants that can tolerate burial and strong salt exposure (e.g, sea oats).

Freeboard
The vertical distance between the water level and the top of a stormwater management structure. Generally used to describe the water storage capacity of landscape stormwater features.

Gabion/Gabion Box
Steel wire-mesh baskets filled with stones, rocks, or crushed masonry and used to protect a bank or bottom from erosion.

Geographic Information System (GIS)
Database of information which is geographically referenced, usually with an associated visualization system.

Geotextile
A synthetic fabric which may be woven or non-woven and is generally used as a filter layer but may also refer to such materials used for temporary erosion control or weed suppression.

Groin
A "hard" coastal stabilization feature that is a narrow strip of armored materials attached perpendicular to an exposed coastline and built out into a tidal waterway to reduce longshore currents and/or to trap and retain littoral sediments.

Groundwater
Water below the surface of the earth, whether it is fresh or saltwater. Fresh groundwater soaks into the soil from rain falling onto pervious surfaces and surficial water bodies where it infiltrates down into the ground and is eventually confined and stored in the tiny spaces (pores) between rocks and particles of soil, often consolidating within discrete geologic formations. This is the natural process by which aquifers are recharged. The vast majority of drinking water supplies in South Florida depend on fresh groundwater. However, groundwater reserves in coastal southeast Florida have become increasingly contaminated with saltwater in recent years (see "Saltwater Intrusion").

Habitat Structure/Habitat Architecture
The level or strength of possible interactions any given species can have with its environment. This includes both the number of physical-behavioral pathways available within the habitat (see "Ecological Niche") as well as the amount of variation in small-scale abiotic conditions (see "Microclimate").

Hard Stabilization
Inflexible/rigid human-made structures designed for coastal protection with the sole purpose of preventing erosion and/or maintaining inland sediments (e.g, seawalls and breakwaters).

Hybrid Stabilization
Some combination of natural and built infrastructural methods for coastal protection.

Hydric Soils
Soils that are saturated, flooded, or ponded with water long enough to develop anaerobic conditions (see "Anoxic") in the upper part of the soil profile and which often support hydrophytic vegetation (see "Hydrophyte").

Hydrophyte
Meaning "water plant", refers to plant species that are highly adapted to growth and reproduction under periodically or permanently saturated conditions during at least a portion of the growing season.

Impervious Area
An area covered by a surface material that does not permit infiltration or percolation of water directly into the ground. This can include building roofs, non-porous concrete and asphalt pavements, as well as some fine grained and/or compacted soils.

Impoundment
Any artificially created lake, reservoir, pond, or other contained surface water occupying a bed or depression and having a discernible shoreline.

Inline
Refers to a system that accepts all of the flow from a drainage basin or catchment area and conveys any larger flows that may occur from those areas through an overflow outlet (see also "Offline").

Intensive Green Roof
A "roof garden" where the purpose is mainly recreation and/or aesthetics in the same sense as an ordinary garden. Such roofs will have deeper soils, be frequently used, require regular maintenance, and may support a wide range of horticultural plants. These types of green roofs are generally much more expensive to install and maintain than other designs (see "Extensive Green Roof").

Intertidal Zone
Refers to the frequently observed gradient of biotic and abiotic patterns found within the space between the low tide and high tide lines along coastlines.

Invasive Species
A non-native species that is established in natural or seminatural areas and threatens native biodiversity, economic or environmental harm or harm to human health.

Karst
Limestone geology that contains numerous pores and solution cavities, and where physical features of the land surface include large and small depressions. A phenomenon common in areas around the world that have a geologic history of both marked changes in sea-level and the formation of calcium carbonate reefs and/or wetlands.

Lagoon
A naturally occurring, shallow, coastal depression and/or body of water body that has a permanent or ephemeral connection with the sea (e.g, an inlet), but which is also protected from the sea by some type of naturally existing barrier (e.g, a barrier island).

Leeward
Specifically refers to the direction toward which the wind is blowing and/or the direction toward which waves are traveling. More generally refers to areas that are on the protected side of some structural feature within a water body (e.g, a barrier island or breakwater), the other side of which is exposed to a region of much greater fetch and so has much higher wind and wave energies (see "Seaward"). This relatively protected area/direction is also simply referred to as the "Lee."

Level-Spreader
A form of stormwater pre-treatment that ensures runoff drains into landscape features as an even sheetflow to reduce or prevent erosion downstream. Useful with vegetated filter strips, bioretention features, and swales.

Littoral
Of or pertaining to a shore or shallow submerged areas near to shore, especially of the sea. Often used as a general term for the coastal zone influenced by wave action, or, more specifically, the shore zone between the high and low water marks.

Littoral Drift
The seaward transport of bottom sediments (see "Sediment Transport") of the areas near to shore in high-energy, coastal environments. Caused by littoral currents, which are any nearshore currents that are primarily incited by regular wave action (see "Littoral").

Living Shoreline
A coastal protection practice that provides erosion control benefits that also protect, restore, or enhance natural shoreline habitats (see "Soft Stabilization"). Usually accomplished through the strategic placement of plants, stone, sand fill, and other naturalistic structural elements.

Longshore
Parallel to and near the shoreline. The "longshore current" runs parallel to shore (see "Longshore Drift").

Longshore Drift
The lateral transport of sediments (see "Sediment Transport") in a direction parallel to shore that is common to coastal environments.

Low-Impact Development (LID)
Broadly refers to a suite of development practices meant to reduce the impact of the built environment on natural landscapes and hydrologic processes.

Managed Realignment
The planned breaching or removal of coastal defenses and/or structures to create new intertidal habitats. Generally meant to improve flood risk management while also adding environmental value.

Mean High Water (MHW)
A line of elevation mathematically defined by averaging the heights of all highest water levels recorded in a given water body over a given time period. For tidally influenced water bodies, this average is specifically taken from the height of all recorded high waters over a nineteen-year period (the "Tidal Epoch"). This value is important as an elevational benchmark with respect to siting coastal and estuarine infrastructure and vegetation (see "Datums").

Mean Higher High Water (MHHW)
A plane of elevation mathematically defined by averaging the observed heights of all the higher of the highest water levels recorded in a tidal waterway over a nineteen-year period (the "Tidal Epoch"). This value is important as an elevational benchmark with respect to siting coastal and estuarine structural setbacks, infrastructure, and vegetation (see "Datums"). "Higher high water" is specifically distinct from "high water" along the east coast of Florida because every "lunar day" produces two distinct high tides and two distinct low tides in this region (see "Semidiurnal Tide"). Of the two high tides that happen every day, the values that represent the higher of the two lowest values are the only records used to derive MHHW, whereas MHW is derived from an average of the highest values recorded.

Mean Higher-High Water (MHHW)
A line of elevation mathematically defined by averaging the heights of the highest of all high water levels for each tidal day, as observed over a nineteen-year period (the "Tidal Epoch"). Specific to tidally influenced water bodies, this value is important as an elevational benchmark with respect to siting coastal and estuarine infrastructure and vegetation (see "Datums").

Mean Low Water (MLW)
A line of elevation mathematically defined by averaging the heights of all the lowest water levels observed in a given water body over a given time period. For tidally influenced water bodies, this average is specifically taken from the height of all recorded low waters over a nineteen-year period (the "Tidal Epoch"). This value is important as an elevational benchmark for siting certain coastal stabilization features and projects with respect to design and permitting considerations.

Mean Lower-Low Water (MLLW)
A line of elevation mathematically defined by averaging the heights of the lowest of all low water levels for each tidal day, as observed over a nineteen-year period (the "Tidal Epoch"). Specific to tidally influenced water bodies, this value is important as an elevational benchmark with respect to maritime navigation and certain sub-tidal infrastructure (see "Datums").

Mean Sea-Level (MSL)
The datum representing the height of the surface of the sea averaged for all stages of the tide, typically computed by taking the sum of local, hourly water-level heights over a 19-year period.

Media
An engineered soil substitute, often associated with bioretention features and green roofs, that is specially formulated from a mixture of various materials to perform one or more specialty functions.

NAVD88
(Acronym) The "North American Vertical Datum of 1988" (see also "Datum"). A vertical system for measuring elevation commonly used in North America and based on a mathematically established, orthometric distance from a point at the center of the Earth to a given point on the surface of the Earth.

Nearshore The zone extending seaward from the shoreline out to a specified depth well beyond where waves tend to break most frequently (the "breaker zone"). The depth where the nearshore zone ends and the offshore zone begins is typically delineated at around 60 ft.

Non-point Source Pollution
Diffuse sources of pollution to receiving water bodies, most often in the form of runoff from adjacent land or atmospheric deposition.

Nutrients Chemical elements that are functionally involved in the key processes of life. Mostly used to refer to those chemical elements or compounds required for the growth of plants and algae (e.g, nitrogen).

Obligate Wetland Plants
Plant species that have specially adapted to thrive in wetland conditions (also see "Hydric Soils") and cannot thrive in any other context.

Offline
Stormwater storage systems designed to handle a specified volume of stormwater so that subsequent runoff in excess of that volume does not overflow from the features storing the initial volume of stormwater. Offline systems will often utilize some combination of flow splitters, bypass channels, piping, weirs, or curb cut-outs to reduce and/or divert inflow rates to help meet target storage volumes.

On-Site
A geographically contiguous property or group of properties under common control. For the purposes of the present work, "on-site" specifically refers to the relevant area of stormwater and/or coastal protection management (see "Catchment").

Outfall
A structure extending into a body of water for the purpose of discharging sewage, stormwater runoff, or cooling water.

Overwash
The flow of water over the crest of a shore or shoreline structure, by whatever mechanism, and the resultant volume that does not flow directly back to the ocean or water body and is retained inland.

Oyster Reef
Large clusters of oysters that form structural habitat in estuaries. Can include naturally produced features and artificially sited structures that are designed to collect and grow oysters in shallow waters.

Patches
Spatially discrete components within a ecosystem that have been separated into physically isolated units due to natural and/or developmental disturbances (see "Habitat Fragmentation").

Percolation
The flow of water through a porous substance.

Permeability
Refers to how well a material transmits water.

Pervious Area
Non-compacted land and/or surface area that allows the uninterrupted passage of water into the ground through infiltration and/or percolation.

pH
A measurement of the acidity or alkalinity of a material or substance, on a scale form 0 to 14. Levels below 6 are considered "acidic" and levels above 8 are considered "alkaline." Levels greater than 6 but less than 8 are considered "neutral." Determined by a measure of hydrogen ion concentrations in a liquid.

Plant Community
An association of native plants that are dominated by one or more prominent species (e.g, mangroves) or a characteristic abiotic attribute (e.g, dialy tidal inundation) and forming a distinct habitat (e.g, mangrove swamp).

Pollution/Pollutants
The presence in outdoor atmosphere or waters any substances, contaminants, noise, or other human-induced alteration or influence that negatively impacts the chemical, physical, biological, or radiological integrity of the environment.

Porosity
Refers to the percentage of the total volume of a sample not occupied by solid particles but by air and/or water.

Recharge
The addition of new water to an aquifer and/or to the subsurface zone of saturation known as "the water table."

Reclaimed Water
Recycled wastewater that has been treated, filtered, disinfected, and repurposed for the irrigation of landscape areas.

Required Treatment Volume (RTV)
A legally defined volume of stormwater required to be routed through either retention features or infiltration features in order to treat the runoff for pollutants, specifically nutrient pollutants.

Retention
The prevention of stormwater runoff from direct discharge into receiving waters through the complete storage of specified volumes of stormwater on-site. This can include features or systems that discharge stormwater through percolation, exfiltration, filtered bleed-down, evaporation, or some combination of these processes. Contrasts with "Detention" in that designs prioritize handling stormwater on-site and discourage discharge to downstream features and/or waterways.

Revetment
An armored covering or facing of erosion-resistant material placed directly on an existing slope, bank, scarp, embankment, or dike to protect the adjacent shoreline and upland areas against scour caused by waves and currents. Consist of an armor layer, filter layer, and toe. They depend on the underlying soil for support.

Right-of-Way (ROW)
Generally used to refer to the marginal public spaces/lands that act as buffers and/or boundaries between properties and important public infrastructure, such as canals and roads. These lands are normally regulated and maintained as open space by relevant public agencies for the purposes of construction and upkeep of the adjacent infrastructure. Requirements of both public and private activities within ROWs can vary widely depending on the administrative structure of the managing agency (e.g, SFWMD or Broward County) and the facility needs of the pertinent infrastructure (e.g, drainage canal or public road).

Riprap
Unconsolidated hard materials, such as boulders, rocks, or concrete rubble.

Roof Assembly
A system designed to provide weather protection and resistance to buildings and architecture. The system consists of a roof covering and roof deck or a single component serving as both the roof covering and the roof deck.

Root Zone
The total surface area and/or the 3-dimensional volume within a given tract of soil, substrate, or media where living plant roots are growing and occupying space.

Runoff
Water from rainfall or irrigation that exceeds the soil infiltration capacity and/or encounters impervious areas and which moves downhill until it is discharged into depressions, water bodies, and landscape features in an un-channelized flow.

Saturated Zone
The zone below the land surface in which soil and rock become completely saturated with groundwater (see also "Water Table").

Seasonal High Water
The elevational plane at which the combined level of both ground and surface waters can be expected to rise in any given year and/or season under normal conditions. Can apply equally to both freshwater and tidal water bodies (also see "High Water Line") but is generally reserved for inland freshwater bodies and wetlands.

Seawall
A vertical, shore-parallel, and often interlocking structure placed between an upland area and a water body for the purposes of erosion control and retaining inland sediments. The term "seawall" is colloquially synonymous with the term "bulkhead" but, in a strict design sense with respect to the stabilization of exposed coasts, "seawall" specifically refers to a structure that is much more massive and capable of resisting much greater wave energy than a bulkhead, which, by way of comparison, is designed for the lower wave energy environment of protected waterways.

Seawall Cap
A concrete box-like structure (usually reinforced) that connects seawall/bulkhead panels, piles, and anchoring system (if present) together at the top.

Sediment
Loose fragments of rocks, minerals or organic materials which are transported from their source and are easily mobilized in water.

Sediment Transport
The movement of sediment by gravity, running water, and sea currents.

Setback
A regulatory consideration that mandates a minimum, horizontal distance between one aspect of the built environment and another or from a natural feature, defined and regulated by various federal, state, or local governments or other management agencies.

Sewer
A pipe or conduit that carries wastewater or stormwater. The central infrastructure element to most conveyance-based stormwater management systems (see "Conveyance"). Generally sited underground.

SFWMD
(Acronym) "South Florida Water Management District." The main water management agency in the South Florida region, spanning all applicable jurisdictions.

Site Plan
A plan (to scale) showing uses and structures proposed for a legal lot or lots of record; or an application for a development permit approving such a plan that is reviewed in accordance with this article.

Slough
A slow-moving water body occupying a shallow, poorly-defined channel that is slightly deeper than the surrounding area.

Soft Stabilization
Flexible constructions for coastal protection that aim to work with nature and enhance habitat, such as living shorelines and beach renourishments.

Species Richness
Refers to the number of species in an area, habitat, community, or ecosystem. Species richness does not take into account the abundances of species or their relative distributions across that given area (see "Biodiversity").

Storm Surge
A rise above normal water level on the open coast due to the action of wind stress on the water surface. Storm surge resulting from a hurricane also includes a rise in water level due to atmospheric pressure reduction as well as that due to wind stress.

Stormwater Utility
The entity (can be public or private) through which funding for a stormwater management program is obtained by assessing the cost of the program to the beneficiaries (normally property owners) based on their relative contribution to its need. It is operated as a typical utility that bills services regularly, similar to water and wastewater services.

Street Tree
A tree which is located within the right-of-way of a street, road, or pavement.

Substrate
Generally refers to an artificial soil replacement made from various materials mixed together to optimize the performance of certain features. This usually refers to a soil substitute specially designed to grow plants (also see "media") but can also refer to prepared soils specifically made to act as a fill layer for certain coastal stabilization features.

Swale
A shallow, linear, trough-like depression that carries stormwater and that provides on-site flood and water quality control.

Tidal Current
The alternating horizontal movement of water associated with the rise and fall of the tide caused by the astronomical tide-producing forces. Is the principal phenomenon driving water movement in protected, tidally influenced water bodies, such as lagoons and estuaries.

Tidal Flat
A tidal flat is a low-gradient surface, underlain by mud, muddy sand, or sand, which is exposed during low tide.

Tidal Range
The vertical difference in height between high and low waters over a tidal cycle.

Tidally Influenced
Any terrestrial land and/or real property adjacent to, or affected by, a waterway with water levels that change in response to the daily tides.

Tides
The regular and predictable rise and fall of the sea caused by the gravitational attraction and rotation of the earth, moon, and sun system.

Tombolo
A sediment deposit at the coast formed by wave refraction and diffraction at the edges of an obstacle (natural or artificial) that was originally detached from the mainland.

Turbidity
A measure of water clarity, or lack thereof, caused by suspended sediments, such as clay, silt, fine particulate organic and inorganic matter, soluble colored organic compounds, plankton, and other microorganisms.

Unsaturated Zone
The soil zone between land surface and the water table where the pores in the soil matrix are filled with both air and water (see "Saturated Zone").

Water Table
The upper surface of the zone of water saturation underground (see "Saturated Zone" – see also "Aquifer").

Watershed
The total upland area that drains surface waters to receiving waters by way of streams, tributaries, and/or other surface features (also see "Drainage Basin").

Waterway
Any stream, canal or body of water, dedicated to public use, publicly owned, or used and available for public travel by boats, not including privately owned bodies of water or drainage ditches.

Wave Diffraction
The phenomenon by which wave energy is transmitted laterally after encountering a barrier, such as a breakwater feature.

Wave Reflection
The process by which the energy of a wave is returned seaward.

Wave Refraction
The process by which the direction of a wave moving in shallow water at an angle to the contours is changed: the part of the wave advancing in shallower water moves more slowly than that part still advancing in deeper water, causing the wave crest to bend toward alignment with the underwater contours.

Wet Detention
Permanently wet ponds which are designed to slowly release a portion of the collected stormwater runoff through an outlet structure (see "Detention").

biblio- graphy

bibliography

Abiy, Anteneh Z, Assefa M Melesse, Wossenu Abtew, and Dean Whitman. 2019. "Rainfall trend and variability in Southeast Florida: Implications for freshwater availability in the Everglades." *PLoS One* 14 (2): e0212008.

Aiken, Christopher M., Rory Mulloy, Gordon Dwane, and Emma L. Jackson. 2021. "Working With Nature Approaches for the Creation of Soft Intertidal Habitats." *Frontiers in Ecology and Evolution* 9. https://doi.org/10.3389/fevo.2021.682349. https://www.frontiersin.org/articles/10.3389/fevo.2021.682349.

Ali, Alaa, Wossenu Abtew, Stuart Van Horn, and Nagendra Khanal. 2000. "Temporal and Spatial Characterization of Rainfall over Central and South Florida 1." *JAWRA Journal of the American Water Resources Association* 36 (4): 833-848.

Almaaitah, Tamer, Madison Appleby, Howard Rosenblat, Jennifer Drake, and Darko Joksimovic. 2021a. "The potential of Blue-Green infrastructure as a climate change adaptation strategy: a systematic literature review." *Blue-Green Systems* 3 (1): 223-248.

—. 2021b. "The potential of Blue-Green infrastructure as a climate change adaptation strategy: a systematic literature review." *Blue-Green Systems* 3 (1): 223-248.

Almarshed, Badreyah, Jens Figlus, Jon Miller, and Henk Jan Verhagen. 2020. "Innovative coastal risk reduction through hybrid design: combining sand cover and structural defenses." *Journal of Coastal Research* 36 (1): 174-188.

Ann Conyers, Zella, Richard Grant, and Shouraseni Sen Roy. 2019. "Sea level rise in Miami Beach: vulnerability and real estate exposure." *The Professional Geographer* 71 (2): 278-291.

Ariza, Eduard, Kenyon C Lindeman, Pallab Mozumder, and Daniel O Suman. 2014. "Beach management in Florida: Assessing stakeholder perceptions on governance." *Ocean & coastal management* 96: 82-93.

Armstrong, Scott B, and Eli D Lazarus. 2019. "Masked shoreline erosion at large spatial scales as a collective effect of beach nourishment." *Earth's Future* 7 (2): 74-84.

Bacopoulos, Peter, and Ralph R Clark. 2021. "Coastal erosion and structural damage due to four consecutive-year major hurricanes: Beach projects afford resilience and coastal protection." *Ocean & Coastal Management* 209: 105643.

Balaguru, Karthik, David R Judi, and L Ruby Leung. 2016. "Future hurricane storm surge risk for the US gulf and Florida coasts based on projections of thermodynamic potential intensity." *Climatic Change* 138 (1): 99-110.

Baldwin, Andrew H. 2004. "Restoring complex vegetation in urban settings: the case of tidal freshwater marshes." *Urban Ecosystems* 7: 125-137.

Bayas-Jiménez, Leonardo, Pedro L Iglesias-Rey, and F Javier Martínez-Solano. 2019. "Multi-Objective Optimization of Drainage Networks for Flood Control in Urban Area Due to Climate Change." *Multidisciplinary Digital Publishing Institute Proceedings* 48 (1): 27.

Bayulken, Bogachan, Donald Huisingh, and Peter MJ Fisher. 2021. "How are nature based solutions helping in the greening of cities in the context of crises such as climate change and pandemics? A comprehensive review." *Journal of Cleaner Production* 288: 125569.

Bean, Eban, Lynn Jarrett, Jennison Kipp Searcy, and Mary Szoka. 2019. *Low-Impact Development & Green Infrastructure: Pollution Reduction Guidance for Water Quality in Southeast Florida.* Program for Resource Efficient Communities (PREC), Center for Land Use Efficiency (CLUE) Department of Agricultural & Biological Engineering (ABE)
Institute of Food and Agricultural Sciences (IFAS) University of Florida (UF) (Office of Florida Department of Environmental Protection and Resilience and Coastal Protection.).

Beck, Travis. 2013. *Principles of ecological landscape design*. Island Press.

Berland, Adam, Sheri A Shiflett, William D Shuster, Ahjond S Garmestani, Haynes C Goddard, Dustin L Herrmann, and Matthew E Hopton. 2017. "The role of trees in urban stormwater management." *Landscape and urban planning* 162: 167-177.

Besser, Lilah M, and Diana P Mitsova. 2021. "Neighborhood green land cover and neighborhood-based walking in US older adults." *American journal of preventive medicine* 61 (1): e13-e20.

Betts, Anthony T, and Kamal A Alsharif. 2014. "Assessment of a countywide stormwater pond improvement program." *Urban water journal* 11 (1): 11-19.

Bilkovic, Donna Marie, Molly M Mitchell, Megan K La Peyre, and Jason D Toft. 2017. *Living shorelines: the science and management of nature-based coastal protection*. CRC Press.

Bloetscher, Frederick, Gerardo Rojas, Anthony Abbate, Tucker Hindle, Jeffery Huber, Richard Jones, Weibo Liu, Daniel Eduardo Meeroff, Diana Mitsova, and Sudhagar Nagarajan. 2021. "A Framework for a Subwatershed-Scale Screening Tool to Support Development of Resiliency Solutions and Flood Protection Priority Areas in a Low-Lying Coastal Community." *Journal of Geoscience and Environment Protection* 9 (10): 180-205.

Bodle, M. 2001. *Waterwise South Florida Landscapes: Landscaping to Promote Water Conservation Using the Principles of Xeriscape*. South Florida Water Management District (West Palm Beach, FL).

Boyden, Patrick, Elisa Casella, Christopher Daly, and Alessio Rovere. 2021. "Hurricane Matthew in 2100: effects of extreme sea level rise scenarios on a highly valued coastal area (Palm Beach, FL, USA)." *Geo-marine letters* 41: 1-13.

Branoff, Benjamin. 2018. "Urban mangrove biology and ecology: Emergent patterns and management implications." *Threats to Mangrove Forests: Hazards, Vulnerability, and Management*: 521-537.

Brathwaite, Angelique, Eric Clua, Ramon Roach, and Nicolas Pascal. 2022. "Coral reef restoration for coastal protection: Crafting technical and financial solutions." *Journal of Environmental Management* 310: 114718.

Brears, Robert C. 2018. *Blue and green cities: the role of blue-green infrastructure in managing urban water resources*. Springer.

Bridges, Todd S, Jane McKee Smith, Jeffrey K King, Jonathan D Simm, Maria Dillard, Jurre deVries, Denise Reed, Candice D Piercy, Boris van Zanten, and Katie Arkema. 2022. "Coastal natural and nature-based features: International guidelines for flood risk management." *Frontiers in Built Environment* 8: 904483.

Broward, MPO. 2015. Broward Complete Streets Evaluation Toolkit: User Manual. Broward Metropolitan Planning Organization, Fort Lauderdale, FL.

Buchanan, Maya K, Scott Kulp, Lara Cushing, Rachel Morello-Frosch, Todd Nedwick, and Benjamin Strauss. 2020. "Sea level rise and coastal flooding threaten affordable housing." *Environmental Research Letters* 15 (12): 124020.

Bureau, US Census. 2020. "QuickFacts: Florida." https://www.census.gov/quickfacts/FL.

Burger, Joanna. 2003. "Perceptions about environmental use and future restoration of an urban estuary." *Journal of Environmental Planning and Management* 46 (3): 399-416.

Busker, Tim, Hans de Moel, Toon Haer, Maurice Schmeits, Bart van den Hurk, Kira Myers, Dirk Gijsbert Cirkel, and Jeroen Aerts. 2022. "Blue-green roofs with forecast-based operation to reduce the impact of weather extremes." *Journal of Environmental Management* 301: 113750.

Butler, William H, Robert E Deyle, and Cassidy Mutnansky. 2016. "Low-regrets incrementalism: Land use planning adaptation to accelerating sea level rise in Florida's coastal communities." *Journal of Planning Education and Research* 36 (3): 319-332.

Capodaglio, Andrea G, Silvia Bolognesi, and Daniele Cecconet. 2021. "Sustainable, decentralized sanitation and reuse with hybrid nature-based systems." *Water* 13 (11): 1583.

Carlson, Douglas B, R Grant Gilmore, and JR Rey. 1985. "Salt marsh impoundment management on Florida's central east coast: reintegrating isolated high marshes to the estuary." Proceedings of the 12th annual conference on wetlands restoration and creation, Tampa, Florida.

Center, UF GeoPlan. 2021. "Florida Geographic Data Library." University of Florida. Accessed 07/22/2021. https://fgdl.org/.

Chen, Chi-Feng. 2013. "Performance evaluation and development strategies for green roofs in Taiwan: A review." *Ecological engineering* 52: 51-58.

Chenoweth, Jonathan, Andrew R Anderson, Prashant Kumar, William F Hunt, Sarah Jane Chimbwandira, and Trisha LC Moore. 2018. "The interrelationship of green infrastructure and natural capital." *Land use policy* 75: 137-144.

Chin, David A. 2017. "Designing bioretention areas for stormwater management." *Environmental processes* 4: 1-13.

Chong, Lisa, Angela B Collins, Holly Abeels, Anna Braswell, Andrew Ropicki, Scott Jackson, and Ed Camp. 2022. "Artificial Reefs in Florida 101–why are they built? Part 1 of an Artificial Reef series: FOR379/FR450, 4/2022." *EDIS* 2022 (2).

Chong, Lisa, Keith Mille, Holly Abeels, Victor Blanco, and Ed Camp. 2021. "Artificial Reefs and People: How We Create Them and How They Affect Us: FA231, 02/2021." *EDIS* 2021 (2): 6-6.

Chávez, Valeria, Debora Lithgow, Miguel Losada, and Rodolfo Silva-Casarin. 2021a. "Coastal green infrastructure to mitigate coastal squeeze." *Journal of Infrastructure Preservation and Resilience* 2 (1): 1-12.

—. 2021b. "Coastal green infrastructure to mitigate coastal squeeze." *Journal of Infrastructure Preservation and Resilience* 2 (1): 1-12.

Colares, Gustavo S, Naira Dell'Osbel, Patrik G Wiesel, Gislayne A Oliveira, Pedro Henrique Z Lemos, Fagner P da Silva, Carlos A Lutterbeck, Lourdes T Kist, and Ênio L Machado. 2020. "Floating treatment wetlands: A review and bibliometric analysis." *Science of the Total Environment* 714: 136776.

Committee, Waterways Advisory. 2018. *Seawall Manual*. City of Marco Island.

Converse, Jordan, Meagan Wengrove, and Pedro Lomonaco. 2020. "Observations of wave attenuation, scour, and subsurface pore pressures across three marsh restoration sill structures on a sandy bed." *Shore & Beach* 88 (3): 14.

Cristiano, Elena, Stefano Farris, Roberto Deidda, and Francesco Viola. 2021. "Comparison of blue-green solutions for urban flood mitigation: A multi-city large-scale analysis." *PLoS One* 16 (1): e0246429.

Dagenais, Danielle, Jacques Brisson, and Tim D Fletcher. 2018. "The role of plants in bioretention systems; does the science underpin current guidance?" *Ecological Engineering* 120: 532-545.

Davis, Luise. 1995. *A handbook of constructed wetlands: A guide to creating wetlands for: agricultural wastewater, domestic wastewater, coal mine drainage, stormwater. In the Mid-Atlantic Region. Volume 1: General considerations.* USDA-Natural Resources Conservation Service.

Dean, Robert G, Renjie Chen, and Albert E Browder. 1997. "Full scale monitoring study of a submerged breakwater, Palm Beach, Florida, USA." *Coastal Engineering* 29 (3-4): 291-315.

Divya, Y, P Gopinathan, Krish Jayachandran, and Ayad M Fadhil Al-Quraishi. 2021. "Color slices analysis of land use changes due to urbanization in a city environment of Miami Area, South Florida, USA." *Modeling Earth Systems and Environment* 7: 537-546.

Domènech, Laia. 2011. "Rethinking water management: From centralised to decentralised water supply and sanitation models." *Documents d'anàlisi geogràfica* 57 (2): 293-310.

Donnelly, Melinda, Michelle Shaffer, Suzanne Connor, Paul Sacks, and Linda Walters. 2017. "Using mangroves to stabilize coastal historic sites: deployment success versus natural recruitment." *Hydrobiologia* 803: 389-401.

Dukes, Michael D. 2022. "Future of urban landscapes: A Florida perspective." *International Turfgrass Society Research Journal* 14 (1): 1030-1034.

Elko, Nicole, Tiffany Roberts Briggs, Lindino Benedet, Quin Robertson, Gordon Thomson, Bret M Webb, and Kimberly Garvey. 2021. "A century of US beach nourishment." *Ocean & Coastal Management* 199: 105406.

Elliott, Alexander H, Sam A Trowsdale, and Sanjay Wadhwa. 2009. "Effect of aggregation of on-site storm-water control devices in an urban catchment model." *Journal of Hydrologic Engineering* 14 (9): 975-983.

Ennenbach, Mounir William, Paulina Concha Larrauri, and Upmanu Lall. 2018. "County-scale rainwater harvesting feasibility in the United States: Climate, collection area, density, and reuse considerations." *JAWRA Journal of the American Water Resources Association* 54 (1): 255-274.

Enwright, Nicholas M, Kereen T Griffith, and Michael J Osland. 2016. "Barriers to and opportunities for landward migration of coastal wetlands with sea level rise." *Frontiers in Ecology and the Environment* 14 (6): 307-316.

Erwin, Kevin L. 2009. "Wetlands and global climate change: the role of wetland restoration in a changing world." *Wetlands Ecology and management* 17 (1): 71-84.

Ewel, John J, and Ronald L Myers. 1990. *Ecosystems of Florida*. University of Central Florida Press.

Extension, UF/IFAS, and FDOT. "Rain Gardens: A Manual for Central Florida Residents." UF/IFAS Extension St. Johns County. http://gardeningsolutions.ifas.ufl.edu/pdf/articles/rain-garden-manual-hillsborough.pdf.

FDEP. 2016. *The Homeowners Guide to the Coastal Construction Control Line Program*. The Florida Department of Environmental Protection Division of Water Resource Management (Tallahassee, FL).

Ferguson, Bruce K. 1991. "Taking advantage of stormwater control basins in urban landscapes." *Journal of Soil and Water Conservation* 46 (2): 100-103.

Fernández-Cañero, Rafael, Luis Pérez Urrestarazu, and Antonio Franco Salas. 2012. "Assessment of the cooling potential of an indoor living wall using different substrates in a warm climate." *Indoor and Built Environment* 21 (5): 642-650.

Fivash, Gregory S, Delia Stüben, Mareike Bachmann, Brenda Walles, Jim van Belzen, Karin Didderen, Ralph JM Temmink, Wouter Lengkeek, Tjisse van der Heide, and Tjeerd J Bouma. 2021. "Can we enhance ecosystem-based coastal defense by connecting oysters to marsh edges? Analyzing the limits of oyster reef establishment." *Ecological Engineering* 165: 106221.

Francis, Robert A, and Michael A Chadwick. 2013. *Urban ecosystems: understanding the human environment*. Routledge.

Friess, Daniel A. 2017. "Mangrove rehabilitation along urban coastlines: a Singapore case study." *Regional Studies in Marine Science* 16: 279-289.

Ghanbari, Mahshid, Mazdak Arabi, Shih-Chieh Kao, Jayantha Obeysekera, and William Sweet. 2021. "Climate change and changes in compound coastal-riverine flooding hazard along the US coasts." *Earth's Future* 9 (5): e2021EF002055.

Ghanbari, Mahshid, Mazdak Arabi, and Jayantha Obeysekera. 2020. "Chronic and Acute Coastal Flood Risks to Assets and Communities in Southeast Florida." *Journal of Water Resources Planning and Management* 146 (7): 04020049. https://doi.org/doi:10.1061/(ASCE)WR.1943-5452.0001245. https://ascelibrary.org/doi/abs/10.1061/%28ASCE%29WR.1943-5452.0001245.

Ghiasian, Mohammad, Jane Carrick, Landolf Rhode-Barbarigos, Brian Haus, Andrew C Baker, and Diego Lirman. 2021. "Dissipation of wave energy by a hybrid artificial reef in a wave simulator: implications for coastal resilience and shoreline protection." *Limnology and Oceanography: Methods* 19 (1): 1-7.

Gibbs, David A, Jordan M West, and Patricia Bradley. 2021. "Incorporating adaptation and resilience into an integrated watershed and coral reef management plan." *Plos one* 16 (6): e0253343.

Goh, Hui Weng, Khe Sin Lem, Nor Ariza Azizan, Chun Kiat Chang, Amin Talei, Cheng Siang Leow, and Nor Azazi Zakaria. 2019. "A review of bioretention components and nutrient removal under different climates—future directions for tropics." *Environmental Science and Pollution Research* 26: 14904-14919.

Guo, J. 2012. "6.18 - Recent Achievements in Hydraulic Research in China." In *Comprehensive Renewable Energy*, edited by Ali Sayigh, 485-505. Oxford: Elsevier.

Hamid, Shahid, BM Golam Kibria, Sneh Gulati, Mark Powell, Bachir Annane, Steve Cocke, Jean-Paul Pinelli, Kurt Gurley, and Shu-Ching Chen. 2010. "Predicting losses of residential structures in the state of Florida by the public hurricane loss evaluation model." *Statistical methodology* 7 (5): 552-573.

Han, Yapan, Qingxu Huang, Chunyang He, Yongqiang Fang, Jiahong Wen, Jun Gao, and Shiqiang Du. 2020. "The growth mode of built-up land in floodplains and its impacts on flood vulnerability." *Science of the Total Environment* 700: 134462.

Hansen, Gail, and Shangchun Hu. 2013. "Florida-Friendly Plants for Stormwater Pond Shorelines: ENH1215/EP476, 5/2013." *EDIS* 2013 (5).

Hardaway Jr, C Scott, and James R Gunn. 2010. "Design and performance of headland bays in Chesapeake Bay, USA." *Coastal Engineering* 57 (2): 203-212.

Harfouche, Antoine L, Daniel A Jacobson, David Kainer, Jonathon C Romero, Antoine H Harfouche, Giuseppe Scarascia Mugnozza, Menachem Moshelion, Gerald A Tuskan, Joost JB Keurentjes, and Arie Altman. 2019. "Accelerating climate resilient plant breeding by applying next-generation artificial intelligence." *Trends in biotechnology* 37 (11): 1217-1235.

Harris, Lee E. 2009. "Artificial reefs for ecosystem restoration and coastal erosion protection with aquaculture and recreational amenities." *Reef Journal* 1 (1): 235-246.

Havens, Karl E. 2018. "The future of harmful algal blooms in Florida inland and coastal waters."

Heimlich, Barry, and Frederick Bloetscher. 2011. "Effects of Sea Level Rise and Other Climate Change Impacts on Southeast Florida's Water Resources." *FLORIDA WATER RESOURCES JOURNAL* (September).

Holanda, Francisco Sandro Rodrigues, and Igor Pinheiro da Rocha. 2011. "Streambank soil bioengineering approach to erosion control." In *Progress in molecular and environmental bioengineering-from analysis and modeling to technology applications*. IntechOpen.

Houle, James J, Timothy A Puls, and Thomas P Ballestero. 2015. "Performance analysis of two relatively small capacity urban retrofit stormwater controls."

Houston, James R. 2020. "Beach nourishment versus sea level rise on Florida's coasts." *Shore & Beach* 88 (2): 3-13.

Huber, Jeffrey E, Keith Van de Riet, John Sandell, and Lawrence Scarpa. 2017. "Salty Urbanism: Towards an Adaptive Coastal Design Framework to Address Sea Level Rise."

Huq, Erfanul, and Omar I Abdul-Aziz. 2021. "Climate and land cover change impacts on stormwater runoff in large-scale coastal-urban environments." *Science of The Total Environment* 778: 146017.

Irizarry-Ortiz, Michelle M, Jayantha Obeysekera, Joseph Park, Paul Trimble, Jenifer Barnes, Winifred Park-Said, and Erik Gadzinski. 2013. "Historical trends in Florida temperature and precipitation." *Hydrological Processes* 27 (16): 2225-2246.

Jahanmiri, Fatemeh, and Dawn Cassandra Parker. 2022. "An overview of fractal geometry applied to urban planning." *Land* 11 (4): 475.

Jane, Robert, Luis Cadavid, Jayantha Obeysekera, and Thomas Wahl. 2020. "Multivariate statistical modelling of the drivers of compound flood events in south Florida." *Natural Hazards and Earth System Sciences* 20 (10): 2681-2699.

Jarden, Kimberly M, Anne J Jefferson, and Jennifer M Grieser. 2016. "Assessing the effects of catchment-scale urban green infrastructure retrofits on hydrograph characteristics." *Hydrological Processes* 30 (10): 1536-1550.

Jayanthi, M, JK Patterson Edward, H Malleshappa, N Gladwin Gnana Asir, G Mathews, K Diraviya Raj, Deepak S Bilgi, TK Ashok Kumar, and SA Sannasiraj. 2020. "Perforated trapezoidal artificial reefs can augment the benefits of restoration of an island and its marine ecosystem." *Restoration Ecology* 28 (1): 233-243.

Jesus, João M, Anthony S Danko, António Fiúza, and Maria-Teresa Borges. 2018. "Effect of plants in constructed wetlands for organic carbon and nutrient removal: a review of experimental factors contributing to higher impact and suggestions for future guidelines." *Environmental Science and Pollution Research* 25: 4149-4164.

Jim, Chi Yung. 2015. "Assessing climate-adaptation effect of extensive tropical green roofs in cities." *Landscape and Urban Planning* 138: 54-70.

Jim, Chi Yung, and Hongming He. 2011. "Estimating heat flux transmission of vertical greenery ecosystem." *Ecological Engineering* 37 (8): 1112-1122.

Jordan, LKB, KW Banks, Louis E Fisher, Brian K Walker, and David S Gilliam. 2010. "Elevated sedimentation on coral reefs adjacent to a beach nourishment project." *Marine Pollution Bulletin* 60 (2): 261-271.

Joyce, Justin, Ni-Bin Chang, Rahim Harji, and Thomas Ruppert. 2018. "Coupling infrastructure resilience and flood risk assessment via copulas analyses for a coastal green-grey-blue drainage system under extreme weather events." *Environmental modelling & software* 100: 82-103.

Joyce, Justin, Ni-Bin Chang, Rahim Harji, Thomas Ruppert, and Sanaz Imen. 2017. "Developing a multi-scale modeling system for resilience assessment of green-grey drainage infrastructures under climate change and sea level rise impact." *Environmental Modelling & Software* 90: 1-26.

Kamali, Babak, and Roslan Hashim. 2011. "Mangrove restoration without planting." *Ecological Engineering* 37 (2): 387-391.

Kazak, Jan K, Jakub Chruściński, and Szymon Szewrański. 2018. "The development of a novel decision support system for the location of green infrastructure for stormwater management." *Sustainability* 10 (12): 4388.

Kennish, Michael J. 2016. *Encyclopedia of estuaries*. Springer Netherlands.

KG, Parvathy, and Prasad K Bhaskaran. 2017. "Wave attenuation in presence of mangroves: A sensitivity study for varying bottom slopes." *The International Journal of Ocean and Climate Systems* 8 (3): 126-134.

Kousky, Carolyn, Billy Fleming, and Alan M Berger. 2021. *A blueprint for coastal adaptation: Uniting design, economics, and policy*. Island Press.

Leyden, Kevin M, Amanda Slevin, Thomas Grey, Mike Hynes, Fanney Frisbaek, and Richard Silke. 2017. "Public and stakeholder engagement and the built environment: a review." *Current environmental health reports* 4: 267-277.

Lund, Nadia Schou Vorndran, Morten Borup, Henrik Madsen, Ole Mark, Karsten Arnbjerg-Nielsen, and Peter Steen Mikkelsen. 2019. "Integrated stormwater inflow control for sewers and green structures in urban landscapes." *Nature Sustainability* 2 (11): 1003-1010.

McIntyre, Tina, Rachel Gutner, Hamutahl Cohen, Tiare Silvasy, and Esen Momol. 2023. "A Florida-Friendly Landscaping™ Approach to Pest Management in Your Edible Landscape: EP629/ENH1365, 1/2023." *EDIS* 2023 (1).

Menéndez, Pelayo, Iñigo J Losada, Saul Torres-Ortega, Siddharth Narayan, and Michael W Beck. 2020. "The global flood protection benefits of mangroves." *Scientific reports* 10 (1): 1-11.

Miller, Debbie, Mack Thetford, Christina Verlinde, Gabriel Campbell, and Ashlynn Smith. 2018. *Dune restoration and enhancement for the Florida panhandle*. United States Fish and Wildlife Service UF/IFAS Extension Florida Sea Grant.

Mitsova, Diana. 2021. "Integrative interdisciplinary approaches to critical infrastructure interdependency analysis." *Risk Analysis* 41 (7): 1111-1117.

Mitsova, Diana, Chris Bergh, and Greg Guannel. 2016. "Suitability Analysis for Living Shorelines Development in Southeast Florida's Estuarine Systems."

Mitsova, Diana, Chris Bergh, Greg Guannel, Caitlin Lustic, Michael Renda, James Byrne, Andrea Graves, Kevin Cresswell, Rayan Alhawiti, and Allison Goldberg. 2018. "Spatial decision support for nature-based shoreline stabilization options in subtropical estuarine environments." *Journal of Environmental Planning and Management* 61 (14): 2468-2490.

Mitsova, Diana, Monica Escaleras, Alka Sapat, Ann-Margaret Esnard, and Alberto J Lamadrid. 2019. "The effects of infrastructure service disruptions and socio-economic vulnerability on hurricane recovery." *Sustainability* 11 (2): 516.

Mitsova, Diana, and Ann-Margaret Esnard. 2012. "Holding back the sea: an overview of shore zone planning and management." *Journal of Planning Literature* 27 (4): 446-459.

Mitsova, Diana, William Shuster, and Xinhao Wang. 2011. "A cellular automata model of land cover change to integrate urban growth with open space conservation." *Landscape and urban planning* 99 (2): 141-153.

Mitsova, Diana, Frank Wissinger, Ann-Margaret Esnard, Ravi Shankar, and Peter Gies. 2013. "A collaborative geospatial shoreline inventory tool to guide coastal development and habitat conservation." *ISPRS International Journal of Geo-Information* 2 (2): 385-404.

Monroe, Martha C, Annie Oxarart, Holly Abeels, Wendy-Lin Bartels, Alicia Bradigan-Betancourt, Crystal Goodison, and Thomas Ruppert. 2020. "Facilitating Community Change: Lessons from Climate Adaptation to Guide Extension Engagement: FR430/FOR361, 11/2020." *EDIS* 2020 (6): 19-19.

Monteiro, Renato, and José Carlos Ferreira. 2020. "Green infrastructure planning as a climate change and risk adaptation tool in coastal urban areas." *Journal of Coastal Research* 95 (SI): 889-893.

Montgomery, JM, KR Bryan, and G Coco. 2022. "The role of mangroves in coastal flood protection: The importance of channelization." *Continental shelf research* 243: 104762.

Moosavi, Sareh. 2017. "Ecological coastal protection: pathways to living shorelines." *Procedia Engineering* 196: 930-938.

Moura, Newton Célio Becker de, Paulo Renato Mesquita Pellegrino, and José Rodolfo Scarati Martins. 2016. "Best management practices as an alternative for flood and urban storm water control in a changing climate." *Journal of Flood Risk Management* 9 (3): 243-254.

Muerdter, Claire P, Carol K Wong, and Gregory H LeFevre. 2018. "Emerging investigator series: The role of vegetation in bioretention for stormwater treatment in the built environment: Pollutant removal, hydrologic function, and ancillary benefits." *Environmental Science: Water Research & Technology* 4 (5): 592-612.

Nelson, Walter G. 1993. "Beach restoration in the southeastern US: environmental effects and biological monitoring." *Ocean & coastal management* 19 (2): 157-182.

Nighswander, Gisele P, Mary E Szoka, Kayla M Hess, Eban Z Bean, Gail Hansen, and Basil V Iannone. 2019. "A New Database on Trait-Based Selection of Stormwater Pond Plants: FOR347/FR416, 6/2019." *EDIS* *UF/IFAS Extension* *University of Florida* 2019 (4): 6-6.

Obeysekera, Jayantha, Jenifer Barnes, and Martha Nungesser. 2015. "Climate sensitivity runs and regional hydrologic modeling for predicting the response of the greater Florida Everglades ecosystem to climate change." *Environmental management* 55: 749-762.

Onnis-Hayden, A, K Johnston, AJ Pinto, and K Vilardi. 2019. "Tidal Flow Constructed Wetland for Water Reuse: Performance Evaluation and Microbial Population." WEFTEC 2019.

Palazzo, Elisa, and Sisi Wang. 2022. "Landscape design for flood adaptation from 20 years of constructed ecologies in China." *Sustainability* 14 (8): 4511.

Pallathadka, Arun, Jason Sauer, Heejun Chang, and Nancy B Grimm. 2022. "Urban flood risk and green infrastructure: Who is exposed to risk and who benefits from investment? A case study of three US Cities." *Landscape and Urban Planning* 223: 104417.

Palm, Risa, and Toby Bolsen. 2021. "The Development of Vulnerable Real Estate in South Florida." In *Housing Market Response to Sea-Level Rise in Florida*, 7-19. Springer.

Pamukcu-Albers, Pinar, Francesca Ugolini, Daniele La Rosa, Simona R Grădinaru, João C Azevedo, and Jianguo Wu. 2021. "Building green infrastructure to enhance urban resilience to climate change and pandemics." *Landscape ecology* 36 (3): 665-673.

Parkinson, Randall W, and Danielle E Ogurcak. 2018. "Beach nourishment is not a sustainable strategy to mitigate climate change." *Estuarine, Coastal and Shelf Science* 212: 203-209.

Pataki, Diane E, Marina Alberti, Mary L Cadenasso, Alexander J Felson, Mark J McDonnell, Stephanie Pincetl, Richard V Pouyat, Heikki Setälä, and Thomas H Whitlow. 2021. "The benefits and limits of urban tree planting for environmental and human health." *Frontiers in Ecology and Evolution* 9: 603757.

Persaud, Ann, Kamal Alsharif, Paul Monaghan, Fenda Akiwumi, Maria C Morera, and Emily Ott. 2016. "Landscaping practices, community perceptions, and social indicators for stormwater nonpoint source pollution management." *Sustainable cities and society* 27: 377-385.

Peterson, Charles H, and Melanie J Bishop. 2005. "Assessing the environmental impacts of beach nourishment." *Bioscience* 55 (10): 887-896.

Peña, Francisco, Fernando Nardi, Assefa Melesse, Jayantha Obeysekera, Fabio Castelli, René M Price, Todd Crowl, and Noemi Gonzalez-Ramirez. 2022. "Compound flood modeling framework for surface-subsurface water interactions." *Natural Hazards and Earth System Sciences* 22 (3): 775-793.

Pilkey, Orrin H, and J Andrew G Cooper. 2012. ""Alternative" shoreline erosion control devices: a review." *Pitfalls of shoreline stabilization: selected case studies*: 187-214.

Pradhan, Snigdhendubala, Sami G Al-Ghamdi, and Hamish R Mackey. 2019. "Greywater recycling in buildings using living walls and green roofs: A review of the applicability and challenges." *Science of The Total Environment* 652: 330-344.

Prevatt, D, G Acomb, and F Masters. 2012. *Comprehensive Wind Uplift Study of Modular and Built-in-Place Green Roof Systems* Department of Civil and Coastal Engineering (Structures Group) Engineering School of Sustainable Infrastructure and the Environment University of Florida (Gainesville, FL).

Pérez-Urrestarazu, Luis, Rafael Fernández-Cañero, Antonio Franco-Salas, and Gregorio Egea. 2015. "Vertical greening systems and sustainable cities." *Journal of Urban Technology* 22 (4): 65-85.

Rendon, Celine, Khalid K Osman, and Kasey M Faust. 2021. "Path towards community resilience: Examining stakeholders' coordination at the intersection of the built, natural, and social systems." *Sustainable Cities and Society* 68: 102774.

Ridge, Justin T, Antonio B Rodriguez, F Joel Fodrie, Niels L Lindquist, Michelle C Brodeur, Sara E Coleman, Jonathan H Grabowski, and Ethan J Theuerkauf. 2015. "Maximizing oyster-reef growth supports green infrastructure with accelerating sea-level rise." *Scientific Reports* 5 (1): 14785.

Ridha, Tamarah, Ashley D Ross, and Ali Mostafavi. 2022. "Climate change impacts on infrastructure: Flood risk perceptions and evaluations of water systems in coastal urban areas." *International Journal of Disaster Risk Reduction* 73: 102883.

Robinson, Jake M, Jacob G Mills, and Martin F Breed. 2018. "Walking ecosystems in microbiome-inspired green infrastructure: an ecological perspective on enhancing personal and planetary health." *Challenges* 9 (2): 40.

Roeland, Samson, Marco Moretti, Jorge Humberto Amorim, Cristina Branquinho, Silvano Fares, Federico Morelli, Ülo Niinemets, Elena Paoletti, Pedro Pinho, and Gregorio Sgrigna. 2019. "Towards an integrative approach to evaluate the environmental ecosystem services provided by urban forest." *Journal of Forestry Research* 30: 1981-1996.

Ruppert, Thomas, and Erin L Deady. 2017. "Climate change impacts on law and policy in Florida." *Florida's climate: Changes, variations, & impacts.*

Ruppert, Thomas, John Fergus, and Enio Russe-Garcia. 2018a. "Managing Property Buyouts at the Local Level: Seeking Benefits and Limiting Harms." *Envtl. L. Rep. News & Analysis* 48: 10520.

—. 2018b. "Managing Property Buyouts at the Local Level: Seeking Benefits and Limiting Harms." *Envtl. L. Rep. News & Analysis* 48: 10520.

Ruppert, Thomas, and Carly Grimm. 2013. "Drowning in place: Local government costs and liabilities for flooding due to sea-level rise." *Fla. Bar J.* 87: 29.

Ruppert, Thomas K. 2008. "Eroding long-term prospects for Florida's beaches: Florida's coastal construction control line program." *Sea Grant L. & Pol'y J.* 1: 65.

Sadler, Jeffrey M, Jonathan L Goodall, Madhur Behl, Benjamin D Bowes, and Mohamed M Morsy. 2020. "Exploring real-time control of stormwater systems for mitigating flood risk due to sea level rise." *Journal of Hydrology* 583: 124571.

Salas, Jose D, and Jayantha Obeysekera. 2014. "Revisiting the concepts of return period and risk for nonstationary hydrologic extreme events." *Journal of hydrologic engineering* 19 (3): 554-568.

Saleh, Firas, and Michael P Weinstein. 2016. "The role of nature-based infrastructure (NBI) in coastal resiliency planning: A literature review." *Journal of Environmental Management* 183: 1088-1098.

Salgado, Karla, and M Luisa Martinez. 2017. "Is ecosystem-based coastal defense a realistic alternative? Exploring the evidence." *Journal of Coastal Conservation* 21: 837-848.

Samal, Kundan, Soham Kar, and Shivanshi Trivedi. 2019. "Ecological floating bed (EFB) for decontamination of polluted water bodies: Design, mechanism and performance." *Journal of environmental management* 251: 109550.

Sealey, Kathleen Sullivan, Esber Andiroglu, Joel Lamere, James Sobczak, and Prannoy Suraneni. 2021. "Multifunctional Performance of Coastal Structures Based on South Florida Coastal Environs." *Journal of coastal research* 37 (3): 656-669.

Semaan, Mary, Susan D Day, Michael Garvin, Naren Ramakrishnan, and Annie Pearce. 2021. "Distributed Rainwater Harvesting: Novel Approach to Rainwater Harvesting Systems for Single-Family Households." *Journal of Water Resources Planning and Management* 147 (10): 04021061.

Setiawan, Irene, Leanne Morgan, Crile Doscher, Kelvin Ng, and Amandine Bosserelle. 2022. "Mapping shallow groundwater salinity in a coastal urban setting to assess exposure of municipal assets." *Journal of Hydrology: Regional Studies* 40: 100999.

SFRCCC. 2020. *Unified Sea Level Rise Projection Southeast Florida - 2019 Update.* Southeast Florida Regional Climate Change Compact Sea Level Rise Work Group (Miami, FL).

SFRPC. 2013. Adaptation Action Areas: Policy Options for Adaptive Planning For Rising Sea Levels. Southeast Florida Regional Planning Council.

SFWMD. 2013a. Environmental Resource Permit Applicant's Handbook Volume II for Use Within the Geographic Limits of the South Florida Water Management District. South Florida Water Management District.

—. 2013b. *Right of Way Criteria Manual for Use of Works and Lands of The District.* South Florida Water Management District.

—. 2020. *Canals, Levees, Lakes and Stormwater Treatment Areas Subject to Right of Way Permittting.* South Florida Water Management District.

—. 2021. "Geospatial Open Data Portal." South Florida Water Management District. Accessed 07/22/2021.

Shafique, Muhammad, Reeho Kim, and Muhammad Rafiq. 2018. "Green roof benefits, opportunities and challenges–A review." *Renewable and Sustainable Energy Reviews* 90: 757-773.

Shaw, JE, and M Zamorano. 2020. "Saltwater Interface Monitoring and Mapping Program." *Water Resources Division, South Florida Water Management District.*

Shi, Shaoyu, Bo Yang, and Wensheng Jiang. 2022. "Numerical simulations of compound flooding caused by storm surge and heavy rain with the presence of urban drainage system, coastal dam and tide gates: A case study of Xiangshan, China." *Coastal Engineering* 172: 104064.

Shishegar, Shadab, Sophie Duchesne, and Geneviève Pelletier. 2019. "An integrated optimization and rule-based approach for predictive real time control of urban stormwater management systems." *Journal of Hydrology* 577: 124000.

Shrestha, Sunita, Ram Devi Tachamo-Shah, Tanya Doody, Susan Cuddy, and Deep Narayan Shah. 2021. "Establishing the relationship between benthic macroinvertebrates and water level fluctuation in subtropical shallow wetlands." *Environmental Monitoring and Assessment* 193 (8): 534.

Simenstad, Charles, Denise Reed, and Mark Ford. 2006. "When is restoration not?: Incorporating landscape-scale processes to restore self-sustaining ecosystems in coastal wetland restoration." *Ecological Engineering* 26 (1): 27-39.

Simmons, Mark T. 2015. "Climates and microclimates: challenges for extensive green roof design in hot climates." *Green roof ecosystems*: 63-80.

Simmons, Mark T, Brian Gardiner, Steve Windhager, and Jeannine Tinsley. 2008. "Green roofs are not created equal: the hydrologic and thermal performance of six different extensive green roofs and reflective and non-reflective roofs in a sub-tropical climate." *Urban Ecosystems* 11: 339-348.

Sinclair, James S, Alexander J Reisinger, Eban Bean, Carrie R Adams, Lindsey S Reisinger, and Basil V Iannone III. 2020. "Stormwater ponds: An overlooked but plentiful urban designer ecosystem provides invasive plant habitat in a subtropical region (Florida, USA)." *Science of The Total Environment* 711: 135133.

Sinha, Palash, Michael E Mann, Jose D Fuentes, Alfonso Mejia, Liang Ning, Weiyi Sun, Tao He, and Jayantha Obeysekera. 2018. "Downscaled rainfall projections in south Florida using self-organizing maps." *Science of the Total Environment* 635: 1110-1123.

Smalls-Mantey, Lauren, and Franco Montalto. 2021. "The seasonal microclimate trends of a large scale extensive green roof." *Building and Environment* 197: 107792.

Smith, Carter S, Morgan E Rudd, Rachel K Gittman, Emily C Melvin, Virginia S Patterson, Julianna J Renzi, Emory H Wellman, and Brian R Silliman. 2020. "Coming to terms with living shorelines: a scoping review of novel restoration strategies for shoreline protection." *Frontiers in Marine Science* 7: 434.

Smyth, A, L Wu, R Muñoz-Carpena, and Y Li. 2018. *Vegetative Filter Strips—A Best Management Practice for Controlling Nonpoint Source Pollution.* U.S. Department of Agriculture
UF/IFAS Extension Service
University of Florida
Florida A & M University Cooperative Extension Program.

Soderlund, Jana, and Peter Newman. 2015. "Biophilic architecture: a review of the rationale and outcomes." *AIMS environmental science* 2 (4): 950-969.

Sonne, J. 2006. "Energy performance aspects of a florida green roof."

Sonne, Jeff, and Danny Parker. 2008. "Energy performance aspects of a Florida green roof part 2."

Strain, EMA, T Kompas, A Boxshall, J Kelvin, S Swearer, and RL Morris. 2022. "Assessing the coastal protection services of natural mangrove forests and artificial rock revetments." *Ecosystem Services* 55: 101429.

St-Hilaire, André, Taha BMJ Ouarda, Marius Lachance, Bernard Bobée, Jocelyn Gaudet, and Claude Gignac. 2003. "Assessment of the impact of meteorological network density on the estimation of basin precipitation and runoff: a case study." *Hydrological processes* 17 (18): 3561-3580.

Sutton-Grier, Ariana E, Kateryna Wowk, and Holly Bamford. 2015. "Future of our coasts: The potential for natural and hybrid infrastructure to enhance the resilience of our coastal communities, economies and ecosystems." *Environmental Science & Policy* 51: 137-148.

Sweet, WV, BD Hamlington, RE Kopp, CP Weaver, PL Barnard, D Bekaert, W Brooks, M Craghan, G Dusek, and T Frederikse. 2022. *Global and regional sea level rise scenarios for the United States: Updated mean projections and extreme water level probabilities along US coastlines.* NOAA Technical Report.

Sánchez, Alejandro. 2008. "Interactions Between Wetlands and Tidal Inlets." 15.

Teo, Hoong Chen, Yiwen Zeng, Tasya Vadya Sarira, Tze Kwan Fung, Qiming Zheng, Xiao Ping Song, Kwek Yan Chong, and Lian Pin Koh. 2021. "Global urban reforestation can be an important natural climate solution." *Environmental Research Letters* 16 (3): 034059.

Thompson, Philip L., M L Corry, Frederick J. Watts, Dennis L. Richards, J. Sterling Jones, and Joseph N. Bradley. 1975. "Hydraulic Design of Energy Dissipators for Culverts and Channels."

Thompson, Philip R., Matthew J. Widlansky, Benjamin D. Hamlington, Mark A. Merrifield, John J. Marra, Gary T. Mitchum, and William Sweet. 2021. "Rapid increases and extreme months in projections of United States high-tide flooding." *Nature Climate Change* 11 (7): 584-590. https://doi.org/10.1038/s41558-021-01077-8. https://doi.org/10.1038/s41558-021-01077-8.

Thompson, SE, CJ Harman, P Heine, and GG Katul. 2010. "Vegetation-infiltration relationships across climatic and soil type gradients." *Journal of Geophysical Research: Biogeosciences* 115 (G2).

Tirpak, R Andrew, Ryan J Winston, Ian M Simpson, Jay D Dorsey, Alec G Grimm, Rachel L Pieschek, Erik A Petrovskis, and Donald D Carpenter. 2021. "Hydrologic impacts of retrofitted low impact development in a commercial parking lot." *Journal of Hydrology* 592: 125773.

Todd, Peter A, Eliza C Heery, Lynette HL Loke, Ruth H Thurstan, D Johan Kotze, and Christopher Swan. 2019. "Towards an urban marine ecology: characterizing the drivers, patterns and processes of marine ecosystems in coastal cities." *Oikos* 128 (9): 1215-1242.

UF/IFAS. 2006. A Guide to Florida-Friendly LandscapingTM: Florida Yards & Neighborhoods Handbook. Gainesville, FL: University of Florida, Institute of Food and Agricultural Sciences.

—. 2021. "Institute of Food and Agricultural Sciences." University of Florida. Accessed 07/22/2021. https://ifas.ufl.edu/.

—. 2023. "Working in Your Florida Soil." Gardening Solutions. University of Florida, Institute of Food and Agricultural Sciences. https://gardeningsolutions.ifas.ufl.edu/care/planting/florida-soil.html#:~:text=You%20can%20improve%20your%20soil,and%20also%20stabilize%20soil%20pH.

USACE. 1984. *Drainage and Erosion Control Mobilization Construction* US Army Corps of Engineers.

—. 1989. Retaining and Flood Walls. Washington, D.C.: US Army Corps of Engineers.

—. 1993. *Engineering design guidance for detached breakwaters as shoreline stabilization structures.* US Army Corps of Engineers.

—. 1995. *Design of Coastal Revetments, Seawalls, and Bulkheads.* US Army Corps of Engineers.

—. 2002. *Coastal Engineering Manual - Appendix A.* US Army Corps of Engineers.

—. 2014. *Engineering and Design: Guidelines for Landscape Planting and Vegetation Management at Floodwalls, Levees, and Embankment Dams.* US Army Corps of Engineers.

—. 2017. *Nationwide Permit (54) Living Shorelines.* US Army Corps of Engineers.

USDA. 1986. *Urban Hydrology for Small Watersheds.* Natural Resources Conservation Service, Conservation Engineering Division.

—. 1993. *Soil Survey Manual.* US Department of Agriculture, Soil Conservation Service.

USDOT. 2001. *Hydraulic Design of Highway Culverts.* US Department of Transportation, Federal Highway Administration.

Verhagen, Henk Jan. 2018. "The beneficial effects of mangrove forest to sea defence structures." *Threats to Mangrove Forests: Hazards, Vulnerability, and Management*: 475-495.

Verhagen, Henk, and Tran Thi Loi. 2012. "The use of mangroves in coastal protection." The 8th International Conference on Coastal and Port Engineering in Developing Countries (COPEDEC) India.

Veri, Albert R, William W Jenna, and Dorothy Eden Bergamaschi. 1975. *Environmental quality by design, South Florida*. University of Miami Press.

Vijayaraghavan, Kuppusamy, Basanta Kumar Biswal, Max Gerrit Adam, Soon Hong Soh, Daryl Lee Tsen-Tieng, Allen P Davis, Soon Hoe Chew, Puay Yok Tan, Vladan Babovic, and Rajasekhar Balasubramanian. 2021. "Bioretention systems for stormwater management: Recent advances and future prospects." *Journal of Environmental Management* 292: 112766.

Völker, Sebastian, Hendrik Baumeister, Thomas Claßen, Claudia Hornberg, and Thomas Kistemann. 2013. "Evidence for the temperature-mitigating capacity of urban blue space—A health geographic perspective." *Erdkunde*: 355-371.

Walsh, Sean, and Robert Miskewitz. 2013. "Impact of sea level rise on tide gate function." *Journal of Environmental Science and Health, Part A* 48 (4): 453-463.

Ward, Donald, and David King Jr. 2011. "Miami Beach, Florida, Reef Ball™ Breakwater Design." In *The Proceedings of the Coastal Sediments 2011: In 3 Volumes*, 122-134. World Scientific.

Williams, MJ. 2007. "Native plants for coastal dune restoration: what, when and how for Florida." *USDA, NRCS, Brooksville Plant Materials Center, Brooksville, Florida.*

Woodruff, Sierra, Sara Meerow, Philip Gilbertson, Bryce Hannibal, Melina Matos, Malini Roy, Matthew Malecha, Siyu Yu, and Phil Berke. 2021. "Is flood resilience planning improving? A longitudinal analysis of networks of plans in Boston and Fort Lauderdale." *Climate Risk Management* 34: 100354.

Wu, Caiyan, Junxiang Li, Chunfang Wang, Conghe Song, Yu Chen, Maroš Finka, and Daniele La Rosa. 2019. "Understanding the relationship between urban blue infrastructure and land surface temperature." *Science of the Total Environment* 694: 133742.

Wu, Y., A. Chung, N. F. Y. Tam, N. Pi, and M. H. Wong. 2008. "Constructed mangrove wetland as secondary treatment system for municipal wastewater." 34 (2): 137-146. https://www.sciencedirect.com/science/article/pii/S092585740800147X.

Wunderlin, R, B Hansen, A Franck, and F Essig. 2021. "Atlas of Florida Plants." Institute for Systematic Botany, University of South Florida. Accessed 07/22/2021. https://florida.plantatlas.usf.edu/.

Wurthmann, Kurt. 2019. "Assessing storage requirements, water and energy savings, and costs associated with a residential rainwater harvesting system deployed across two counties in Southeast Florida." *Journal of Environmental Management* 252: 109673.

Xiao, Kai, Jiapeng Wu, Hailong Li, Yiguo Hong, Alicia M Wilson, Jiu Jimmy Jiao, and Meghan Shananan. 2018. "Nitrogen fate in a subtropical mangrove swamp: potential association with seawater-groundwater exchange." *Science of the total environment* 635: 586-597.

Yang, Bin, Zhihan Lv, and Faming Wang. 2022. "Digital Twins for Intelligent Green Buildings." *Buildings* 12 (6): 856.

Yang, Jiachuan, and Elie Bou-Zeid. 2019. "Scale dependence of the benefits and efficiency of green and cool roofs." *Landscape and urban planning* 185: 127-140.

Yao, Lan, Abdol Chini, and Ruochen Zeng. 2020. "Integrating cost-benefits analysis and life cycle assessment of green roofs: a case study in Florida." *Human and Ecological Risk Assessment: An International Journal* 26 (2): 443-458.

Zahina, John G, Winifred Park Said, Rachelle Grein, and Michael Duever. 2007. "Pre-development vegetation communities of southern Florida." *Technical Publication HESM-02. South Florida Water Management District, West Palm Beach*: 227.

Zedler, Joy B, and Mark K Leach. 1998. "Managing urban wetlands for multiple use: research, restoration, and recreation." *Urban Ecosystems* 2: 189-204.

Zhai, Jun, Jing Ren, Miao Xi, Xiaonan Tang, and Yixin Zhang. 2021. "Multiscale watershed landscape infrastructure: Integrated system design for sponge city development." *Urban Forestry & Urban Greening* 60: 127060.

Zhao, Mingjie, Paulo Cesar Tabares-Velasco, Jelena Srebric, Sridhar Komarneni, and Robert Berghage. 2014a. "Effects of plant and substrate selection on thermal performance of green roofs during the summer." *Building and Environment* 78: 199-211.

—. 2014b. "Effects of plant and substrate selection on thermal performance of green roofs during the summer." *Building and Environment* 78: 199-211.

Zheng, Xinzhu, Yicheng Zou, Amanda W Lounsbury, Can Wang, and Ranran Wang. 2021. "Green roofs for stormwater runoff retention: A global quantitative synthesis of the performance." *Resources, Conservation and Recycling* 170: 105577.

Zuniga-Teran, Adriana A, Chad Staddon, Laura de Vito, Andrea K Gerlak, Sarah Ward, Yolandi Schoeman, Aimee Hart, and Giles Booth. 2020. "Challenges of mainstreaming green infrastructure in built environment professions." *Journal of Environmental Planning and Management* 63 (4): 710-732.

contributors and collaborators

Brooks + Scarpa
Jeffrey Huber, FAIA, ASLA
Lawrence Scarpa, FAIA
Angela Brooks, FAIA
Kun Li, Project Designer
Fan Wu, Project Designer
Arty Vartanyan, Project Designer
Pieter Conradie, Project Designer
Heather Akers, Project Designer
Aren Castro, Project Designer
Mason Millner, Project Designer
Claudia Perdomo, Intern
Alyssa Scherger, Intern

Florida Atlantic University
School of Architecture
Jeffrey Huber, FAIA, ASLA, Professor
John Sandell, Associate Professor
Anthony Abbate, AIA, Professor
Francis Lyn, Associate Professor
Henning Haupt, Associate Professor
Kun Li, Research Assistant
Pieter Conradie, Research Assistant
Gerardo Ormachea, Research Assistant
Ian Fennimore, Research Assistant
Heather Akers, Research Assistant
Chance Stillman, Research Assistant
Dogus Oren, Research Assistant
Dane Quist, Research Assistant
Nicholas DiMattia, Research Assistant

Architecture Students:
German Avila, Pieter Conradie, Hernan D'Angelo, Nicholas DiMattia, Eduardo Ecenarro, Hassan El Wazzan, Austin Fox, David Gillis, Cody Gosier, Laetitia Lamarre, Francys Liscano, Olga Marin, Haleng Mustafo, Javier Mendoza, Rodrigo Navarro, Kevin Ortega, Carlos Tejado, Emily Peters, Gilberto Pujols, Dane Quist, Jessie Robles, Maria Rodriguez, Ricardo Rodriguez, Kathleen Valdez, Maria Valero, Kyle Vayda, Rollson Virgile, Katja Whyte, Nadia Zuta, Heather Akers, Luis Ardila, Juanita Bernal, Laren Buss, Cristin Courtney, Christopher Emile, Christie Garcia, Noah Illes, Fadia Jawhari, Daniel Justiniano, Carlos Justiniano, Maria Kokalias, Tyler Laforme, Jonathan Llampay, Amber Lewis, Rebeca Machado, Angela Menah, Lisa Munoz, Michael Olitsky, Dogus Oren, Michael Ospina, Elizabeth Parry, Connor Peede, Daniel Shareef, Deshay Sinclair, Chance Stillman, Anthony Talavera, Diego Valencia, Kevin Van Osterom.

Florida Center for Environmental Studies (CES)
Dr. Colin Polsky, Director and Professor
Richard Jones, Senior Research Associate (co-led publication efforts)*

College of Engineering and Computer Science
Dr. Fredrick Bloetscher, Professor

School of Urban and Regional Planning
Dr. Diana Mitsova, Professor
Rayan Alhawiti, Research Associate
Connor Bailey, Research Associate

University of Southern California School of Architecture
Lawrence Scarpa, FAIA, Adjunct Professor
Esther Margulies, ASLA, Associate Professor of Practice of Landscape Architecture

Architecture Students:
Norah Altwaijri, Chase Ashley, Danut Bidasca, Jennifer Brozozowski, Milioni Doshi, Christian Estrada, Hieu Huynh, Yangxiaoxia Li, Yu Liu, Jen Yu (Jason) Lo, Zhuo Wang, Mengyu Wu, Yufei Liu , Sarah De La Cruz, Wan Sin Lan, Can Derman, Tyler Gates, Jun Jun Wang, Zachary Bergmann, Chi In Wong, Jerry Ta, Yuan Pu, Manwei Li, Shu Wei, Sneha Ravani, Ai-Ju Liu, Jing Sun, Ziqiong Liu, Xiaolu Song, Liang Zhao, Shuwei Liu, Jiayu Liang, Lin Cheng, Clara Yoshihara, Yuliang Jiang.

University of Kansas School of Architecture
Dr. Keith Van de Riet, Associate Professor

Architecture Students:
Nicholas Bontrager, Camille Cieutat, Anna Collins, Patrick Griffin, Jake Lester, Pennie Liu, Zachary Overschmidt, Kevin Purdom, Quentin Rabu, Nicolas Rakowski, Spencer Reed, Emma Riordan, Hannah Rupprecht, Claire Ryan, Joseph Schaefer-Glick, Mitchell Starrs, Hannah Underwood.

With additional support from the City of Fort Lauderdale and Broward County Natural Resources and Management Division.

A special acknowledgement for Richard Jones from the Florida Center for Environmental Studies at Florida Atlantic University who took on the major responsibility and push to see this publication through completion. His efforts and all other contributors and collaborators were instrumental in seeing this publication come to fruition.

ORO Editions
Publishers of Architecture, Art, and Design
Gordon Goff: Publisher

www.oroeditions.com
info@oroeditions.com

Published by ORO Editions.

Author: Jeffrey E. Huber, FAIA, ASLA
Book Design: Florida Atlantic University and Brooks + Scarpa,
with Pablo Mandel / CircularStudio
Project Manager: Jake Anderson

10 9 8 7 6 5 4 3 2 First Edition

ISBN: 978-1-957183-75-6

Color Separations and Printing: ORO Editions Inc.
Printed in China

ORO Editions makes a continuous effort to minimize the overall carbon footprint of its publications. As part of this goal, ORO, in association with Global ReLeaf, arranges to plant trees to replace those used in the manufacturing of the paper produced for its books. Global ReLeaf is an international campaign run by American Forests, one of the world's oldest nonprofit conservation organizations. Global ReLeaf is American Forests' education and action program that helps individuals, organizations, agencies, and corporations improve the local and global environment by planting and caring for trees.

This publication was supported by the National Sea Grant College Program of the U.S. Department of Commerce's National Oceanic and Atmospheric Administration (NOAA), Grant No. NA 14OAR4170108. The views expressed are those of the authors and do not necessarily reflect the view of these organizations. Additional information is available by contacting Florida Sea Grant, University of Florida, PO Box 110409, Gainesville FL, 32611-0409, tel. (352) 392.2801, www.flseagrant.org.

Sans limites

Le judo

John Crossingham et Bobbie Kalman

Photographies de Marc Crabtree

Traduction : Josée Latulippe

Le judo est la traduction de *Judo in Action* de John Crossingham et Bobbie Kalman (ISBN 0-7787-0362-2).

Catalogage avant publication de Bibliothèque et Archives nationales du Québec et Bibliothèque et Archives Canada

Crossingham, John, 1974-

Le judo

(Sans limites)
Traduction de : Judo in action.
Comprend un index.
Pour les jeunes de 8 à 12 ans.

ISBN 978-2-89579-318-2

1. Judo - Ouvrages pour la jeunesse. 2. Judo - Ouvrages illustrés - Ouvrages pour la jeunesse. I. Kalman, Bobbie, 1947- . II. Crabtree, Marc. III. Titre. IV. Collection : Sans limites (Montréal, Québec).

GV1114.C7614 2010 j796.815'2 C2010-940727-X

Dédicace de Kathy Kantor
Dla mojej kochanej Babci Zosi (À ma grand-mère bien-aimée Zosi)

Recherche de photos
Crystal Foxton

Consultant
Sensei Kawasaki Kodokan, Shichidan (7e dan),
Académie de judo Kawasaki Rendokan, www.kawasakirendokan.com

Remerciements particuliers à
Sensei Kawasaki pour sa grande contribution à ce livre ; McKenzie Arner, Anastasia Balach, Andrew Balach, Jay Campbell, Amanda Felker, Jean-Lucas Ferreira, Delaney Forsyth, Barbara Karpinski, Melanie Knezevic, Steve Knezevic, Raeanne McAlpine, Karlie Pereira, Nicklaus Tessaro, Vincent Tessaro, Madison Varga et tous leurs parents

Illustrations
Katherine Kantor : pages 6, 29, 30
Trevor Morgan : page 8
Bonna Rouse : pages 9, 10, 11, 14

Photos et reproductions
Toutes les photos sont de Marc Crabtree, sauf : Conception de Marco Gagnon, © martialgraphics. com : page 4 (en bas)

Nous reconnaissons l'aide financière du gouvernement du Canada par l'entremise du Programme d'aide au développement de l'industrie de l'édition (PADIÉ) pour nos activités d'édition.

Conseil des Arts du Canada Canada Council for the Arts

Bayard Canada Livres inc. remercie le Conseil des Arts du Canada du soutien accordé à son programme d'édition dans le cadre du Programme des subventions globales aux éditeurs.

Cet ouvrage a été publié avec le soutien de la SODEC.
Gouvernement du Québec – Programme de crédit d'impôt pour l'édition de livres – Gestion SODEC.

Dépôt légal –
Bibliothèque et Archives nationales du Québec, 2010
Bibliothèque et Archives Canada, 2010

Direction : Andrée-Anne Gratton
Graphisme : Mardigrafe
Traduction : Josée Latulippe
Révision : Sophie Sainte-Marie

4475, rue Frontenac
Montréal (Québec)
Canada H2H 2S2
Téléphone : 514 844-2111 ou 1 866 844-2111
Télécopieur : 514 278-0072
Courriel : **edition@bayardcanada.com**
Site Internet : **www.bayardlivres.ca**

Imprimé au Canada